The Geography of Money

THE GEOGRAPHY OF MONEY ∿

BENJAMIN J. COHEN

CORNELL UNIVERSITY PRESS   ITHACA AND LONDON

First published 1998 by Cornell University Press
First printing, Cornell Paperbacks, 2000

Printed in the United States of America

Library of Congress Cataloging-in-Publication Data

Cohen, Benjamin J.
    The geography of money / Benjamin J. Cohen.
    p. cm.
    Includes index.
    ISBN 0-8014-3513-7 (cloth : alk. paper)
    ISBN 0-8014-8513-4 (pbk. : alk. paper)
    1. International finance. 2. International trade. I. Title.
HG3881.C5856   1998
332'.042—dc21   97-32860

Cornell University Press strives to use environmentally responsible suppliers
and materials to the fullest extent possible in the publishing of its books. Such
materials include vegetable-based, low-VOC inks and acid-free papers that are
recycled, totally chlorine-free, or partly composed of nonwood fibers. Books
that bear the logo of the FSC (Forest Stewardship Council) use paper taken
from forests that have been inspected and certified as meeting the highest standards for environmental and social responsibility. For further information, visit
our website at www.cornellpress.cornell.edu.

Cloth printing   10 9 8 7 6 5 4 3 2 1

Paperback printing   10 9 8 7 6 5 4 3 2 1

For Jane—

always a new world to explore

Contents

Tables

Preface

Money is much on our minds these days. In Europe, debate rages over the pros and cons of a new common currency to replace existing francs, lire, and pesos. In the former Soviet bloc and many parts of the developing world, governments agonize over how to respond to the widespread circulation of popular foreign moneys, most notably the U.S. dollar, within their territorial frontiers. In the Far East, Asians ponder the risks and opportunities of a possible new bloc in the region based on the Japanese yen. And in the United States, Americans worry about threats to the proud greenback's traditional preeminence in international monetary affairs.

Though seemingly technical in nature, these questions are anything but neutral in their implications for the distribution of global wealth and power. In fact, they go to the very essence of what we mean by state sovereignty in the world today. All carry implications for geopolitical relations that go well beyond the simple economics of who uses what currency and where. At issue is a breakdown of the territorial monopolies that national governments have historically claimed in the issue and management of money. Underlying all these challenges is a growing, market-driven competition between currencies that is increasingly indifferent to the presence of political boundaries or even the nation-state itself.

Responses to these challenges, however, remain mired in outmoded myths about the spatial organization of currency relations: the traditional but increasingly obsolete notion that each money's circulation is—or should be—confined solely to the sovereign domain of its issuing government. Such ways of thinking merely perpetuate misunderstanding and hinder practical policy remedies. What we need is a new lens through which to view the revolutionary changes in currency space wrought by accelerating cross-border competition. The purpose of this book is to provide a corrective for our defective vision.

The immediate impetus for the book was an article I wrote in 1993 for a collection of essays on European monetary unification (B. Cohen 1993a). Reviewing the historical experience of six experiments in monetary union, three of them still in existence, I began to ponder the broader question of how currency spaces are organized. Gradually I became more and more absorbed by what I came to call the geography of money.

Once embarked, however, I came to realize that this project's roots really go much further back—indeed, to the very first article I ever published in a professional journal, about a third of a century ago (B. Cohen 1963). "The Euro-Dollar, the Common Market, and Currency Unification" explicitly addressed the complex relationship between geography and sovereignty in monetary matters. The seeds sown then have now, many years later, finally come to fruition. In a sense, this is a book that I have been waiting to write all my life.

The Geography of Money is rooted as much in economics, the discipline in which I received all my formal university training, as it is in political science, my adopted profession. Although addressed primarily to students of the politics of money, a subcategory of the now recognized specialty of International Political Economy, the book will, I hope, have broader significance for the study of international relations and may have some resonance in related fields, including economic history, sociology, and geography. With luck I may even pique the interest of a few economists, who among social scientists are likely to experience the most difficulty in adjusting their thinking to the perspectives I develop here. The language of the book is designed to be accessible to the widest possible audience.

Preparation of *The Geography of Money* has benefited from the generous assistance of a large number of colleagues around the world, including Pierre-Richard Agenor, Stanley Black, Karen Donfried, Barry Eichengreen, Edgar Feige, Jeffrey Frankel, Michael Frenkel, Loren Gatch, Charles Goodhart, Jiming Ha, Ruth Judson, Jonathan Kirshner, Russell Krueger, Andrew Leyshon, Peter Lindert, Paul Masson, Robert McCauley, Paul Mizen, Bettina Peiers, Jean Pisani-Ferry, Richard Porter, Richard Portes, Angela Redish, Wolfgang Rieke, Miguel Savastano, Garry Schinasi, Franz Seitz, Robert Solomon, Linda Tesar, Van Can Thai, Niels Thygesen, Horst Ungerer, Carlos Vegh, and Charles Wyplosz. I sincerely thank them all for their help.

Earlier versions of portions of the book were presented at colloquia at UC Berkeley, UC Santa Barbara, University of Chicago, Georgetown University, and Stanford University; at the Institut d'Études Politiques de Paris and the London School of Economics; and at conferences at the Claremont Graduate School, Columbia University, the College of Europe (Bruges, Belgium), and the Istituto Affari Internazionale (Rome, Italy). In all of these discussions I received helpful commentary and suggestions.

I have also received valuable advice and counsel from friends who read earlier segments of the book, including Leslie Armijo, Henning Bohn, Marc Flandreau,

Jeffry Frieden, Judith Goldstein, Daniel Gros, Stephan Haggard, Philipp Hartmann, Randall Henning, Fabienne Ilzkovitz, Miles Kahler, Peter Kenen, Stephen Kobrin, Stephen Krasner, David Lake, Charles Lipson, Helen Milner, John Odell, Pier-Carlo Padoan, Daniel Philpott, George Tavlas, Geoffrey Underhill, Stephen Weatherford, and Ngaire Woods. To all of them I feel a deep debt of gratitude.

The full penultimate manuscript was read by David Andrews, Joanne Gowa, Eric Helleiner, Louis Pauly, and Susan Strange. I am particularly grateful to these five eminent scholars for their incisive comments and suggestions, which have undoubtedly improved the final product enormously.

I am grateful as well to several of my students at UCSB who provided valuable research assistance. These include Kelley Hwang and Steven Reti, who contributed importantly at the earliest stages of this project, and Ben Pettit, who helped out at the end. Most especially, I thank Kathleen Collihan, without whose industrious support and initiative I might never have been able to carry the enterprise through to completion.

Sincere thanks also to Roger Haydon of Cornell University Press. One could not hope to find a better or more knowledgeable editor.

Finally, this book is dedicated to my wife and soulmate, Jane Sherron De Hart, who did not let the pressure of her own latest book project prevent her from offering the support and counsel needed to see my ambitions realized.

BENJAMIN J. COHEN

Santa Barbara, California

Abbreviations

ACU	artificial currency unit
BENELUX	Belgium, Netherlands, and Luxembourg
BIS	Bank for International Settlements
BLEU	Belgium-Luxembourg Economic Union
CBR	Central Bank of Russia
CFA	Communauté Financière Africaine (African Financial Community)
CI	currency internationalization
CMA	Common Monetary Area
CS	currency substitution
DM	Deutschemark
EAC	East African Community
EC	European Community
ECB	European Central Bank
ECCA	East Caribbean Currency Area
EC92	European Community 1992 Project
ECU	European Currency Unit
EMI	European Monetary Institute
EMS	European Monetary System
EMU	Economic and Monetary Union
ERM	Exchange Rate Mechanism
EU	European Union
EUA	European Unit of Account
IMF	International Monetary Fund
LMU	Latin Monetary Union
OCA	optimum currency area
PLO	Palestine Liberation Organization
SDR	Special Drawing Right
SMU	Scandinavian Monetary Union
UN	United Nations

The Geography of Money

Introduction: Money in International Affairs

"One of the hallmarks of national sovereignty through the ages has been the right to create money. . . . The ability to create its own domestic money is the key financial distinction of a sovereign state."

Fred Hirsch, *Money International*, 1969

How should we think about money in international affairs? Ask the proverbial man or woman in the street, and the answer will be straightforward. All currencies are national: One Nation/One Money. America has its dollar, the British their pound, Japan the yen, each money exclusive within its own sovereign domain. The geography of money coincides precisely with the political frontiers of nation-states.

Even professionals who should know better, like the late Fred Hirsch, a noted international economist, share the One Nation/One Money myth. Economists in particular find it difficult to think of currency relations in anything other than traditional territorial terms. In the words of the research director of the International Monetary Fund: "Virtually all of the world's nations assert and express their sovereign authority by maintaining a distinct national money and protecting its use within their respective jurisdictions. Money is like a flag; each country has to have its own" (Mussa 1995:98). The vice president of the Federal Reserve Bank of Boston concurs: "Currency independence rules the waves" (Fieleke 1992:17).

In fact, nothing could be further from the truth. Currency use is by no means confined by the territorial limits of individual states. Quite the contrary. As a French economist, Pascal Salin, writes, in a rare dissent from the conventional wisdom: "The production of money, like the production of law, is not an essential attribute of state sovereignty, despite what the mythology says" (1984:3). The geography of money is far more complex than we generally assume.

As a practical matter, a surprising number of moneys have come to be employed outside their home country for transactions either between nations or within foreign states. The former is usually called "international" currency use or currency "internationalization"; the latter is typically described as "currency substitution" and may be referred to as "foreign-domestic use." An even larger number of moneys now routinely face domestic competition from currencies that originate abroad. It is simply wrong to deny that several currencies may circulate in the same state; the phenomenon has become commonplace. The time has come to adjust our thinking to the new reality of cross-border currency competition.

Both international and foreign-domestic currency use result from intense market rivalry—a kind of Darwinian process of natural selection, driven by the force of demand, in which some moneys such as the U.S. dollar and German mark (the Deutschemark) come to seem more attractive than others for various commercial or financial purposes. Once, before the emergence of the modern nation-state system, cross-border circulation of currencies was quite common. The phenomenon has now reappeared as barriers to market exchange have come down since World War II, greatly expanding the array of currency choice. Competition between national moneys, a market-driven process in which transactors are free to choose among alternative currencies, is accelerating rapidly. As a result, the domains within which individual currencies serve the standard functions of money now diverge ever more sharply from the legal jurisdictions of issuing governments.

Does it matter? Again ask the person in the street, and the answer may be no more than a shrug of the shoulders. For national governments, however, intensely jealous of their sovereign authority, the question is anything but uninteresting. To those responsible for public policy, currency competition poses a clear and present danger. The production of money may not in fact be an essential attribute of state sovereignty, but along with the raising of armies and the levying of taxes it has long been regarded as essential. Genuine power resides in the privilege that money represents. The ability to monopolize monetary issue, excluding all other currencies from circulation, promises abundant access to real resources—goods and services of all kinds—and a powerful instrument of command over the operation of the national economy. Such advantages are lost when a government no longer exercises effective control over the creation and management of money. As one observer has argued, with only a touch of sarcasm: "A government that does not control money is a limited government. . . . No government likes to be limited. . . . Governments simply must monopolize money if they are to control it and they must control it if they really are to be governments" (O'Mahony 1984:127).

Like it or not, the changing geography of money *does* matter—for governments, whose powers are diluted, and hence for those in whose name the state ostensibly rules. Political regimes differ, of course. The relationship between state and society, the public sector and the private sector, runs the gamut from purest democracy to the most arbitrary forms of authoritarianism. A government may act solely as agent for the electorate or as a principal in its own right. Public policy may serve the interests of the many or merely line the pockets of a few. The nature of the political regime, however, is not the issue here. Whatever the political regime—however representative or unrepresentative it may be—private citizens are vitally affected when public decisionmaking is compromised. Indifference to cross-border currency competition is a luxury that people in the street simply cannot afford.

The aim of this book is to reconsider the role that money plays in today's world. This means looking beyond finance in the conventional sense of the term—the processes and institutions responsible for the mobilization of savings and allocation of credit—to focus on the underlying supplies of currency in which investments and other transactions are conducted. My starting point is the widespread and growing use of currencies outside their country of origin. My central thesis is that international relations, political as well as economic, are being dramatically reshaped by the increasing interpenetration of national monetary spaces. Market-driven currency competition alters the distribution of resources and power around the globe. It generates mounting tensions and insecurities—potential threats to global stability as well as promising opportunities for cooperation.

The impact on public policy is visible everywhere: from the European Union's heated debates about a new common currency to the still-unresolved fallout from the breakup of the old Soviet ruble zone; from Latin American concerns about the hegemonic implications of "dollarization" to anxieties sparked by the looming possibility of a yen bloc in the Asian Pacific. The United States worries about how to preserve the privileges associated with global use of the greenback; the British worry about whether to preserve the pound itself. Former Soviet republics seek to establish credible new currencies to go with their newfound political independence; inflation-prone developing economies struggle to sustain confidence in old currencies threatened with displacement from abroad. Governments on every continent fret about the risks involved in increased dependence on other states; even more, policymakers fear a growing vulnerability to unpredictable pressures from the market. A fresh wind is blowing across traditional boundaries, dramatically altering established patterns of global wealth and influence. The stakes could not be higher.

Analytically, what we need is a new understanding of the spatial organization of currency relations—the geography of money. To date, monetary geography has been woefully underexplored in the social sciences. Indeed, the very term "monetary geography" remains unknown to all but a few academic specialists. In a world of increasingly competitive currencies, such thoughtless disregard is inexcusable.

The issues are clear. If currency domains are no longer confined by territorial frontiers, what shape do they take? How are they determined? And what are their economic and political effects? If national monetary sovereignty can no longer be assured, how in practice are monetary affairs governed, and what can or should we do about it? Such questions affect us all. One does not have to be a geographer to appreciate the need for a better grasp of monetary geography.

Toward a New Mental Map

The central argument of this book may be briefly summarized. The traditional myth of One Nation/One Money inaccurately privileges the interests of governments in relation to other societal actors, perpetuating a misleading image of the structure of power in global currency relations. In reality, competition across borders transforms the role of the state in monetary governance, threatening a major crisis of legitimacy in this vital realm of political economy.

At issue is a growing gap between image and fact: between the way we conceive monetary geography in our minds—the imaginary landscapes that make up our mental maps of money—and the way currency spaces have come to be configured in actual practice. Representations of space are socially constructed. Such cognitive images matter because they embody specific understandings of underlying political relationships—who has power and how it is exercised. Our choice of particular spatial images automatically lends legitimacy to particular forms of dominion or authority. Clinging to an outmoded vision of monetary geography makes it more difficult for us to come to grips with the real problems of currency relations today.

One Nation/One Money is derived from the conventions of standard political geography which, ever since the seventeenth-century Peace of Westphalia, has celebrated the nation-state, absolutely sovereign within its own territory, as the basic unit of governance in world politics. Just as political space was conceived in terms of those fixed and mutually exclusive entities we call states, so currency spaces came to be visualized in terms of the separate sovereign territories where each money originated. I call this the Westphalian model of monetary geography.

In this state-centered model, national governments exercise monopoly control over the issue and management of their own money. As a result, power in monetary matters is concentrated decisively in the hands of the state. Not every government may be able to avail itself of all the advantages of monetary monopoly; compromises may be required that lead to either a subordination or a sharing of currency sovereignty among states. But even then, monetary governance remains, it is assumed, the privileged mandate of governments.

The Westphalian model may have been largely accurate once upon a time—but no longer. What was once a reasonable approximation of reality has now become an outmoded and misleading caricature. Today, market-driven competition has greatly altered the spatial organization of monetary relations, significantly eroding the monopoly powers of the state. We need an updated model, in order to bring perceptions more in line with contemporary developments. At a time when currencies increasingly are employed outside their country of origin, penetrating other national monetary spaces, we need an image defined not by political frontiers but rather by the full range of each money's effective use and authority. Monetary geography needs to be reconceptualized in functional terms, to focus on evolving networks of currency transactions and relationships. Seen in this light, the traditional Westphalian model is in fact a very special case. A strictly territorial money is a transactional network confined exclusively to the borders of a single state. We need to comprehend a much wider range of possible currency configurations.

In this new imaginary landscape, power has been redistributed not only between states but, even more important, from states to market forces. Government is no longer automatically privileged in relation to societal actors. States remain influential, of course, through their continuing jurisdiction over the supply of national moneys. But their role in monetary governance has been transformed, evolving in effect from Westphalian monopolist to something more akin to an industrial oligopolist. Now authority must be shared with other market agents, in particular the users on the demand side of the market. Currency spaces now are shaped not by political sovereignty but by the invisible hand of competition— governments interacting together with societal actors in the social spaces created by money's transactional networks.

The principal advantage of this new system of governance is that it provides a check on the arbitrary exercise of governmental authority. The state now, as oligopolist, is far less likely to abuse or mismanage its monetary powers than it was when it enjoyed a monopoly. The main disadvantage is also clear: market actors are less accountable than politicans to the general electorate, raising serious questions about legitimacy and representation in decisionmaking. Should markets be permitted to rule without the formal consent of the governed? Governments have not entirely lost their capacity to act on behalf of their own citizens. But without an accurate mental map to guide them, politicians may be unable to respond effectively to the many problems they face in making public policy today.

Exploring Monetary Geography

I explore the meaning of monetary geography, as a socially constructed "regime of representation," in Chapter 1. Traditional geographic approaches, it is evident, provide little guidance for an accurate conceptualization of monetary spaces in today's world, in which currencies have become effectively deterritorialized. I outline an alternative approach, a flow-based model founded on a clear analytical distinction between physical and functional notions of space: "spaces-of-flows" rather than "spaces-of-places." Critical to the flow-based model is the concept of a money's authoritative domain, which combines the influence of state-imposed territoriality with that of market-generated transactional networks. Using this alternative approach, it becomes clear why the traditional Westphalian model is indeed a special case, not a normal state of affairs.

The nature and implications of that case are the subject of the next three chapters, beginning in the first half of Chapter 2 with a brief discussion of its historical antecedents and development. Contrary to popular belief, the tradition of One Nation/One Money really is of recent origin. Only during the nineteenth century, in fact, did national governments, first in Europe and then elsewhere, begin to consolidate their monopoly control over the creation and management of money. Before that historical moment, no one was surprised to find a multiplicity of currencies circulating within or between political jurisdictions. Monetary spaces were understood to be effectively deterritorialized. In that sense, today's reemergence of market-driven competition between moneys is simply a rediscovery of the past.

We then look at the principal benefits to be derived from a territorial currency: first, a potent political symbol to promote a sense of national identity; second, a potentially powerful source of revenue to underwrite public expenditures; third, a possible instrument to manage macroeconomic performance; and finally, a practical means to insulate the nation against foreign influence or constraint. All four boons privilege the interests of the state in relation to societal actors.

In practice, of course, states have not always been in a position to avail themselves of all the benefits of a monetary monopoly. Many governments have at times found it necessary either to subordinate themselves to or to share monetary sovereignty with other states. Variations on the former strategy, ranging from outright adoption of a foreign currency or a currency board to diverse forms of exchange-rate peg, are examined in Chapter 3. Variations on the latter, ranging from simple exchange-rate unions to a complete merger of national moneys, are addressed in Chapter 4. In both strategies, politics appears to dominate economics in the decisionmaking of governments.

Alternatives to the state-centric Westphalian model occupy us in the remaining four chapters. Chapter 5 is primarily empirical, bringing together data to demonstrate the impressive scale and growth of cross-border use of currencies in the contemporary era. Available statistics, drawn from both published and unpublished sources, offer us a composite map of money's imaginary landscape which is strikingly at variance with conventional understandings of currency space. Unlike in the Westphalian model, we find ourselves in a world of far-reaching competition and broad hierarchy among moneys—not a simple two-dimensional field of neatly divided territorial currencies but something more like a three-dimensional pyramid existing in the virtual reality created by market-generated transactional networks. The flow-based image of a currency pyramid best captures the meaning of monetary geography today.

What are the implications of currency deterritorialization for power and governance in monetary relations? Going back to the four benefits of a monetary monopoly surveyed earlier, Chapter 6 traces the impact of cross-border competition on the distribution of resources and capabilities in monetary affairs, both among states and between states and markets. Some governments may gain power at the expense of others, but elements of the private sector look to be the biggest winners of all. Through the choices they make among alternative transactional networks, key societal actors gain a new form of leverage over policy behavior in the public sector.

A redistribution of power, however, is not the same thing as a total abdication of authority. Chapter 7 shows that governments have not become an anachronism in the governance of monetary affairs: they continue to dominate the supply of currencies around the world. Rather, their role has been transformed, from privileged local monopolist to strategic oligopolist, competing more or less consciously for the allegiance of users on the demand side of the market. Nor does authority simply dissolve because impersonal market forces grow in influence. Governance survives but, unlike in the Westphalian model, is now exercised jointly, by both sides of the market, not by states alone. The chapter concludes by outlining the crisis of legitimacy that is threatened by recent changes in money's spatial organization.

Finally, I consider some major policy challenges in monetary affairs in light of our improved understanding of today's currency relations. Issues addressed include the future of the dollar, the potential impact of European monetary union, prospects for a yen bloc, and the difficulties of economic management in highly dollarized economies. Practical realities preclude any easy return to the Westphalian model of the past. Some degree of cross-border competition is here to stay. Governments, therefore, have little choice: they have to adapt to the dialectical interaction of state and society which increasingly shapes the global geography of money. Policymakers must now learn how to accommodate themselves to a dramatically new structure of monetary power and governance.

The Meaning of Monetary Geography

"Image is everything."
> Andre Agassi, in a TV ad for Canon
> EOS Rebel cameras

What do we mean by monetary geography? Although the term is not conventional, it actually encompasses much of what discussions of global monetary relations are all about. Most fundamentally, "monetary geography" refers to the spatial organization of currency relations—how monetary domains are configured and governed. Whether we recognize it or not, we all carry around cognitive images of how currency spaces are organized; and these images, or mental maps, in turn shape the way we routinely think about the role of money in world affairs. In a sense, tennis star Andre Agassi is right: image *is* everything. The problem is that currency competition has accelerated in recent years, and so our traditional representations of monetary geography have grown increasingly obsolete. We need a new model to improve our understanding.

The Meaning of Geography

We begin with the meaning of geography. Representations of geography are essentially symbolic—part of "the daily acts of imagination through which space and human identity are constructed" (Shapiro 1996:3). They are imaginary landscapes that we use to order our perceptions of the confusing, often disorderly world in which we live. Geographers speak of the geographical imagination, which permits us to see regularity and even intention in what might otherwise seem overwhelming chaos and void—"a way of making sense of complexity and of helping us get a grip on where we are" (Massey 1995:26).

Representations of geography thus are about far more than just mountains and valleys, rivers and oceans, cities and countries. Most fundamentally, they are about people: who we are and how we organize our lives. As one source notes, "it is through our geographical imagination that we develop a sense of the global nature of places in which we live; that is, we develop a sense of *how* we are connected, in what ways and to which places."[1] In effect, geography is about society as we ourselves conceive it: human geography.

The social content of our geographical imagination is increasingly appreciated by students of world politics, inspired in part by the critical insights of poststructural theorists such as Michel Foucault and Jacques Derrida.[2] The essential message of poststructuralism—also known as "postmodernism"—is the determinative power of discourse: the manner in which language shapes the way we see the world. Developed initially in the 1970s, poststructuralism made its first impact in literary studies and the humanities. More recently social scientists too have begun to stress its significance, even if they do not necessarily subscribe to all aspects of poststructuralist doctrine, putting particular emphasis on perceptions of space in political relations. "In the social sciences," remarks one observer, "spatial metaphors are gaining in currency, and talk is increasingly of boundaries, locations, positions, situations, place-images, and mapping" (Drainville 1995:51). Scholars talk about reimagining political space, remapping the world, and challenging boundaries. Imaginary landscapes have in fact become central to how we think about political relationships.

It is now widely accepted not only that our representations of political space matter but also that they are in fact *socially* constructed—not handed down by the gods but built up from our own ideas and experiences. John Ruggie captures the point in his notion of social epistemes, which he defines as "the mental equipment that people draw upon in imagining and symbolizing forms of political community" (1993:157).[3] Foucault, building on the traditional French notion of *mentalités collectives,* speaks of the "fundamental codes of a culture . . . the already encoded eye" (1970:xx–xxi). Others imply much the same when they talk about models or paradigms; social psychologists, likewise, when they talk of "cognitive mapping." Our understanding of world politics ultimately rests on a foundation of such mental images.

The geographical imagination must be anchored in some empirical reality, of course. Spatial representations cannot be totally arbitrary if they are to remain useful. On the other hand, though we may exclude obvious fantasies, there can be no appeal to a single, objective truth in choosing among alternative social constructs. Geographic representations are inevitably subjective—more properly, intersubjective—each proceeding from a particular perspective, based on social interaction, and embodying one of many possible interpretations. None may lay claim to being either absolutely neutral or definitively true. All, in a sense, are acceptable if they do not depart too radically from observed facts. As David Elkins writes: "Socially constructed worlds . . . are not natural or 'given'. . . . [They] should be viewed as malleable, as constitutive of our environment but ultimately derived from shared social experience" (1995:18–19).

Nonetheless, choices are necessary if we are to make sense of the politics involved. Politics is about power and authority: how rules are made for the allocation of values in society and how they are implemented and enforced—in short, how societies are governed. It is not a radical or a revolutionary notion to recognize that such matters involve elements of interest. Nor would it be unfair or innocent to assume that most prevailing geographic images tend, whether by design or not, to reflect the underlying influence of those who conceive and promote them. As one observer suggests, such representations are "social products . . . which reflect a balance of power" (Massey 1995:41). In choosing among alternative images, we not only privilege one reading of reality over others, we privilege one structure of power over others—one system of governance and not another. Our choices are by no means without consequence, as Edward Soja reminds us: "We must be insistently aware of how space can be made to hide consequences from us, how relations of power and discipline are inscribed into the apparently innocent spatiality of social life, how human geographies become filled with politics and ideology" (1989:6).

In effect, geography *is* politics. How we conceive of space has a real impact on how we think about rulemaking and enforcement, lending legitimacy to particular forms of dominion or authority. This insight is effectively captured by the apt term "regime of representation," as broached in a recent commentary:

> Structures of power are embedded in "regimes of representation." These structures of power are stored in the process of identity formation, in conceptions of space . . . as well as in the political structures that help sustain different forms of production (Murphy and Rojas de Ferro 1995:63–64).

It is in this spirit, tying conceptions of space to regimes of representation, that this book seeks the meaning of monetary geography. We will study money's spatial organization in order to better understand the politics of money: the system of governance embedded in currency relations. We will ask how monetary spaces are organized. The answer will tell us much about who has power, how monetary authority is exercised, and what the impact is on contemporary economics and politics.

The Meaning of Money

Consider next the meaning of money.[4] At its most basic, money is defined by the functions it performs. As a once-prominent British economist wryly observed, many years ago: "Money is one of those concepts which, like a teaspoon or an umbrella, but unlike an earthquake or a buttercup, are defined primarily by the use or purpose which they serve" (Hawtrey 1928:1). Money is anything, regardless of its physical or legal characteristics, that customarily and principally performs certain specific functions.

Three particular functions are traditional: medium of exchange, unit of account, and store of value. As a medium of exchange, money is synonymous with the circulating means of payment. In this role, its key attribute is its general acceptability to satisfy contractual obligations. As a unit of account, money provides a common denominator, or numéraire, for the valuation of diverse goods, services, and assets. Here, its key attribute is its ability to convey pricing information both reliably and expeditiously. As a store of value, money offers a convenient means for holding wealth. In this role, its key attribute is its ability to preserve purchasing power, bridging the interval, however transitory, between receipts from sales and payments for purchases.[5]

The invention of money was one of the most important steps in the evolution of human civilization—"comparable," one writer has suggested, "with the domestication of animals, the cultivation of the land, and the harnessing of power" (Morgan 1965:11). Before money there was only barter. The archetypal economic transaction requires an inverse double coincidence of wants for exchange to occur. Each of two parties has to desire what the other is prepared to offer—a manifestly inefficient system of trade, since much time has to be devoted to the necessary process of search and bargaining. With the introduction of money, the single transaction of barter split into two separate transactions, sale and purchase, reducing the costs of acquiring information. A seller can accept money instead of goods or services for immediate delivery, hold it until needed for a purchase, and in the meantime use it to judge value in the marketplace. One consequence was to facilitate multilateral exchange, promoting specialization in production and an increasingly efficient division of labor.

The invention of money would have been impossible, however, without a minimal degree of social cohesion—some group of agents, located somewhere, with sufficient reason to believe in an instrument's future reusability to accept its present validity for both payment and accounting purposes. The key to all three of money's roles is *trust:* the reciprocal faith of a critical mass of like-minded transactors. No rational individual willingly takes a mere instrument in exchange for goods or services without at least some assurance that it will subsequently be accepted at face value by others. Indeed, money has no meaning at all except with reference to the mutual confidence that makes its use possible.

Where does that bond of mutual confidence come from? It could derive from state action, as the German economist George Knapp argued early in the twentieth century. According to Knapp's "state theory of money," all money was a product of law and dependent on legal ordinances for its validity. But this is an unduly restrictive view of actual practice, as even a casual glance at monetary history makes clear. Acceptability may also stem from a variety of nonstate sources—indeed, from nothing more than the slow accumulation of market practice, reflecting all manner of social beliefs and influences. The roots of the trust embodied in money are in fact many and to some extent mysterious, as the economist W. T. Newlyn has noted:

> The necessary condition for the performance of [money] is general acceptability in settlement of debt. General acceptability may come about as a result of a number of different factors operating singly or in combination; it falls within that perplexing but fascinating group of phenomena which is affected by self-justifying beliefs. If members of a community think that money will be generally acceptable, then it will be; otherwise not. (1962:2)

The generic term for such a community, held together by the cement of social relationships, is *network*—a concept increasingly used by social scientists to study behavior at all levels of analysis, from the local to the global. The network idea stresses a fundamental complementarity and commitment among diverse individuals and organizations. It also emphasizes coordination and self-control through nothing more than an ongoing process of mutual accommodation. In a network, relationships are decentralized and may be both long-distance and impersonal: cohesion is unconstrained by either physical location or a need for face-to-face encounters. Relationships may also be intermittent, involving only occasional and often quite brief episodes of interaction. Networks demand neither formal institutional design nor explicit rules to be effective. They require only a sufficient degree of intra-group reciprocity and trust.

In the case of money, the cement is a web of *transactions*—mutual exchanges among autonomous agents who may otherwise have little or nothing in common and who might even be located in vastly different places. The salience of money's transactional networks, long ago noted by George Simmel (1900) and even earlier by Karl Marx (1864), is frequently cited by scholars today. Indeed, for sociologists such networks have become the very essence of an otherwise abstract economic concept. Money, wrote one early analyst, "is a social fact."[6] Put differently, money is best understood as a coherent and evolving social institution, based on real historical circumstances—a product of self-reinforcing patterns of market practice and behavior. In the more contemporary language of sociologist Nigel Dodd:

> The information implicit in monetary transaction provides the most fundamental point of distinction between monetary exchange and barter. Significantly, this distinction arises not from comparison of monetary and non-monetary forms but from examination of the network of social relationships integral to each as a type of exchange. . . . It follows that to understand what is distinctive about money requires reference to the network of social relationships which makes its transaction possible. (1994:xxiii)

Economists also emphasize the importance of transactional networks, particularly as they explain the origins and material benefits of money. Central to economic analysis of money is the issue of transactions costs—the expenses associated with search, bargaining, uncertainty, and enforcement of contracts. Transactions costs clearly are reduced by the use of monetary exchange rather than barter. The magnitude of the savings will be directly related to the number of actors willing to accept a given money in payment. The larger the size of the money's transactional network—what one analyst calls the "thickness" of its market (Alogoskoufis 1993)—the greater will be the economies of scale to be derived from its use. Monetary theorists variously describe these gains as money's network externalities, thickness externalities, and, simply, the network value of money. Network externalities may be understood as a form of interdependence in which the practices of any one actor depend strategically on the practices adopted by others in the same network of interactions.

In effect, transactional networks define the functional domains of individual currencies: the range of their effective use for various monetary purposes. Monetary geography, we shall see, is fundamentally grounded in these key social structures.

Political Geography

Mental maps of monetary geography require a conscious choice among alternative conceptualizations, or models, each one embodying a different regime of representation. As Robert Gilpin has reminded us: "Despite the belief . . . that the monetary system is a neutral mechanism, every monetary regime imposes differential costs and benefits" (1987:119). Traditional representations, based on the One Nation/One Money myth, effectively privilege the interests of the state over private market actors. In an era of accelerating cross-border currency use, however, such views look obsolete. A new model is called for.

The territorial trap

The simplest way to represent monetary geography is in elementary territorial terms, the analog of traditional political geography.[7] Just as we are all conditioned to see the world's surface, first and foremost, in terms of fixed and mutually exclusive entities called nation-states, so we might think of currencies in terms of the separate sovereign domains in which they originate. Politically, the globe is divided into territorially based national jurisdictions. Why not conceptualize money in the same state-centric way?

The answer is that such an approach obscures far more than it reveals—just like the political geography from which it is derived. Territoriality, we know, is a primary geographical expression of social power among humans, as it is among many other animals, and it traces back to the very origins of our species as a breed of naked ape. In the words of the geographer Robert Sack: "Territoriality in humans is best understood as a spatial strategy to affect, influence, or control resources and people, by controlling area" (1986:1).[8]

In recent years, however, geographers and political scientists alike have begun to emphasize the severe limitations, even distortions, introduced by the conventional territorial imagery of international relations—the deceptively innocent notion that world politics can best be understood in terms of "neatly divided spatial packages."[9] The territorial perspective, as a way to map politics, has always been to some extent misleading. Today it is becoming increasingly remote from the real world in which we live. As Robert Jackson has written:

> Sovereign statehood . . . is now so ingrained in the public life of humankind and imprinted in the minds of people that it seems like a natural phenomenon beyond the control of statesmen or anyone else. When schoolchildren are repeatedly shown a political map of the world which represents the particular locations of named states in different continents and oceans they can easily end up regarding such entities in the same light as the physical features such as rivers or mountain ranges which sometimes delimit their international boundaries. It is nevertheless the case that not only the map itself but also the sovereign jurisdictions it represents are a totally artificial political arrangement which could be altered or even abolished. (1990:7)

The notion of sovereign statehood, based on exclusive territoriality, has a long and reputable lineage, going back at least to the Peace of Westphalia of 1648. Westphalia is generally recognized as a watershed in world politics—in the eyes of many, not just the first treaty to define modern international law but, more fundamentally, the crucial moment in the evolution of human affairs from medievalism to modernism. The ostensible purpose of Westphalia was to end the Thirty Years War. A complicated document, it contained provisions to address a variety of contentious issues, including diverse dynastic claims, divisions of territory, religious practice, and the constitution of the Holy Roman Empire. The Peace is remembered most, however, for its assertion of the norm of sovereignty for each state within its own geographical frontiers. In effect it formally established territoriality as the sole basis for Europe's political map.[10] Henceforth power was embodied in the independent, autonomous state. No government might intervene in the internal affairs of any other.

Before Westphalia, during the medieval era, matters had been more complicated. There were as yet no fixed or exclusive sovereignties in Europe. Power and authority were diffuse, often shifting, and certainly more permeable. Political domains were scattered and mingled in a vast patchwork of overlapping and incomplete rights of government in which "different juridical instances were geographically interwoven and stratified, and plural allegiances, asymmetrical suzerainties, and anomalous enclaves abounded" (P. Anderson 1974:37–38). The arcane intricacies and ambiguities of legitimacy that resulted were accepted as part of the natural order of the universe. No one thought of territory per se as the dominant criterion for organizing political space. In Ruggie's words: "The medieval system . . . was a form of segmental territorial rule that had none of the connotations of possessiveness and exclusiveness conveyed by the modern concept of sovereignty. It represented a heteronomous organization of territorial rights and claims—of political space" (1983:173).

Westphalia, by contrast, enshrined territory as the central organizing principle of world politics. In the self-consciously modern epoch that succeeded medievalism, legitimate systems of governance took the form of territorially defined, fixed, and mutually exclusive national entities, all essentially similar in functional terms.[11] Sovereignty was in principle both absolute and unambiguous—a *homonomous* rather than a *heteronomous* mode of organizing political space.[12] The territorial state was generally accepted as the basic unit of political authority, privileging government over society. Global politics was conceived in terms of the familiar nation-state system—the so-called Westphalian model of political geography.

More recently, however, the notion of the sovereign territorial state as an accurate representation of political reality has come under increasingly critical scrutiny.[13] The Westphalian model was clearly a product of a particular time and place. It can lay no claim to general truth or eternal validity. As one observer summarizes the point:

> A little comparative history goes a long way. It shows us that the sovereign state is not naturally occurring. In fact, by comparison with other forms of rule and ways of organizing space, it is historically exceptional . . . a distinctively modern way of conceiving and organizing space. . . . No other civilization either imagined or organized the known world in this way. (Rosenberg 1994b:99, 103)

The limits of the Westphalian model are by now well recognized. Absolute state sovereignty may yet prevail as a juridical norm, a core constitutive rule enshrined in international law. The authority of governments over a defined geographic space is still, in principle, inviolate. But in terms of actual practice the concept at best has always and only been a convenient fiction—a "territorial trap" (Agnew 1994a) for the unwary.[14] Some four decades ago John Herz (1957), addressing the increasingly difficult challenge of defending the "hard shell" of state sovereignty in time of war, was already speaking of the "demise of the territorial state." In truth, power has never been wholly unconstrained within fixed geographic frontiers. In some degree practical sovereignty has always been more contingent than categorical: contested rather than conceded, pliant rather than immutable, diffuse rather than indivisible. De facto, states are perpetually engaged in negotiating or renegotiating elements of their nominal national authority. Sovereignty, in Stephen Krasner's blunt phrase, has always been "up for grabs" (1993:260).

And never in the centuries since Westphalia has that observation been more true than in our own time, as states find themselves increasingly challenged by the economic phenomenon known as globalization. Linkages among national economies are clearly on the rise. As a result, pressures today come not only from other governments but even more critically from a widening array of influential societal actors, multinational corporations and others that operate across national frontiers through the mechanisms of the global marketplace. The growing disjuncture between a political system based on sovereign territory and a transnational economy that is becoming more newly worldwide in scope has become a cliché of the scholarly literature.[15] Market integration, it is clear, problematizes the question of economic governance. Power is increasingly drained from national governments and shared, formally or informally, with private agents. Authority, more and more, is exercised jointly through diverse and hybrid structures of governance. In the words of one recent commentary: "The state now finds itself confronted by ever more elaborate layers of organization which criss-cross its territorial boundaries. . . . The image of a world where space is appropriated and exclusively controlled by sovereign states is a conceptual tool of doubtful utility" (Camilleri and Falk 1992:4, 250).

Our global system now is nowhere near as simple as the state-centric maps we learned as schoolchildren would have us believe. Quite the contrary, in fact. As a practical matter, the organization of political space today is far more like the heteronomous world of the Middle Ages than the homonomous Westphalian model. Ours is now a world of diffuse and permeable structures of power, "governance mechanisms whose authority is not centered in the state" (Sassen 1996a:16). Some scholars, harking back to those earlier days, label these developments the new medievalism or neomedievalism. Others, more in tune with contemporary intellectual fashion, adopt flashy labels: postmodern, postinternational, post-Westphalian, or plurilateral. All agree, however, that political geography has become to an important extent "deterritorialized," to use Arjun Appadurai's apt term.[16] World politics clearly needs to update its imagery.

Avoiding the territorial trap

Money is no different. The same limits that apply to a territorial imagery of politics are relevant to currency relations too. The notion that, like global politics, the world of money can be naively represented by a system of neatly divided spatial packages—what we may call the Westphalian model of monetary geography—is equally deceptive and, given today's accelerating pace of cross-border currency competition, perhaps even more remote from reality.

For a currency to be truly territorial, its functional domain would have to coincide precisely with the political jurisdiction of its issuing state—increasingly, in the contemporary era, a very special case.[17] That currency would have to exercise an exclusive claim to all the traditional roles of money in the domestic economy. No other money could be accepted for transactions purposes or used for the denomination of contracts or financial assets. And the government would have to be able to exercise sole control over the operation of the monetary system, dominating market agents. In matters of commerce, the equivalent would be autarky, national self-sufficiency. In truth, however, autarky is no more common today in monetary matters than it is in trade.

Of course, monetary sovereignty, like political sovereignty, continues to exist as a constitutive rule. It is the exceptional government that does not still seek to preserve, as best it can, an effective monopoly over the issue and management of money within its own territory. What matters, however, is actual practice not formal principle—and practice depends on the *demand* for money, over which governments have relatively little control, not just *supply*. States exercise direct jurisdiction only over the stock of national currency in circulation. Indirectly they may manipulate market demand by means of pecuniary incentives or legal restrictions. But in a world of rapidly integrating markets, not even the most authoritarian government can ensure that its money alone will be used in preference to currencies originating elsewhere. As in other areas of national policy, the monetary authority of governments today is increasingly challenged by a wide array of powerful market forces.

The notion of simple territorial currencies, therefore, is at best a convenient fiction. The organization of currency space, no less than political space, has become to some extent deterritorialized.[18] The state-centric imagery of monetary geography needs updating too.

Economic Geography

If traditional political geography is of limited use as a guide to mapping monetary relations, what about *economic* geography—the field of inquiry devoted explicitly to the spatial organization of economic activity? Money obviously plays a central role in the production, distribution, and consumption of material wealth. Might studies of economic geography, therefore, provide a more apt analog for the representation of currency spaces?

Still the territorial trap

Regrettably, the usefulness of economic geography is also limited, for our purposes, by a preoccupation with the overarching importance of territory. "Fundamentally," one leading textbook informs us, "the economic geographer is concerned with the *spatial organization* of economic systems: with *where* the various elements of the system are located, *how* they are connected together in space, and the *spatial impact* of economic processes."[19] True, territory in economic geography does not mean neatly divided spatial packages. The very nature of economics demands a focus on the links among physically separate entities, not their mutual exclusivity. Nor are all economic geographers necessarily resistant to alternative "topological presuppositions," as one recent commentary phrases it, embodying "different sets of coordinates" (Thrift and Olds 1996:321). Nonetheless, for most scholars working in the field, the core imagery remains tightly bound to place.

This general tendency is certainly evident in standard location theory, the oldest analytical tradition of economic geography, which was developed specifically to explain how and why various activities come to be situated where they are. Based on the principles of conventional neoclassical economics, location theory addresses such matters as the spatial pattern of agriculture, the distribution of towns and cities, and within urban areas the location of individual households. It emphasizes the importance of distance and accessibility as determinants of production costs. Outcomes are analyzed in terms of spatial diffusion or agglomeration economies (the increasing returns derived from concentrating operations in close proximity). Effects are described in terms of spread or polarization, trickledown or uneven growth.

The same orientation is also evident in newer, structural approaches to economic geography, often based on Marxist or neo-Marxist theory, which add an emphasis on the underlying structures of capitalism to help explain the spatial organization of activity.[20] In contrast to standard location theory, which is often criticized for its static abstractions, structural approaches stress issues of global change and the key role of historical processes. They merge traditional economic geography with newer theories of economic and political development. The world is conceptualized, typically, as an economic hierarchy comprising a rich core, an economically impoverished periphery, and frequently a semiperiphery in between.

In principle, structural models focus on process rather than place. As one leading exponent has written: "This core-periphery pattern . . . refers to complex processes and not directly to areas, regions, or states. . . . Space itself can be neither core nor periphery in nature. Rather there are core and periphery processes which structure space." (Taylor 1993:19). In practice, however, dialogue is almost always conducted in territorial terms, focusing on how or when various areas, regions, or states move from one rank of the hierarchy to another. The role of physical location remains central.

These different approaches thus provide little direct help to aid us in deterritorializing the study of money. Indirectly, however, studies of economic geography, particularly of the structural variety, do offer two important insights. One is that the notion of place may be detached from a strict equivalence with nation-states. Location may refer to areas as small as a neighborhood, as large as a continent, not just to sovereign entities defined by fixed political frontiers. The other is that a homonomous mode of spatial organization is not inconsistent with behavioral links and core-periphery relationships based on power, influence, and authority. Spaces may be structured hierarchically, not just in terms of functional equivalence. Both ideas, as we shall see, contribute to a more accurate representation of the geography, of money today.[21] But we are still some way from a truly satisfactory model of global currency relations.

The end of geography?

What of more specialized studies within the tradition of economic geography focusing specifically on money and finance? Although the notion of monetary geography is not part of the customary language of social science, it is not wholly unknown either; and in recent years a scattering of younger scholars, particularly in the English-speaking world, have begun to think seriously about what new insight might be gained by reconceptualizing issues of money and finance in terms of their spatial organization.[22] Unfortunately most of these efforts too, for all the ingenuity involved, have remained tightly bound to traditional territorial imagery.

The immediate inspiration for this new work has been the remarkable revival of global financial markets in recent decades, spurred by both technological innovation and government deregulation and manifested in massive movements of currency and capital across national frontiers. The globalization of finance, we are told, has dramatically altered the geography of the world system. Monetary spaces are being systematically and fundamentally transformed by the greatly expanded array of currency choice. Yet most questions continue to be phrased in a territorial vocabulary, touching on such familiar topics as the distribution of power among states or the allocation of market activities among financial centers.[23] For many studies, in fact, the term "geography" serves as little more than stylistic windowdressing for otherwise conventional analysis.

One author, however—Richard O'Brien, an international banker—has managed to inspire some fresh thinking with a single pithy phrase: *The End of Geography*.[24] According to O'Brien, the worldwide integration of financial markets inevitably means geography's demise. In his words: "As markets and rules become integrated, the relevance of geography and the need to base decisions on geography will alter and diminish. Money, being fungible, will continue to try to avoid, and will largely succeed in escaping, the confines of the existing geography. . . . The closer we get to a global, integrated whole, the closer we get to the end of geography" (1992:2–5). O'Brien's thesis is provocative. It has spawned a vigorous debate.[25] Is he right?

At least three interpretations can be attached to his proposition. At its simplest (and least interesting) it can be construed in purely territorial terms, to mean a decline in the importance of physical location as markets are integrated by the forces of competition and technical innovation. New communications and information technologies already permit market actors to operate with impunity across national frontiers. A future can be imagined where financial services are provided and transactions conducted solely in cyberspace. This appears to be the meaning that O'Brien himself had in mind. Again in his words: "The end of geography, as a concept applied to international financial relationships, refers to a state of economic development where geographical location no longer matters" (1992:1). In effect, all the world's markets will collapse into a single organic entity, and business will be done anywhere and everywhere, regardless of place.

Such a scenario, however, strains credulity. The importance of place will not be erased completely so long as agglomeration economies can be gained from locating related production and service operations in close proximity. Benefits include the more efficient use of information where contact between market agents is facilitated, the spreading of costs of needed public utilities and infrastructure, and the ready availability of specialist skills and support functions. Even O'Brien admits that "certain activities will still be transacted within a relatively limited physical area, in which a collection of expertise is valuable. . . . Where deals require the personal touch . . . location of the players will still matter" (1992:76). It is no accident that financial markets historically gather together in a few select locales; nor that financial centers, once established, generally resist encroachment by newer rivals for long periods of time. As Ron Martin has argued, "global integration does not spell the 'end of geography' as far as the overwhelming locational and trading influence of the world's financial centres is concerned."[26] Rational actors will continue to be attracted to certain specific places so long as gains exceed the costs of congestion.

In a second sense the End of Geography can be understood in political terms, referring to the decline of state authority that many scholars attribute to financial globalization and the growing influence of "stateless" markets in monetary affairs.[27] The more public policy is hemmed in by the actions of private actors, the less relevant are the legal borders traditionally drawn between political jurisdictions. Ultimately, all power might be drained off in favor of transnational capital. The territorial state, as Charles Kindleberger once predicted, would then be "just about through as an economic unit" (1969:207). But this interpretation too strains credulity. As I have argued elsewhere (B. Cohen 1996), the more plausible scenario is rather less dramatic—a world of shared governance and persistent tension on both sides of the state-market divide. National monetary authority is undoubtedly under challenge, but it is not yet ready to be tossed into the dustbin of history.

Finally, in a third sense, the End of Geography may be interpreted in cognitive terms, as a shorthand expression for a long-term shift in the way we think about monetary spaces. Herein lies the real value of O'Brien's arresting proposition. The spatial organization of finance is clearly about more than just the location of business activity or the constraints on state authority (both matters essentially grounded in traditional territorial imagery). Fundamentally, it is about the transactional networks that undergird the world's markets for money and capital—the functional domains within which individual currencies operate. The issue is not that borders have become less relevant; it is that their very meaning has been transformed. O'Brien compels us to reconsider how to conceptualize the structure and governance of monetary relations.

More than a quarter-century ago the futurologist Alvin Toffler anticipated O'Brien when he too spoke of the "demise of geography"—caused, he said, by the marked rise of personal and professional mobility in the global economy after World War II. Loyalties and commitments were "shifting from place-related social structures (city, state, nation or neighborhood) to those (corporation, profession, friendship, network) that are themselves mobile, fluid, and, for all practical purposes, place-less." The mobility of the "new nomads," in effect, "stirred the pot so thoroughly that the important differences between people are no longer strongly place-related" (1970:84). Is the mobility of capital any different? With financial globalization comes increased cross-border currency use and competition, diminishing the importance of place in determining who uses what money, when, and for what purpose. Geography does not end as a result; O'Brien and Toffler are wrong about that. But geography is effectively deterritorialized, freed from strict dependence on physicial location. O'Brien's contribution is to underscore the critical limitations of conventional territorial interpretations of currency space.

A Flow-Based Model

To deterritorialize the study of monetary geography, we need a clear distinction between physical and functional notions of space—the former tied to location or place, the latter to networks of transactions or relationships. Currency domains, properly speaking, are *social* spaces, defined not by political frontiers but by the range of each money's effective use and authority: "spaces-of-flows," to use an increasingly popular expression, rather than the more conventional "spaces-of-places."[28] Such a distinction is crucial to a new and more useful model of monetary geography, what we may call a *flow-based model* of currency relations. The dimensions of currency space are more accurately measured not by the standard coordinates of longitude and latitude but by supply and demand: the behavior and decisions of diverse agents, including governments, in the global marketplace for money.

Admittedly, a flow-based model is not easy to visualize. A kind of "virtual geography," it certainly cannot be drawn easily on a map.[29] But the network idea offers a sounder basis for understanding money's spatial organization than does the traditional territorial state; and it certainly provides greater insight into the underlying structures of power and governance in currency relations.

Spaces as networks

The distinction between physical and functional space is not new. Fully half a century ago, the economic historian François Perroux was highlighting the contrast between "banal" notions of physical space and more abstract ideas of *economic* space, which he defined primarily as a "field of forces." "Modern mathematics," he wrote, "has become accustomed to consider the abstract relations which define mathematical beings, and so to give the name 'spaces' to these structures of abstract relations" (1950:91). Economists should learn to do the same lest they seriously misrepresent the world they purport to explain. In Perroux's words: "A banal sense of space location creates the illusion of the coincidence of political space with economic and human space. . . . Thus it comes about that pathological doctrines . . . present themselves as supported by the admitted facts of a sound common sense" (1950:90).

More recently, a new generation of economic geographers, concerned that their field was becoming increasingly stale, has begun to stress the same point. Traditional, place-bound "topological presuppositions," they argue, need to be supplemented or replaced by newer imageries more functional than physical in nature. Thrift and Olds (1996) predict that much future work in economic geography will indeed focus on such abstractions as networks and flows, just as Perroux had urged.

Interestingly, among the most important of the abstract economic spaces emphasized by Perroux was *monetary* space—a field of forces "seen more easily in terms of a 'network' of payments." Given the central importance of money in human civilization, he maintained, the notion of monetary space "deserves to be scrutinized and analyzed" (1950:97–98). Yet in practice his advice has long been neglected.[30] Only recently have some rudimentary attempts been made to escape the limits of the Westphalian model of monetary geography.

The anthropologist Appadurai, for example, writes of "finanscapes"—imaginary landscapes generated by the movement of vast amounts of capital "through national turnstiles at blinding speed" (1990:8). Similarly, the geographers Andrew Leyshon and Nigel Thrift talk of "actor-networks" created by market agents interacting through the medium of money, which they characterize as "the chief structures of governance in the international financial system" (1997:298). Elsewhere, Thrift describes the world of money as a "skein of networks," a "new topology that makes it possible to go almost anywhere that networks reach" (1995:29, 33). A sociologist, Nigel Dodd, emphasizes "the utility of the monetary network for empirical and analytical purposes" (1994:xxiii). And Stephen Kobrin, a management professor, describes the world financial market as a construct "in electronic rather than geographic space . . . a network integrated through electronic information systems" (1997a:158).

Unfortunately, in most such discussions the concept of network remains underdeveloped, serving in effect as little more than a convenient metaphor for each author's particular intellectual concerns. None of these observers makes use of the new literature on the economics of networks, developed largely in France, where theorists have finally begun to explore systematically the practical implications of a functional approach to the organization of spatial relations. Just two sources, to my knowledge, have so far tried to apply this new network theory directly to the analysis of currency issues.[31] What we need is more work along these lines, to refine the notion of monetary networks and to spell out in detail their potential economic and political consequences.

The notion of authoritative domain

To formalize the notion of monetary networks, we need to distinguish clearly among three possible meanings of currency domain:

(1) *Territorial domain.* This is a money's traditional "space-of-place," defined by the political jurisdiction of issuing governments. It corresponds to the conventional physical imagery of political geography and is the basis of the standard, state-centric Westphalian model.

(2) *Transactional domain.* This is money's relational "space-of-flows," defined by the range of each currency's direct use for various monetary purposes, whether in its country of origin or elsewhere. It corresponds directly to the alternative, functional imagery of transactional networks and appears to be the basis for the rudimentary suggestions of Arjun Appadurai and others.

(3) *Authoritative domain.* This is a new concept, meant to combine transactions and territoriality—the functional dimension as well as the physical—in a single amalgam of use and authority. The notion captures the critical role of not just one but both major influences on monetary geography, markets and governments.[32]

The notion of authoritative domain serves as the core variable in a flow-based model of monetary geography. To be fully comprehensive, analysis cannot focus alone on the direct use of currency for various purposes—transactional domains—any more than it can on traditional territorial domains. A purely transactional domain is the approach typical of empirical studies of international money,[33] and it certainly seems to capture a functional conception of geography. But such an approach, in fact, is partial and potentially misleading, since it neglects the indirect connections among monetary spaces that result from competition and hierarchical relationships. We cannot forget the systems of power and governance that are implicit in alternative configurations of monetary space.

Currency relations, being competitive, are a matter not just of use but also of *authority*. Elements of dominance and dependence clearly enter the picture too, as a result of either market forces or political decision. A complete model must take due account of such indirect influences and not just of the more obvious direct determinants of monetary geography.

Conceptually, therefore, we need to think of more than just the range of transactions for which a given currency may perform the standard functions of money. We must, in addition, think of transactions over which the currency may exercise a significant degree of effective influence, either formally or informally. That is what the notion of authoritative domain captures, encompassing hierarchical links between currencies as well as their individual networks of use. Authoritative domains may be either greater or smaller than transactional domains, depending on the links that exist between separate moneys.

To illustrate, consider a country where for one reason or another residents begin to favor a foreign currency for various domestic purposes. The process is known as currency substitution. In effect, the home money's transactional domain is correspondingly diminished. International competition directly erodes its authoritative domain while enhancing the authoritative domain of the foreign currency. Much the same effect, however, can be achieved indirectly, even in the absence of overt substitution, if external financial linkages are sufficiently strong. Imagine, for instance, that financial markets at home are functionally tied to those of a larger and wealthier neighbor; or that the home government has chosen to peg its exchange rate, formally or informally, to a stronger foreign currency. Either way, a degree of control over the domestic money has in effect been ceded to a dominant currency elsewhere. Local money may continue to function normally within the national economy, preserving its transactional domain. But the money's authoritative domain is nonetheless eroded by the expansion of the foreign currency's influence.

In a competitive and hierarchical world, the notion of authoritative domain is more suitable than either territorial or transactional domain for formal analytical purposes. Admittedly, it cannot be easily operationalized for empirical research. The data simply do not exist to accurately report all cross-border use of currencies, let alone more subtle authority relationships. But neither is authoritative domain just another convenient metaphor for talking about money; and it is plainly superior to traditional approaches as a way to explore structures of governance and the role of power in currency relations.

The Westphalian model in perspective

Formalization of the concept of authoritative domain not only generalizes our mental map of monetary geography. It also enables us to put the conventional Westphalian model in perspective.

The hallmark of the state-centric Westphalian model, the strictly territorial currency, is the equivalent of a transactional network confined exclusively to the borders of a single sovereign state—a condition that I have already described as, increasingly, a very special case. Monetary domains would be neatly divided spatial packages only if each government were able to maintain monopoly control over not just the issue of money but also its use; that is, over demand as well as supply. But we know that is no longer true. Governments today are less and less capable of preserving even a modicum of monetary autarky; in a world of extensive cross-border competition among currencies, authority is not exercised solely by the state. On the contrary, private actors too play a key role, through their choices among vehicles to use for various monetary purposes. Generally, therefore, markets and governments share power in the shaping and governance of money's spaces. As one source has commented:

> In the international economy demand factors play a much more important role in the determination of which currencies are being used. . . . Since there is no supranational authority that can impose the use of a single currency, these issues are decided in the market place, by the decisions and actions of public and private agents of all countries. (Alogoskoufis and Portes 1992:274)

Governments may not welcome this role of markets, of course. States generally are no less concerned about their ability to manage money than they are about other dimensions of their putative national sovereignty. Hence within the limits set by resource capabilities and the strategic environment of interstate rivalry, most governments do actively seek to preserve as much monopoly control as possible, either on their own or in cooperation; and they do so whatever the nature of the domestic political regime. A sovereign money is valued everywhere, for reasons we will explore in the next chapter. For now, it is enough to note that if governments had their way, most currency spaces would indeed be defined in strictly territorial terms. Such spaces would be coterminous with national boundaries and as numerous as states themselves decide.

Markets, on the other hand, prefer the efficiency benefits of competition, as the growing pervasiveness of cross-border currency use around the globe amply demonstrates. If market actors had their way, the number of separate moneys would certainly be smaller than governments prefer, and the boundaries of their domains would by no means coincide with established political frontiers. The reasons for these prefences also will be explored in later chapters.

Ultimately, as we shall see, monetary geography depends on market behavior as well as on political authority, each side playing a critical role in an ongoing process. We shall also see that governance is not a matter of state *versus* society, as students of monetary relations so often pose the issue,[34] but rather of state (whether functioning as principal or as agent) *interacting with* societal forces in the social spaces created by money's transactional networks. Logically, therefore, we can conceive of a broad range of alternative configurations.

In this context the Westphalian model, enforced solely by governments, can be seen for what it really is—a limiting case at one extreme. At the opposite extreme is a world of unrestricted currency competition, a system of effectively deterritorialized money shaped exclusively by market forces—"denationalized" money as the idea was called by its best known advocate, the Austrian Friedrich Hayek, a Nobel laureate in economics (Hayek 1976, 1990). Hayek's influential laissez-faire views have been echoed by monetary specialists in both Europe and the United States, who question why governments should have any role at all in the creation and management of money.[35] The Westphalian model is a special case because it absolutely privileges state power over society. Denationalized money is an equally special case because it does the reverse, absolutely privileging markets over governmental authority.

In practice, of course, outcomes fall somewhere between these two polar opposites, with transactional networks embodying the reciprocal impacts of both state and market behavior. Political and economic implications, accordingly, are apt to be quite different from those suggested by either the Westphalian model or its equally extreme free-competition counterpart. The great advantage of a flow-based model is that it can encompass all possible spatial variations, including the two special cases of territorial and denationalized money, within a single framework. It is also unbound by time: it is general enough to be used to study monetary geography in any historical period, not just in our own day. Much new insight, I submit, can be gained from this reformulation of our standard mental images.

A new and more comprehensive model of monetary geography is indeed possible, if we build on the key distinction between physical and functional notions of currency space. A traditional territorial imagery, it is clear, conceals more than it reveals about structures of power and governance in a world of currency competition. By contrast, the alternative notion of authoritative domain, based on deterritorialized networks of transactions and relationships, offers us a major opportunity to improve our understanding of the politics of money today.

Territorial Money

"There are few examples of national governments that have not sought to enforce a single monetary standard within their domain of political authority."
Michael Mussa, "Macroeconomic Policy Implications of Currency Zones," 1991

Although it is fast becoming obsolete, the Westphalian model continues to dominate our thinking about international monetary relations. Even most specialists, IMF research director Michael Mussa among them, still mislead us by basing their discussions on a mental image of strictly territorial currencies.[1] The advantage of the One Nation/One Money myth is clear. Like the assumption of perfect competition in standard economic theory, it provides a convenient starting point for analysis. Facts to the contrary can be treated simply as awkward devia- tions. But the disadvantage is equally evident. By insisting on an imaginary landscape populated by mutually exclusive sovereign moneys, the conventional approach in effect privileges the power of national governments over all other actors. Implicitly it endorses a state-centric system of governance, however much it may misrepresent reality in the process.

A Look Back

Let us begin with a brief look back, in order to place current representations in proper historical perspective. Few observers seem to realize just how recent the Westphalian model's origins are. As Robert Zevin has written: "In our modern myopia, we usually forget that a world of separate national monies was not the primeval economic garden from which we evolved" (1992:46). In fact, the idea of a strictly territorial currency was, like the nation-state itself, a very late invention. It was really only during the 1800s that governments first claimed the legitimate right to monopolize control over the issue and management of money.

The practice of sovereign coinage, of course, goes back much further—indeed, to the very dawn of modern civilization.[2] In the Western world, coins initially appeared in the Greek city-states of Asia Minor (in western Turkey) during the eighth and seventh centuries B.C.E. and were to be found everywhere in the eastern Mediterranean by 500 B.C.E. Most historians credit the first of these coins to Gyges, king of Lydia (687–652 B.C.E.), around the year 670. In the Far East, the oldest known coins originated even earlier, during the Chou dynasty that commenced in 1022 B.C.E. (Kann 1937). Once invented, coins quickly came to dominate all other instruments then in use for standard monetary purposes.

Before the nineteenth century, however, the sovereign right of coinage was hardly ever interpreted in exclusively territorial terms. Few states expected—or even, in principle, claimed—a monopoly for their own coins within their own frontiers. Quite the contrary, in fact, as has been amply documented. "The general rule," one source notes, "was that coins circulated everywhere without consideration for frontiers" (Boyer-Xambeu at al. 1994:105). Foreign coins could be used interchangeably with local money, and restrictions were only rarely imposed on what could be treated as legal tender. Currency choice was virtually unlimited. In the words of Carlo Cipolla, noted economic historian:

> Monetary sovereignty is a very recent thing. As late as the nineteenth century no western state enjoyed a complete monetary sovereignty. . . . In previous centuries . . . the basic tenet of monetary organization [was] that foreign coins had the same rights as national coins and that they could freely come in and freely circulate without any particular limitation. (1967:14).

In brief, monetary geography reflected and closely replicated the diffuse and permeable political order that we associate with the premodern era—the heteronomous world of the Middle Ages and before. Until the nineteenth century, currencies were effectively deterritorialized, and cross-border competition was the rule not the exception.

The emergence of international moneys

Not every currency circulated everywhere, of course. Most coins were of the small, fractional variety—"petty" coins generated to serve in local transactions. Minted of base metals like copper or bronze alloy, their metallic content of little intrinsic value, these tokens were not often accepted and so were rarely found outside the limited area where they were issued. Widespread use was limited to bigger "full-bodied" coins of silver or gold ("specie")—moneys whose usefulness as a medium of exchange or a store of value could be more readily assured.

Among these full-bodied moneys competition for the allegiance of users was keen, for two reasons. On the one hand there was the possibility of debasement: depreciation of the intrinsic value of coinage, accidental or otherwise, through erosion of weight or fineness. On the other hand, there was also the possibility of a shift in the commodity price of silver or gold, which would alter the relative attractiveness of coins minted from either metal. From these contingencies arose the famous proposition known as Gresham's Law, "Bad money drives out good," which predicts that where the intrinsic values of separate moneys, as determined by market forces, diverge from their nominal values, the money of higher intrinsic value will be withdrawn from circulation and hoarded in anticipation of a rise in price.[3] No one wants to give up a coin that is likely to be worth more in the future.

Over time, however, as everyone sought the same "good" money, market favorites tended to develop, creating a hierarchy among full-bodied moneys. Typically, just one coin would eventually emerge as the dominant international money—the winner in a demand-driven process of natural selection.[4] This Darwinian favorite would enjoy an authoritative domain extending far beyond the jurisdiction of the sovereign entity that issued it. Other moneys would then offer the ultimate flattery, imitation, patterning themselves on the principal features of the dominant coin. As Cipolla writes:

> If one looks more closely at the mass of existing and circulating big coins, at their types and their characteristics, one realizes that indeed they were all more or less international currencies, but (1) that there always existed one among them that predominated as the international currency and everywhere enjoyed much more prestige, being much more eagerly demanded and much more easily accepted, and (2) that most of the other big coins in circulation and issued in the different states were nothing but a more or less faithful copy of the prevailing one, imitating its weight, its fineness, and often even the design and inscriptions. (1967:15)

The first genuinely international currency, the silver drachma of Athens, established its predominance as early as the fifth century B.C.E. (Ederer 1964: chap. 6; Chown 1994: chap. 12). With the head of Athena on one side and an owl, the sign of the goddess, on the reverse, the "owl" was by far the most prestigious coin of its day. It continued to be widely circulated and imitated long after the influence of Athens itself had faded—indeed, well into the time of the Roman Empire, whose own (frequently debased) currency, the denarius, was generally considered suspect. According to the historian Elgin Groseclose:

> The Athenian drachma . . . became the standard coin of Greek trade, and through the Alexandrine conquests the standard for Asia. Athenian drachmas moreover found their way into such distant parts of the world as India and northern Europe. Following the absorption of Greece into the Roman Empire, it became the model for the Roman denarius, which was originally minted at an equivalent weight and fineness

. . . [H]owever, the Greek drachma was preferred to the fluctuating Roman coinage, particularly for the Indian trade, and consequently we find it minted, under imperial auspices, far into the period of Roman imperialism. While the Roman denarius was constantly being depreciated . . . the drachma, by the purity of its standard, kept alive the institutions of commerce. (1976:20–21)[5]

Following the fall of the Roman Empire, no coin was more widely accepted than the Byzantine gold solidus—later also called the nomisma and still later, under Italian influence, the bezant—which was first struck by Constantine the Great in the early fourth century. For nearly eight hundred years, the bezant could properly be called, in the words of Robert Lopez (1951), the "dollar of the Middle Ages"—the premier international currency of its time. Its circulation, according to one authority, stretched "from Ceylon to the Baltic. . . . Bezants struck with the imperial seal became the accepted medium of exchange throughout the civilized world" (Groseclose 1976:49–50). Other sources quote a sixth-century Greek monk who proudly boasted that the bezant "is accepted anywhere from end to end of the earth. It is admired by all men and in all kingdoms, because no kingdom has a currency that can be compared to it" (Lopez 1951:209; Cipolla 1967:16). Although it was partially supplanted from the seventh century onward by the dinar of the new Muslim empire—which, true to form, was designed in its likeness, though with Muslim inscriptions[6]—not until the collapse of the last shreds of the Byzantine Empire in the fifteenth century was the bezant finally and definitively eclipsed.[7]

With the Renaissance came a new generation of international currencies, starting with the golden florin of Florence, first issued in the year 1252. So called because it was stamped with the city-state's emblem, a lily (*fiorino*), the florin reigned supreme for nearly a century, until the great European crisis triggered by the Black Death of the 1340s (Cipolla 1989). "Like the drachma, denarius, and the bezant of earlier days, the florin took its place as the international money of the day," as Ederer notes (1964:90), until replaced by its Venetian rival, the golden ducat (*ducato*) named for the dukes of Venice, which first appeared in 1284. By the middle of the fourteenth century Venice's money, though similar in intrinsic value to the florin, had already overtaken the latter as the principal medium of international exchange. By the end of the century, Cipolla tells us, "even in Florence the florin, though unchanged in weight, fineness, or design, was often referred to as a ducato" (1989:13). Over the next three hundred years the ducat and its predecessor, the florin, were widely imitated elsewhere in Europe, from France, England, and the Netherlands in the west to Poland, Hungary, and even Russia in the east (Pond 1940; Groseclose 1976: chap. 5; Vilar 1976: chap. 3).

Following colonization of the New World, yet another coin arose to international preeminence—the Spanish-Mexican silver peso or *real* ("royal"), later known as the Spanish or Mexican dollar. From 1535, when the first Mexican mint was established, until well into the nineteenth century, nearly all additions to the world's silver supplies came from Spanish America, particularly Mexico. Pesos, typically in the multiple unit "pieces of eight," poured forth to become a virtually universal money, circulating widely throughout not only the Western Hemisphere but, by way of the Philippines and Goa, much of the Far East as well. For the English colonists of North America, they were almost the only coin in use and served as an explicit model for the U.S. Congress when, after the Revolutionary War, it chose to make the dollar America's basic monetary unit. (The new U.S. dollars were to be equal in value to existing pieces of eight, and so a quarter was, in popular parlance, worth "two bits.")[8] As late as 1830, according to one nineteenth-century source,[9] pesos accounted for some 22 percent of the value of all coins in use in the United States. Circulation of the Mexican dollar began to decline after the middle of the century, as it was increasingly eclipsed by its northern counterpart, and by the start of the twentieth century the silver peso was clearly destined to disappear completely from international commerce (Andrew 1904; Pond 1941b).

Dominant in the nineteenth century, of course, was Britain's pound sterling, which benefited not only from the British economy's leadership in international trade but also from the role of the City of London as the world's foremost financial center. With the end of the Napoleonic Wars in 1815, foreigners increasingly found themselves earning large incomes in Britain or in countries making payments to Britain; or alternatively making payments to Britain or to countries earning incomes there. It was only natural that commercial debts would come to be cleared through London and be denominated in sterling; and as London's capital exports grew, eventually to overshadow all other financial centers, network externalities made the pound more appealing as a longer-term store of value as well. Especially after 1860, even as much of the developed world moved toward consolidation of a global gold standard, sterling gained acceptance nearly everywhere for both transactions and investment purposes. As one early history of the currency has explained:

> In general the more connexions a country has and the stronger they are, the more connexions she is likely to attract. This meant that because Britain had very extensive trading . . . connexions, sterling would be all the more useful to a country which chose to use it; and as more people came to use it, sterling would be all the more attractive as a means of international payments to everyone. The very strength and importance of sterling attracted more strength and more importance.[10]

One of the most unusual coins to attain broad international circulation was the Maria Theresa thaler, an Austrian silver coin first minted in Vienna in 1751 for trade with the Middle East and Asia, and until recently still to be found in circulation in parts of Africa and the Arab world (Pond 1941a). The thaler (from which we derive the label *dollar*) is the classic example of a so-called trade coin—a money created solely to pay for imports and not intended for domestic use. Literally hundreds of millions were struck over the course of the nineteenth century, all bearing the date 1780 when Empress Maria Theresa died. Following the disintegration of the Austro-Hungarian Empire in 1918, rival copies were produced by enterprising Italian and Swiss manufacturers, and curiously even by Britain's Royal Mint, until the Austrian monopoly was restored by international agreement in 1961 (Hirsch 1969:297–98). More recently, however, even Austria has finally terminated its output. Today, the Maria Theresa thaler is nothing more than a collector's item.

Whatever money happened to dominate at any particular time, and however faithful its imitation by others, many other coins remained in circulation with diverse features and uncertain rates of exchange. In principle, this should have caused confusion—not to say chaos—in commercial and financial markets. How could one judge the meaning of prices with so many currencies in circulation? How could consistent accounts be maintained? In practice, however, many difficulties, though by no means all, were resolved by the more or less spontaneous emergence of so-called imaginary or ghost moneys—abstract units of account that could be used to compare the values of real currencies in actual use.[11] Most popular were diverse variations on the silver pound unit, such as the livre (French), lire (Italian), peso (Spanish), and pfund (German) as well as the British pound sterling. In effect, a distinction was created between two functions of money: the medium of exchange and the unit of account. Any number of coins could pass from hand to hand in daily transactions. Ghost moneys simplified transactions in a world of competing currencies.

The emergence of territorial moneys

Truly fundamental changes in the geography of money did not occur until well into the nineteenth century, as national governments, eager to consolidate their emerging powers, started to assert greater control over the creation and management of money. For the first time in history, the goal of a strictly territorial currency—One Nation/One Money—came to seem both legitimate and attainable.

The transformation of currency space, once begun, took hold quickly and spread rapidly. Even before the century's end, it was clear that premodernism in monetary affairs was over. The era of territorial money—the Westphalian model—had arrived.[12]

Monopoly over monetary powers was a natural corollary of broader trends in global politics at the time. The nineteenth century, greatly influenced by the experience and ideals of the American and French revolutions, was a period of rising nationalism and the general centralization of political authority within state borders. Throughout the Western world, the principles embodied in the Peace of Westphalia—above all, the concept of absolute sovereignty based on exclusive territoriality—achieved a new level of tangible expression in the emergence of increasingly autonomous and homogeneous nation-states. National governments deliberately undertook to suppress all threats to their rule, whether from powers abroad or rivals at home. Their goal was to build up the nation, as far as possible, as a unified economic and political community led by a strong central authority.

Control of money was simply a logical part of that process. As one author has commented: "Just as all rival centers of power were absorbed into one monopoly of power so too all rival sources of money were absorbed into one monopoly of money creation" (O'Mahony 1984:127). Half a century ago, in *The Great Transformation*, Karl Polanyi spoke of the intimate connection between the emergent, "crustacean" nation-state and what he called "monetary protectionism":

> Protectionism everywhere was producing the hard shell of the emerging unit of social life. The new entity was cast in the national mold, but had otherwise only little resemblance to its predecessors, the easygoing nations of the past. The new crustacean type of nation expressed its identity through national token currencies safeguarded by a type of sovereignty more jealous and absolute than anything known before. . . .
>
> Actually, the new national unit and the new national currency were inseparable . . . (1944:202–3).

Creating new territorial currencies was not easy. In fact, an enormous and sustained governmental effort was required to overcome market forces and centuries of monetary tradition. Control was implemented in two principal ways—first, by promoting the development of a robust national money; and second, by limiting the role of rival foreign currencies. One might say that these were two sides of the same coin.

On the first side, governments tried to consolidate and unify the domestic monetary order. Standardization was promoted, not only in coinage but also in the new paper banknotes that were then just coming onto the scene. In addition, all forms of money were now fixed in relation to one another and tied to a uniform metallic standard, eliminating the need for ghost moneys to alleviate confusion. The national unit of account now corresponded directly to real money in circulation. And ultimate authority over the supply of money was firmly lodged in a government-sponsored central bank, newly created or empowered to sustain both currency convertibility and the well-being of the commercial banking system (Braudel 1982, chap. 5; Goodhart 1988; Goodhart et al. 1994).

On the reverse side, increasingly prohibitive restrictions were imposed on the free circulation of foreign currencies. Most prominent were new legal-tender laws and so-called public receivability provisions. "Legal tender" is any money that a creditor is obligated to accept in payment of a debt. "Public receivability" refers to what currency may be used for remittance of taxes or to satisfy other contractual obligations to the state. As the nineteenth century progressed, coins that previously had been permitted, or even specifically authorized, to serve as legal tender had the privilege gradually withdrawn. At the same time, public receivability was gradually confined to domestic money alone. Also, and with increasing frequency, governments curtailed or suspended their commitment to accept foreign coins freely for conversion at the national mint. And ultimately, in most countries, the local circulation of foreign currency was banned altogether, at least formally.

The experience of the United States was typical. Until mid-century, the Mexican dollar and several other foreign currencies (including the gold coins of Britain, France, Portugal, and Brazil) not only circulated widely in the United States but were even explicitly protected by Federal legislation that dated back to 1793. During the 1850s, however, new U.S. silver and copper coins were introduced; they were supposed to eliminate all foreign elements from the money supply. In 1857 rates were fixed at which, for a limited time, the Treasury would accept foreign money for reminting into U.S. currency. After 1861 the dollar became the country's sole legal tender, although it was to be another half-century before the country's paper money would be standardized—with the creation of the Federal Reserve System, America's own central bank.

In Britain this process started even earlier, with coinage reforms enacted after the Napoleonic Wars and later with the Bank Charter Act of 1844, which finally consolidated the central position of the Bank of England in the national financial system. Fully fledged territorial currencies also began to emerge elsewhere in Europe, and in Japan, during the second half of the century; and later, in the early 1900s, in the British Empire and throughout Latin America. By the middle of the twentieth century, the exclusive monetary authority of national governments had become universally recognized and enshrined in international law. When the great wave of decolonization got under way after World War II, ultimately bringing dozens of new states onto the global stage, few even questioned the assumption that each nation might legitimately aspire to create its own central bank and territorial money.

The Political Economy of Territorial Money

In historical terms the Westphalian model of monetary geography has enjoyed a short life. From its beginnings in the nineteeth century, it reached its apogee during the Great Depression and the years following World War II, when exchange and capital controls were widely used to reinforce the exclusive role of each state's currency within its own borders. Never before had governments come so close to autarky in the management of their monetary affairs. In more recent years, by contrast, as currency barriers have come down and financial markets have expanded across the globe, the array of currency choice has greatly widened; and monetary sovereignty, as a result, has as in earlier times become increasingly diffuse and permeable. The transience of the historical experience cannot be overemphasized. In Robert Zevin's words: "The century from 1870 to 1970 was an episode in which national governments briefly held the high ground in their struggle to control money" (1992:46). Today, once more, we find ourselves in a world of currency competition and dynamic change—a far cry from the fixed and strictly territorial organization of currency spaces we still conventionally assume.

The intimate connection between political nationalism and territorial money, so heavily stressed by Polanyi and others, serves to highlight the state-centric regime of representation implicit in the Westphalian model. The interests of sovereign governments, whatever the nature of the domestic political regime, are clearly privileged in relation to other societal actors. Power is derived from a monetary monopoly through at least four different channels.

Political symbolism

First, a territorial currency promotes a sense of collectivity useful to rulers who may be wary of internal division or dissent. It is easier to centralize political authority insofar as citizens all feel themselves bound together as members of a single social unit—all part of the same "imagined community," in Benedict Anderson's resonant phrase. Anderson stresses that states are made not just through force but through loyalty, through voluntary commitments to a joint identity. A nation, someone once quipped, is "a people with a common confusion as to their origins and a common antipathy to their neighbors" (Harmelink 1972). The critical distinction between Us and Them can be heightened by all manner of tangible symbols: flags, anthems, postage stamps, public architecture, even national sports teams. Among the most potent of these tokens is money, as the Italian economist Tommaso Padoa-Schioppa has noted:

> John Stuart Mill once referred to the existence of a multiplicity of national moneys as a "barbarism". . . . One could perhaps talk of a tribal system, with each tribe being attached to its own money and attributing it magical virtues . . . which no other tribe recognizes (1993:16).

A currency's magical virtues were appreciated even in the earliest days of minted coins, which used images of monarchs and emperors to celebrate sovereign majesty and often were designed by the best artists of the day. During the nineteenth century, national money was similarly employed to advance the revolutionary ideals of community, equality, and unity. In the newly independent United

States, for instance, coins bore the inscription "E Pluribus Unum"—From Many, One. In revolutionary France, the franc replaced the coinage of the ancien régime, with inscriptions written in the French language rather than in Latin. And throughout the world, as paper money grew in popularity, notes were decorated with various kinds of nationalist emblems and images.

Eric Helleiner (1996a, 1997b) highlights two key ways in which an exclusive territorial currency served to enhance a sense of national identity. First, because the currency was issued by the central government or its central bank, money acted as a daily reminder to citizens of their connection to the state and their oneness with it. And second, by virtue of its universal, daily use, it underscored the fact that everyone was part of the same social entity—a role not unlike that of a single national language, which many governments also actively promoted in the new age of nationalism. A common money helped to homogenize diverse and often antagonistic social groups. It was, in the words of Karl Marx, a "radical leveller" that "does away with all distinctions" associated with traditional societal relations (1864:132). In a short time, the notion of a national money became virtually inseparable from the idea of sovereign statehood.

Nor has the symbolic value of money faded in more recent times despite the growth of cross-border currency use. In the popular mind, there is still a strong bond between money and nation. Witness, for example, the haste with which a variety of brand new currencies, however unsound, were introduced by the successor states of the former Soviet Union after the disintegration of the Evil Empire in 1991. Though other factors were involved in the breakup of the ruble zone, as we shall see in Chapter 4, a foremost motivation was clearly to assert a new national identity. A national money represented tangible proof of one's rightful place in the family of nations. Old Soviet rubles were quickly replaced with new paper notes carrying, in the words of the *New York Times* (Berliner 1995), "images of mosques, Madonnas and musicians [instead of] workers, soldiers and farmers." Commented a former director of the U.S. Bureau of Engraving and Printing: "Money is history in your hands. . . . New governments want to represent the history of their country and show that they have had a significant change of administration."[13]

Witness likewise the widespread popular resistance that has persisted across much of the European Union, particularly in Britain and Germany, to the prospect of a new common currency replacing existing moneys. Though other factors are involved here, one consideration surely is the political symbolism involved. As the Archbishop of Canterbury, a determined foe of monetary union, reportedly insisted: "I want the Queen's head on the banknotes. . . . The point about national identity is a very important one. For me, being British is deeply important. I don't want to become French or German."[14]

For precisely this reason, the officials responsible for planning Europe's joint currency, to be called the Euro, have had a difficult time coming up with a design for the new banknotes which would not offend existing national sensibilities. "European symbols are not easy to find," the head of the EU's embryonic central bank is reported to have said. "What is really European, without raising nationalistic objections? Even birds are not exactly the same from one country to another."[15] In the end, after extensive discussion and research, officials agreed to avoid anything that might even hint of specific national identity. Neither historical figures nor identifiable physical locations are to be pictured on the new bills. Rather, all images—bridges, windows, gateways, etc.—will be strictly fictitious, and the notes themselves will bear a single word: Euro. A small space will be reserved, however, for individual governments to print a national symbol on the Euros that they themselves issue.

Resistance to the Euro has also grown in Germany, where the DM has been revered since 1948, when it replaced the older Reichsmark inherited from Hitler's Nazi regime. For Germans, the new mark was not only the foundation stone of their postwar economic recovery; it has also become the most visible symbol of the new respectable Germany that was born from the ashes of World War II—"an indispensable talisman of the 'good' Germany," as one observer puts it (Shlaes 1997:188). In the words of Hans Tietmeyer, president of Germany's central bank: "The German people have a broken—an interrupted—relationship with their own history. They can't parade like others. They can't salute their flag with the same enthusiasm as others. Their only safe symbol is the mark."[16] The Euro, conversely, "has become a token, for various reasons, of everything that is seen as politically, economically and socially unpleasant," according to a prominent German journalist.[17]

Indeed, resistance to the Euro extends even to prospective EU members, such as the Balkan republic of Slovenia, which gained its independence from Yugoslavia in 1991. Despite their eagerness to join the European Union, Slovenian officials express great wariness about giving up their newly created currency, the tolar. Their nascent currency is seen as "a badge of national identity," says *The Economist* (1996d). "Having just recovered sovereignty from one federation, Slovenia is prickly about losing too much of it to what it senses may turn out to be another."

Another instructive example of currency nationalism comes from 1994, involving the peace process between Israel and the Palestine Liberation Organization (PLO). In November 1993, following the celebrated Oslo accord, Israeli and PLO diplomats had begun intensive negotiations over economic ground rules to govern rapprochement between the two sides. Before agreement was finally reached in April 1994, the talks nearly foundered on a single controversial issue: should the areas to come under PLO control, occupied by Israel since 1967, be permitted their own currency? The question was manifestly political and had little to do with economic necessity. The West Bank and Gaza Strip had been comfortably using the Israeli shekel, Jordanian dinar, and U.S. dollar for years, and there was no obvious reason why they could not continue doing so. As a news report commented at the time: "The currency debate appears more a question of principle, revolving more around Palestinian demands for symbols of sovereignty than economic reality. Economists from donor nations have said they see no economic justification for printing Palestinian money" (Simons 1994:4). In the end, to avoid deadlock, the Palestinians agreed to shelve the idea for the duration, though they did persuade Israel to accept creation of a Palestinian monetary authority to regulate banks and foreign-currency transactions—in effect, the nucleus of a future central bank.

The Israelis may have been particularly sensitive to the symbolism involved in this debate because of their own unpleasant experience of hyperinflation just a few years earlier, which had led some observers to question why Israel needed its own national money. Why not use some more stable currency, like America's dollar, instead? Such suggestions proved, to say the least, unpopular. As economist Lawrence Klein (1993:113) later wrote: "When an Israeli minister [Finance Minister Yoram Aridor] suggested . . . that Israel 'dollarize' in order to cope with uncontrolled inflation and other economic ills, that minister had to leave the government. It was unthinkable that a proud independent nation could be without its own currency." Another source (Glasner 1989:31–32) reports the suggestion of one politician, not at all unusual at the time, that if the idea were to be implemented Israel might as well start flying the American flag and singing the "Star-Spangled Banner"!

In Africa the symbolic power of money was demonstrated in Zaire (since renamed the Democratic Republic of the Congo), where the rebellious province of East Kasai long showed its resistance to the authority of the central government by refusing to make use of the official Zairian currency (French 1996). Indeed, before its overthrow in 1997 the crumbling regime of President Mobutu Sese Seko could get hardly anyone to accept its newly printed banknotes, contemptuously referred to as "prostates" after the site of the ailing dictator's advanced cancer (French 1997). In Turkey, money's symbolic power was demonstrated in 1996 by the eventual winner of the national parliamentary election, Necmettin Erbakan, leader of the Islamist Welfare Party. Perhaps inspired by the dinar of the first Muslim empire, Erbakan campaigned on a platform that included a prominent pledge to seek creation of a new "Islamic currency."

Perhaps the most vivid recent example, however, involved the Republic of Croatia, another former Yugoslav republic, following its success in fending off military forces from its arch-enemy, Serbia, and Serbia's Montenegrin allies. In 1994 the Croatian government decided to replace the Yugoslav dinar, then still the principal money circulating in Croatia,[18] with a newly created currency of its own—hardly a controversial decision in itself, given that Croatia's Serbian foes in Belgrade still controlled the dinar supply. "Dependence on the Yugoslav dinar meant dependence on Belgrade," the Croatians argued, not unreasonably

(Brozovic 1994:3). Zagreb, Croatia's capital, did not want its access to currency controlled by an enemy.

Highly controversial, however, was the decision to label the new currency the "kuna"—a Croatian word for the marten, a small forest animal with a valuable fur—which just happened to be the name used for the money of the fascist Ustashe regime that Nazi Germany set up to rule Croatia during World War II. The decision was defended by Zagreb as a legitimate exercise of national sovereignty. "Money is . . . the mark of national sovereignty and it mirrors the state which issues it. The symbolic role of money is one of its essential characteristics, and the name of the currency is its salient feature" (Brozovic 1994:3). For many centuries, marten pelts had played an important role in Croatia for payment in kind and even as a unit of account. But the choice brought strong protests from Croatia's Serbs and Jews, both groups whose members had been massacred in large numbers by the Ustashe between 1941 and 1945. The kuna, they pointed out, despite its long tradition, had never actually been used as the formal name of a currency—except during World War II. According to the *New York Times* (R. Cohen 1994), revival of the kuna was "certain to inflame relations with the Serbs, who have argued since the 1991 Serbian-Croatian war that their [attack against Croatia was] a necessary defense against a repetition of the ethnic persecution by the Ustashe regime." In short, a seemingly technical financial matter could become grounds for renewed war. What better illustrates the magical qualities of money?

Seigniorage

A second source of power is seigniorage, the capacity that a monetary monopoly gives national governments to augment public spending at will. Technically defined as the excess of the nominal value of a currency over its cost of production, seigniorage is an alternative source of revenue for the state, beyond what government can raise through taxation or borrowing from financial markets. Public spending financed by money creation in effect appropriates real resources at the expense of the private sector, whose purchasing power is correspondingly reduced by subsequent inflation—a privilege for government if there ever was one.

The term goes back to the Middle Ages, when coins were freely and widely minted by feudal lords—"seigneurs"—and referred originally to the difference between the circulating value of a coin and the cost of its bullion and manufacture. Any difference involved a once-for-all gain to its issuer. Later, when the privilege of minting money was centralized in national governments, the term was extended to include any duty levied by the state for converting precious metals into coinage. Such charges were intended not only to cover the cost of minting but also, and quite explicitly, to serve as a source of public revenue, which sovereigns claimed as their prerogative. And yet later, when paper money began to appear, it was generalized to describe the gain, over and above costs of production, to the issuer of any kind of currency. In the nineteenth century, when banknotes increasingly replaced coins in the money supply, governments could capture seigniorage "the old-fashioned way"—simply by running the printing presses. In the twentieth century, when most money takes the form of transferable bank deposits, seigniorage is attained more indirectly by borrowing from the central bank, which in turn creates new deposits in commercial banks. Because the effect of such money creation is almost inevitably inflationary, the process is also known popularly as the "inflation tax."[19]

The logic of the inflation tax was explained early by the English economist Sir John Hicks, speaking of the motivations of monarchs to take over the monetary franchise:

> Use of the King's money . . . was so clearly an advantage to him that . . . he would not abandon it. He had a direct profit from minting (a profit which became more considerable whenever token coinage was acceptable); but the indirect advantage that accrued was surely more important. If he could get his revenue in the form of money . . . he would be able to spend it, through the channels of trade, so as to get a flow of real goods, that had greater variety, and therefore greater "utility," than he could get directly from taxation paid in kind. (1969:68)

More recently, that same logic has blossomed into a formal theory of optimal seigniorage, by now a staple of the specialized literature in public finance.[20] The basic idea is that collection of any form of public revenue is likely to produce market distortions (so-called deadweight losses of economic welfare); moreover, the degree of distortion typically rises with use. Hence an optimizing government will exploit all available sources of revenue, including inflation as well as ordinary taxation and public borrowing, up to the point where the marginal cost of raising revenue via each of them is equalized—a practice known as "tax spreading." Seen through the lens of economic theory, inflationary finance is not necessarily an irrational public policy.

The privilege of seigniorage also makes sense from a political perspective, as a kind of insurance policy against risk—an emergency source of revenue to cope with unexpected contingencies, up to and including war (Glasner 1989; chap. 2). Decades ago John Maynard Keynes (1924) wrote: "A government can live by this means when it can live by no other." Generations later another noted British economist, Charles Goodhart (1995:452), described seigniorage as the "revenue of last resort"—the single most flexible instrument of taxation available to mobilize resources in the event of a sudden crisis or threat to national security. As Barry Eichengreen has noted: "Money can be printed to pay soldiers, to purchase war matériel, and to underwrite the other costs of a war of national defense without having to wait for tax returns to be filed or for a foreign loan to be extended" (1994:89). It would be an exceptional government that would *not* wish to retain something like the option of an inflation tax.

In practice, most governments do indeed take advantage of the revenue potential of the printing press. Estimates of seigniorage revenues as a percentage of national output among industrialized nations have ranged as high as 2–4 percent or more in Greece, Italy, Portugal, and Spain,[21] though as European inflationary pressures have receded lately, the general trend there has clearly been downward.[22] In the developing world, where inflation rates are often higher and more persistent, seigniorage revenues tend to be correspondingly greater, rising at times (again as a percentage of national output) even into the double digits (Edwards and Tabellini 1991). For some countries, especially in Latin America and sub-Saharan Africa, seigniorage has accounted for more than one-fifth of total government revenues (Fischer 1982; Cukierman, Edwards, and Tabellini 1992).

To some extent, this greater use of seigniorage by developing countries reflects familiar economic plights, such as an inefficient tax structure and primitive financial markets, both of which raise the cost of alternatives to the inflation tax. As one source has commented: "Issuing money is often a less costly way of taxing the public, especially if the administrative fiscal apparatus is inadequate or corrupt or cumbersome" (Aliber 1987:159). But behind the economics lies politics, as recent studies have demonstrated (Edwards and Tabellini 1991; Cukierman, Edwards and Tabellini 1992; Al-Marhubi and Willett 1996). The difficulties of tax collection in developing economies tend to be closely associated with political instability and polarization, which raise enforcement costs and encourage evasion. Unstable and divided polities, *faute de mieux,* generally turn to seigniorage to finance public spending more than do relatively stable and homogeneous nations. Put differently, political cohesion reduces a government's incentive to exploit its monetary monopoly to the disadvantage of its own citizenry.

Ultimately, exercise of seigniorage rests on two institutional prerequisites. First, monetary policy must be effectively subordinated, formally or informally, to fiscal policy, since in contemporary circumstances it is normally the central bank that underwrites public spending through its loans to government rather than the government itself via the printing press. For the money created by the central bank to become revenue for the state, it must be available for appropriation. That is, fiscal officials must be able to tap the resources of the monetary authority more or less on demand; in the specialist jargon, the central bank must be "dependent" (answerable to the government or vulnerable to political influence) rather than "independent." Empirical studies strongly suggest that, all else being equal, inflationary financing of public expenditures is indeed greater in countries with dependent central banks than where monetary policy is effectively autonomous (Eijffinger and De Haan 1996).

Second, there must be no convenient substitute for the domestic currency. Consistent with the state-centrism of the Westphalian model, the government's local monopoly in money must be unchallenged, and if necessary buttressed by capital controls or other measures of financial repression.[23] Only where cross-border currency competition is suppressed can fiscal authorities resort to the inflation tax unimpeded, free to erode the public's purchasing power at will. Should we be surprised, therefore, if governments do all they can to preserve their control over monetary affairs? One observer suggests that "it is the national bureaucracy who is the only loser from the loss of the right to devalue the national currency" (Jovanovic 1992:133). The view may be a bit cynical, but it is not far off the mark. Governments would not be governments if they did not seek to retain as much practical authority as possible.

Macroeconomic management

A third source of power derives from money's potential impact on "real" economic performance—aggregate output and employment. Once governments seized control of currency supply within their own territory, they gained the capacity—in principle, at least—to influence and perhaps even manage the pace of market activity. Money could be used to promote the broad prosperity and strength of the state as well as the government's own narrowly drawn fiscal requirements.

Currency territorialization equips government with two potent policy instruments. First is the money supply itself, which can be manipulated to increase or decrease levels of expenditure by domestic residents. Monetary expansion or contraction not only puts more or less money directly into the hands of individuals, to spend as they wish; it also influences outlays indirectly, via its impact on interest rates. More money means lower interest rates, encouraging credit expansion; less money, the reverse. Economists call monetary policy an "expenditure-changing" instrument—like fiscal policy, it is a tool that can be used to move the economy by altering the *total* of aggregate demand.

Second is the exchange rate—the price of home currency in terms of foreign currency—which can be manipulated to increase or decrease spending in the national economy. Lowering the official price of a currency is known as devaluation; raising it, revaluation. Market-driven variations of the exchange rate are known, correspondingly, as depreciation or appreciation. Devaluation or revaluation tends to drive up or down the local price of imports, discouraging or encouraging spending on foreign goods. It also tends to lower or raise the external price of home goods, stimulating or dampening foreign demand for exports. Both locally and abroad, expenditures are redirected either toward or away from the country's output. Economists call the exchange rate an "expenditure-switching" instrument—like the tariff, it is a tool that can be used to move the economy by altering the *direction* of aggregate demand.[24]

Early in the era of territorial money, before World War I and the Great Depression, governments mainly used their new-found management capacity to promote financial stability and fend off occasional crises in banking or capital markets. Currency supply and interest rates were used to defend the convertibility of national money at established prices in terms of gold or silver (thus fixing exchange rates internationally). Newly created or empowered central banks were encouraged to act as lenders of last resort and to provide direction to monetary affairs. Out went the old faith in money's intrinsic value. In came the widely quoted new dictum of the English journalist Walter Bagehot: "Money will not manage itself" (1873:20).

Ambitions remained comparatively modest, however, until the Keynesian revolution in economic theory, triggered by publication in 1936 of Keynes's pathbreaking *General Theory of Employment, Interest and Money.* As the economist Lawrence White has noted:

> When central banks were established in the nineteenth and early twentieth centuries, it was certainly not for the purpose of manipulating macroeconomic variables according to the full-employment precepts of recent decades. The Keynesian notion of demand management did not yet exist. (1988:302).

With his *General Theory*—which in effect invented macroeconomics—Keynes for the first time provided a systematic and intellectually persuasive rationale for monetary activism. Breaking with the past, he showed how output and employment could now be viewed as operational variables amenable to policy guidance rather than as exogenous conditions determined automatically by Say's Law that "supply creates its own demand."[25] From now on, governments might legitimately aspire to manage the "real" economy and not just financial markets. Monetary policy and the exchange rate, often bolstered by exchange and capital controls, might be used to counteract the business cycle and perhaps even fine-tune the overall pace of activity, unencumbered by concerns about the sanctity of currency values or convertibility into precious metals or even other moneys. The territorial state could assert an authority greater than ever.

More recent theoretical developments—following the so-called monetarist counter-revolution of the 1960s and 1970s—have tempered that optimism. For variations of the money supply or exchange rate to have a sustained impact on the real economy, it is now clear, there must be a lasting trade-off between inflation and unemployment.[26] That is, it must be possible to use expansionary policy, despite its potentially inflationary consequences, to reduce unemployment on a sustained basis. But that convenient assumption has been cast into some doubt, first by Milton Friedman's natural-rate hypothesis—the idea that an economy over time gravitates toward a natural rate of unemployment that is independent of inflation and cannot be changed by monetary policy—and then by rational-expectations theory, which emphasizes the alleged ability of markets to anticipate any systematic effort by government at countercyclical policy. Money is said to be strictly neutral with respect to real output over the long term, influencing only prices. At its most extreme monetarism denies the existence of any inflation-unemployment trade-off at all, even in the short term (Cagan 1992).

As in most such debates, the truth appears to lie somewhere between the more extreme versions of Keynesian and monetarist theory. In practice, empirical evidence suggests that the monetary-neutrality argument is valid, if at all, only over the very long haul. Over the shorter time horizons that interest public officials, monetary policy does in fact retain substantial influence as a tool for macro-economic management. The capacity for activism promised by a monetary monopoly may not be as ample as governments once hoped, but neither is it trivial.

Monetary insulation

Finally, power is also derived in a negative sense—from the ability a national money gives government to avoid dependence on some other provenance for this critical resource. Currency territoriality draws a clear economic boundary between the state and the rest of the world. Such boundaries enhance political authority: government is insulated from outside influence or constraint in formulating and implementing policy.

That sovereign states might use monetary relations coercively should come as no surprise. As Jonathan Kirshner recently reminded us: "Monetary power is a remarkably efficient component of state power . . . the most potent instrument of economic coercion available to states in a position to exercise it" (1995:29, 31). Money, after all, is simply command over real resources. If a nation can be denied access to the means needed to purchase vital goods and services, it is clearly vulnerable in political terms. Kirshner lists four ways in which currency dependence may be exploited by a foreign authority: (1) enforcement—manipulation of standing rules or threat of sanctions; (2) expulsion—suspension or termination of privileges; (3) extraction—use of the relationship to appropriate real resources; and (4) entrapment—transformation of the dependent state's interests. All four risks can be avoided by maintaining an autonomous money of one's own.

The hazards of relying on a foreign power for domestic currency were clearly on the minds of the Croatians after their secession from Yugoslavia in 1991, as well as the Palestinians in their negotiations with Israel in 1994; and, as we shall see in Chapter 4, quite plainly played a role in the hasty breakup of the ruble zone, too. But perhaps the most blatant example of such vulnerability in recent times involves Panama. Since its independence early in this century—in a notable exception to the Westphalian model—the country has used the U.S. dollar as legal tender for most domestic monetary purposes. Panama owes its existence to the United States, which encouraged secession from Colombia to facilitate construction of a canal across the isthmus, and it has always maintained a special relationship with Washington. Although a national Panamanian currency, the balboa, exists in principle, only a negligible amount of balboa coins actually circulates in practice. The bulk of the money supply, including all paper notes and most bank deposits, is accounted for by the dollar.[27] In the late 1980s, Panamanians learned just how exposed they were to external coercion under this monetary scheme.

In economic terms, most observers have had only praise for Panama's currency arrangement. Reliance on the dollar has created an environment of stability that has both suppressed inflation—a bane of most of Panama's hemispheric neighbors—and helped to establish the country as an important offshore financial center. In the words of one recent study:

> The system had virtually guaranteed monetary and price stability, enabling Panama to avoid the crippling bouts of inflation that have afflicted the rest of Latin America. It has also facilitated international transactions, largely because the dollar eliminates any exchange risks. And finally, the use of the dollar and consequent absence of exchange control greatly supported the growth of the international banking center (Zimbalist and Weeks 1991:68).[28]

In political terms, on the other hand, Panama was extremely vulnerable in its relations with Washington, which could of course sour at any time. Finally, in 1988, following accusations of corruption and drug smuggling against General Manuel Noriega, commander of the Panamanian armed forces, the United States used the weapon. In March, Panamanian assets in U.S. banks were frozen, and all payments or other dollar transfers to Panama were prohibited, as part of the Reagan administration's determined campaign to force Noriega from power. The impact was swift: most local banks were compelled to close, and the economy was squeezed by a severe liquidity shortage. The effect was devastating despite rushed efforts by the Panamanian authorities to create a substitute currency, mainly by issuing checks in standardized denominations that they hoped recipients would then treat as cash. The country was effectively demonetized. In the words of one former U.S. ambassador to Panama, Washington's coercive actions had done the most damage "to the Panamanian economy since Henry Morgan, the pirate, sacked Panama City in 1671."[29] Over the course of the year domestic output fell by nearly one-fifth.

The sanctions, as it happens, were not enough to dislodge Noriega on their own. Ultimately, in late 1989, Washington mounted a military invasion and temporarily occupied the country before a new, friendlier government could be installed. But there can be no doubt that the liquidity squeeze was painful and contributed greatly to pressures on Noriega. The lesson is obvious, as Lawrence Klein has prudently suggested:

> Panama . . . uses US dollars for its monetary units. As long as relations remain cordial, this is not a bad arrangement. . . . But for Panama the risk price is very high for having the convenience of US dollars. The small country would be in a better and more independent position if it had not let some of its monetary actions be governed by foreigners. (1993:112–13)

In short, if you want political autonomy, don't rely on someone else's money.

~

Recent as its origins are, the Westphalian model still exercises a strong influence on the way we think about monetary geography. It also harbors a distinctly state-centric view of the governance of world politics. Should we be surprised, then, that national governments resist any departure from strict territoriality in the organization of currency space? Though today no more than a myth, the idea of One Nation/One Money still promises much to reinforce the power of the sovereign state—a political symbol to promote national unity, an alternative source of public revenue, a tool for macroeconomic management, and insulation against foreign coercion. These are hardly boons to be given up lightly.

Subordinating Monetary Sovereignty

"There is nothing especially exotic about an economy that does not use its own money."

> Stanley Fischer, "Seigniorage and the Case for
> National Money," 1982

Even during its heyday, the Westphalian model was never absolute. One Nation/One Money may have become the standing norm, reflecting the logic of a system centered on the nation-state. But it was not necessarily expected to prevail everywhere, in every sovereign state. Governments cannot always avail themselves of all the boons of a monetary monopoly. Circumstances sometimes dictate trade-offs, requiring sacrifices of some policy goals to assure the attainment of others.

Important to note, however, is that even when unorthodox species have been admitted to money's imaginary landscape, they are usually creatures of state choice rather than market forces. Governments are still seen as the principal determinants of monetary geography: currencies are in effect akin to a child's building blocks, passive playthings to be manipulated or combined at will by political authority. Governments are assumed to behave as rational unitary actors, calculating the advantages and disadvantages of alternative monetary configurations and choosing accordingly. Gains and losses, risks and opportunities, are measured in terms of the four elements of power associated with a conventional national money: political symbolism, seigniorage, macroeconomic management, and monetary insulation. In the most formal theory, state decisionmaking is explicitly modeled as a constrained optimization problem.

Variations on the conventional Westphalian model may be classified as con-figurations that embody a vertical *hierarchy* among sovereign states and those that involve a horizontal *alliance* of national currencies. Examples of hierarchy include countries that formally use another nation's money or tie their currency to a stronger foreign money. The states at the top of the hierarchy are said to play the role of hegemon; that is, they exercise influence (hegemony) over those lower down the totem pole. The hierarchical relationship itself is typically described as a monetary bloc or a zone. Examples of alliance include countries that formally freeze their mutual exchange rates in a cooperative endeavor or replace existing national moneys with a single merged currency. Common labels for such arrangements include exchange-rate union, currency union, and monetary union.[1]

These two types, hierarchy and merger, may be called the Two Ss: respectively, *subordination* of monetary sovereignty and *sharing* of monetary sovereignty. The two are similar in that they loosen the tight bond between political nationalism and territorial money, though they continue to stress the central role of governments in shaping currency spaces. They differ substantially, however, in their underlying implications for economic and political relations. The first S is discussed in this chapter, the second in Chapter 4.

Surrender of Sovereignty

The most extreme form of subordination of monetary sovereignty—in effect, more like an unconditional surrender—is outright use of another nation's currency in lieu of a money of one's own. Panama is by no means the only state in the contemporary era to adopt a foreign currency as domestic legal tender. Similar cases have long existed in Europe, including Liechtenstein, which formally employs the Swiss franc; the nominally sovereign entities of San Marino and the Vatican, both of which rely on the Italian lira; and Monaco, where the French franc is the circulating medium. Perhaps most interesting is the Republic of Andorra, high in the Pyrenees, where both the French franc and the Spanish peseta are legal tender, reflecting the official role that neighboring France and Spain play as joint protectors of Andorran independence.

A parallel case can also be found in West Africa, where Liberia, like Panama, for many years used the U.S. dollar for most monetary purposes. Like Panama, Liberia owes its existence to U.S. initiatives; and similarly, from its conception in 1847, it maintained a special relationship with Washington, which persistently supported the country's efforts to preserve its independence in the face of French and British encroachments. During World War II, as the United States built up its military presence in Liberia, Monrovia made the dollar sole legal tender, replacing the British West African colonial coinage that had previously dominated the local money supply (Bixler 1957). Though supplemented by some small-denomination Liberian coins (also named the dollar) beginning in the 1960s, America's currency maintained its dominant role until the mid-1980s, when political turmoil and fiscal deficits led Monrovia to issue large amounts of higher-denomination coins as well as notes—a classic example of a government resorting to seigniorage as a revenue of last resort. Also true to form, Gresham's Law quickly went to work. By the end of the 1980s the U.S. dollar had almost completely disappeared from circulation, though the monetary agreement with Washington remains nominally in effect. Technically, the dollar is still the principal currency of Liberia, though it no longer actively circulates as a medium of exchange.

Other instances can be found in southern Africa, where the South African rand functions as legal tender both in Lesotho, a former British colony entirely surrounded by South Africa, and in neighboring Namibia, which received its independence from South African stewardship in 1990. In the Pacific the island republics of Kiribati, the Marshall Islands, and Micronesia still rely on foreign currencies for all domestic purposes.[2] In Asia the Indian rupee remains legal tender in the landlocked mountain kingdom of Bhutan. Interesting cases are also provided by Belarus and Tajikistan, the only two successor states of the Soviet Union that by 1998 had still not formally replaced the Russian ruble with a currency of their own. Both briefly flirted with the idea, each introducing an "interim" national ruble to circulate side by side with Russia's, but neither has yet established exclusive legal-tender status for its money. Once known as White Russia or Little Russia, Belarus has never made up its mind whether it wishes to separate from mother Russia. Tajikistan, splintered by civil war, has been effectively occupied by the Russian army since attaining nominal independence in 1991.

All of these, of course, appear to be special cases—tiny enclaves or the deferential wards of powerful patrons. All are examples of what political scientist Robert Jackson (1990) calls "quasi-states": countries whose sovereignty is more juridical than empirical.[3] Though legally constituted as nation-states and formally recognized by the international community, they lack the means or the will to provide all the elements of practical governance or to insulate themselves effectively from foreign influence. Their political independence has always been much less than absolute. Hence they lose little more in surrendering formal monetary authority beyond the symbolism of a national currency and the privilege of seigniorage. Giving up the standard instruments of macroeconomic management, money supply, and the exchange rate means little in the absence of a capacity to use such tools effectively.

On the other hand, much may be gained in at least two respects. First, administrative costs are reduced. That saving is apt to be of particular significance to poorer and diminutive sovereignties because of the diseconomies of small scale involved in an infrastructure dedicated solely to the production and management of a separate currency. Even more important, a stable relationship is achieved with a more widely circulated and generally accepted currency—one whose authoritative domain is far greater than any that these quasi-states might hope to attain with a money of their own. Management of local financial conditions is ceded to a foreign power. With luck, resulting improvements in the economic environment—as in the case of Panama for most of the twentieth century—will more than compensate for a heightened vulnerability to foreign influence.

That these are special cases does not mean that they are irrelevant. In fact, their experience holds lessons for many sovereign states, for at least three reasons. First is the great acceleration of currency use across borders in recent years—the subject of this book—which has already challenged the authoritative domain of many nominally independent moneys. As we shall see in Chapter 5, the number of local currencies now routinely facing serious competition from abroad is by no means small. In many instances, in fact, a good part of effective monetary sovereignty has *already* been surrendered. As long as governments continue to take an interest in money, therefore, the cost-benefit calculus cannot be avoided. Policymakers must decide whether the gains from increased reliance on a foreign currency, which are mainly economic, are worth the various risks or losses implied, most of which are political. Or should they take active measures to preserve or restore a domestic monopoly on money?

This dilemma has been growing for decades, at least since the emergence of the market for foreign-currency deposits—popularly known as the Euro-currency market—back in the late 1950s.[4] As the name implies, the market originated in Europe (first in London, later on the European continent) and initially involved U.S. dollars, labeled Euro-dollars, almost exclusively. Already by the 1960s, for the emerging European Community, the Euro-dollar had acquired some of the characteristics of a common currency—"the informal common currency of the Common Market," as I called it in an early discussion.[5] In effect, the Community was becoming part of the dollar's authoritative domain. But because this would mean reliance on a currency supply managed by America's Federal Reserve rather than by Europe's own central banks, it was bound to reduce the effectiveness of European monetary policies. "The problem," I wrote in 1963, "is not one of geography but of sovereignty. . . . Because the borders of the area within which the Euro-dollar circulates do not coincide with the borders of the Common Market, efforts to control liquidity within the union must inevitably [be compromised]." The Europeans, like many others, are still wrestling with the consequences of that type of challenge.

A second reason is the lack of credibility of many present-day national moneys—especially those in East-Central Europe and the former Soviet republics, the so-called transition economies where in most cases adequate banking facilities and experience at monetary management are still in short supply. In such circumstances, many observers have asked, why insist on a national currency at all? Why not use some other country's money instead? For these states, the challenge has been not to preserve monetary stability but to create it. And what better way than to "hire" some widely accepted foreign currency, such as the dollar (with or without the "Euro–" prefix), for the job? In the words of James Meigs: "Solutions to many of the monetary problems of the former Soviet Union and Eastern Europe that Western advisors agonize over are right under their noses in the Euro-currency markets. . . . Using Euro–dollars, without exchange controls, would greatly speed up the clearing of international trade and capital transactions."[6] Even if only an interim device, to aid the transition to a national money, such an approach would surrender the presumed benefits of nominal sovereignty—including political symbolism, seigniorage, and monetary insulation—for the gains of financial stability and a savings in administrative costs. Surely the experiences of countries that have already chosen to hire a foreign currency would be relevant to such a decision.

A final reason, more specific to today's European Union, is suggested by the EU's current efforts to create a new joint currency, the Euro—not to be confused with the Euro–dollar[7]—even as it negotiates to add up to a dozen new partners in an area stretching from the eastern Mediterranean (Malta, Cyprus) through East-Central Europe to the Baltics (Estonia, Latvia, and Lithuania). As we shall see in Chapter 4, not even all of the EU's present members will join the anticipated Economic and Monetary Union (EMU) when it begins. Only Germany, France, the Benelux countries (Belgium, Luxembourg, and the Netherlands), and Austria—often labeled EMU's "hard core"—have always been thought sure to be among the initial "ins." How then might the "outs," especially those countries not yet formally admitted to the EU, enhance their prospects for eventual participation? For some observers, the optimal solution lies in a unilateral surrender of monetary sovereignty: voluntary adoption of the EU's new joint money in place of existing currencies (Frankel and Wyplosz 1995/96; Dornbusch 1996). For any government contemplating such a course, the precedents established by Panama and others are anything but special.

Subjugation of Sovereignty

Other possibilities exist, of course. Choices are not restricted simply to the stark alternatives of your own money or someone else's. Between these extremes there are further options based on a more or less firm bond to a strong foreign currency—an anchor currency or reserve currency. Rather than surrender monetary sovereignty unconditionally, a government might embrace a more limited degree of subordination: an exchange-rate rule of some kind. Domestic money remains in existence, but its value is tied directly to a more widely circulated counterpart elsewhere. Possibilities fall along a continuum, ranging from the tight linkage of a formal currency board to flexible and informal pegged-rate arrangements. Each configuration has its particular trade-offs between potential gains and losses.

Currency boards

Formally closest to outright use of a foreign money is the currency board, an institutional arrangement constructed in effect to sustain the *illusion*, even if not the *reality*, of national monetary sovereignty. A country with a currency board retains the privilege of issuing a money of its own, to function for all the usual purposes inside the territorial frontiers of the state. The supply of local money, however, is strictly tied to the availability of a designated foreign currency. The authoritative domain of the local currency, therefore, is a good deal smaller than its nominal domain and, depending on how the currency board actually operates, may even be zero. In effect, local money simply becomes foreign money by another name—"a proxy for the reserve currency," as one source puts it (Osband and Villanueva 1993:215).

The essence of the currency board, in its purest form, is a clear and publicly observable monetary rule, usually backed by formal legislative mandate. The rule normally combines three key features: (1) a fixed exchange rate against an anchor currency, (2) unrestricted convertibility into that currency, and (3) full foreign-currency backing for any increase in the liabilities of the central monetary authority—what economists call "high-powered money" or "base money," comprising notes and coins and the cash reserves of commercial banks.[8] Together, these three features mean that unlike a central bank, a currency board can neither devalue its currency nor create money at will. Indeed, in principle, it has no discretionary powers at all. No money may be generated by purchasing domestic assets. No inflation tax may be imposed by lending to the government. No exchange-rate adjustment is possible in the event of a capital outflow or a current-account deficit. Instead, the currency board is wholly passive, accommodating any variation in the supply of or demand for foreign currency. The country can neither manage its own macroeconomic affairs nor insulate itself from external influence. Its effective monetary authority is minimal.[9]

Such passivity was of course precisely the point of currency boards when they were first developed by the British government, in the nineteeth century, to help stabilize London's financial relations with its overseas dependencies. Like the Empire itself, currency boards were a product not of deliberate design but of haphazard experimentation.[10] Although a prototype was set up for the Indian Ocean island of Mauritius as early as 1849, the definitive form was attained only in 1912 with establishment of the West African Currency Board for the Gambia, Gold Coast (now Ghana), Nigeria, and Sierra Leone. The West African scheme subsequently served as a model for London's other overseas possessions. By guaranteeing the convertibility of local currency into the pound sterling on demand at a fixed rate, currency boards eliminated all foreign-exchange risk from trade with the mother country and effectively integrated colonial financial institutions into Britain's domestic banking system. British banks could operate as if foreign dependencies were nothing more than localities of the United Kingdom. This British model was subsequently emulated by other colonial powers as well as by some nominally sovereign states, among them the free city of Danzig in 1923–24 and Ireland from 1928 until 1943.

But such passivity was renounced once the great epoch of decolonization began after World War II. Currency boards may have assured former colonies some degree of monetary stability, but they were widely resented as symbols of imperial oppression. The absence of a central bank with discretionary powers served, it was thought, merely to perpetuate dependency and stifle development. The requirement that all currency-board assets be held in a foreign money seemed to mean fewer resources for domestic investment; fixed conversion rates into foreign money precluded flexibility in the management of local monetary conditions. So why not seize control of the creation of money, just as the colonial powers had themselves done in the nineteeth century? As the monetary historian Anna Schwartz has written: "It became an article of faith that independence would enable former colonies, once freed from imperial control, to utilize their resources more productively and thereby achieve faster economic development. . . . Currency boards did not fit this vision" (1993:170).

In any event, as a matter of principle, continued monetary dependence seemed inconsistent with newly won political independence. The Westphalian model now reigned supreme, and every state's sovereign right to its own exclusive currency had become a universal norm. Very quickly, therefore, currency boards were abandoned in favor of indigenous arrangements, most often based on One Nation/One Money. The only exceptions of any note were in East Asia, where both Singapore and Brunei chose to preserve a form of currency board even after attaining independence;[11] and in Djibouti, a former colony of France in East Africa, a currency board has existed since 1949 (though, curiously, it is linked to the U.S. dollar not the French franc). Except for a brief interlude in the 1970s, a currency board was also maintained in the former crown colony of Hong Kong, even after its return to Chinese sovereignty in 1997. Elsewhere, the currency board was rejected as a relic of a bygone era.

More recently, however, currency boards have made something of a comeback. The first new such arrangement in decades was adopted by Argentina in 1991, as part of a stabilization program dubbed the Convertibility Plan. The scheme was intended to reverse persistent domestic inflation that had reached hyperinflationary proportions in 1989–90.[12] Although the central bank was retained, its discretionary powers were severely curtailed by a law stipulating full convertibility of a "new" peso (Argentina's fourth currency in six years)[13] at a fixed parity to the U.S. dollar and mandating full coverage of the monetary base by dollar reserves.

Since then formal currency boards have been established by two successor states of the Soviet Union, Estonia in 1992 and Lithuania in 1994;[14] and in wartorn Bosnia & Herzegovina under the Dayton Peace Accord signed in December

1995.[15] In late 1996 Ecuador temporarily flirted with the idea (*Economist* 1996c), and in mid-1997 an Argentine-style initiative was implemented in Bulgaria (IMF 1997). Currency boards have been advocated for a variety of others states as well.[16]

Why would sovereign states be willing to reconsider the case for a currency board? Clearly, a major attraction is the financial stability promised by a firm link to a popular foreign money. Where confidence in the national currency is lacking, because of past inflationary excesses as in Argentina and Ecuador or uncertainty about the future of a newly created money as in Estonia and Lithuania, credibility may in effect be borrowed from abroad by tying one's own hands.[17] The policies of a respected foreign central bank (e.g., the Federal Reserve or Germany's Bundesbank) become the country's policies as well. Hegemonic discipline is imported through the guarantee of convertibility at a fixed exchange rate. As the Federal Reserve Bank of Cleveland summarizes: "The currency-board country acquires credibility at the expense of losing monetary sovereignty" (Humpage and McIntire 1995:5).

So why not just hire another government's money? Why bother with a proxy at all? Compared with outright use of a foreign money, a currency board offers two distinct advantages. First, the option preserves the symbolic value of a currency to call one's own. Second, it has an incidental side-effect: it generates a potentially lucrative stream of seigniorage income for the monetary authority. When a foreign money circulates domestically, all the real-resource benefit of its creation goes to the country of issue. But when a domestic money is used, seigniorage revenue is gained from the difference between the zero interest paid on the currency board's liabilities (base money) and the positive interest to be earned on its foreign-currency assets. In practice, the net gain may be quite substantial, depending on the level of yields on the anchor currency. A conservative estimate by economist John Williamson (1995:20) suggests potential income equal to about 0.5 percent of gross domestic product in the typical case.

In setting up a currency board, moreover, it is always possible to leave a limited amount of "wiggle room" for discretionary monetary policy.[18] Under Argentina's Convertibility Plan, for example, which ostensibly made any expansion of base money contingent on purchases of dollars, a loophole permitted the central bank to hold as much as one-third of its assets in Argentine government debt. A similar flexibility, long characteristic of surviving arrangements in East Asia, was built into the Estonian and Lithuanian currency boards as well.

There is nothing inherently contradictory about a currency board that allows some leeway for independent decisionmaking. Indeed, other than Britain's earlier colonial arrangements, it is difficult to find a historical example of a pure currency board. At times, room for maneuver has proved immensely valuable. It certainly did for the Argentine authorities in 1995, as they struggled to cope with a devastating capital outflow triggered by financial crisis in Mexico—a contagion effect in international capital-market behavior that was quickly dubbed the tequila effect. In the words of one commentator: "As the Duke of Wellington often observed, victory is the avoidance of being crushed by an onslaught, and Argentina's currency board–like system has certainly kept Argentina from being crushed by the tequila effect" (Hanke 1996:71).

But there is also a risk in giving policymakers some leeway—that flexibility will be used to evade the discipline of a currency board, in turn eroding the confidence that is the very object of the exercise. Lithuania's government discovered that danger, to its regret, in late 1994, six months after its currency board was introduced. Attempts by public officials to use it indirectly to augment fiscal revenues led to nearly disastrous capital flight, which ended only when the authorities renewed pledges to accept the constraints of the system. Plainly, care must be taken not to kill the goose that lays the golden eggs. As one source has remarked, commenting on the Lithuanian experience:

> Currency board arrangements are often introduced when the authorities' policy credibility has been compromised and the introduction of clearly visible rules promises more stable monetary conditions. Under these circumstances, making use of the flexibility available in a currency board arrangement can threaten the credibility gains from the arrangement. . . . The experience of Lithuania . . . illustrates the danger of pursuing flexibility too far. (Camard 1996:2, 19)

How far is too far? The calculus is a fine one, since there is no easy way to know just what may be the trade-off between credibility and flexibility in any given circumstance. In practice, few governments with troubled moneys have proved willing to tie their hands quite as thoroughly as even a looser form of currency board requires, despite what the choice might mean for confidence in the national currency. Most prefer less demanding monetary commitments. The goal of a stable currency may remain paramount. But by imposing a weaker discipline on their own policies, most hope to purchase stability at a lower cost in terms of the subordination of monetary sovereignty.

Pegged exchange rates

Like a currency board, an exchange-rate peg also creates a hierarchical bond between home money and a strong foreign currency, in effect expanding the authoritative domain of the latter at the expense of the former. But unlike a currency board, a standard exchange-rate rule demands neither full convertibility nor a formal constraint on the creation of domestic money. Hence some of the reality of monetary sovereignty, not just the illusion, may be preserved. All the approach involves is a commitment, more or less qualified, to maintain a stable price relationship between home money and anchor currency. Discipline is imported through the exchange-rate link alone.

How much monetary authority may be preserved by an exchange-rate peg? It is difficult to say. The critical issue, long familiar to economists, is best summarized in terms of what I have elsewhere labeled the Unholy Trinity—the intrinsic incompatibility of currency stability, capital mobility, and national policy autonomy.[19] The dilemma is simply stated:

> In an environment of formally or informally pegged rates and effective integration of financial markets, any attempt to pursue independent monetary objectives is almost certain, sooner or later, to result in significant balance-of-payments disequilibrium, and hence provoke potentially destabilizing flows of speculative capital. To preserve exchange-rate stability, governments will then be compelled to limit either the movement of capital (via restrictions or taxes) or their own policy autonomy (via some form of multilateral surveillance or joint decisionmaking). If they are unwilling or unable to sacrifice either one, then the objective of exchange-rate stability itself may eventually have to be compromised. Over time, except by chance, the three goals cannot be attained simultaneously. (1993c:147)

An exchange-rate peg subordinates monetary sovereignty less than a currency board does, but to a degree that is quite unknowable—neither boundless nor predictable. It does provide greater leeway, but only within limits set by the ever-present risk of capital flight. Confidence in the national currency may still be promoted, but only if policymakers exercise their independence with moderation and prudence. Pegging provides no magic formula to escape the stringent logic of the Unholy Trinity. Governments must still find some way to balance credibility and flexibility. In the economics literature, this issue is known as "rules versus discretion."[20]

Not surprisingly, therefore, pegged-rate arrangements come in many shapes and sizes, as each state struggles to find its own working solution to this pressing policy dilemma. An exchange link may be rigidly maintained or frequently varied, managed within narrow limits or allowed to fluctuate between wide margins, sustained in nominal terms or changed periodically according to some predetermined indicator, defined in terms of a single anchor or tied to a broader index ("composite") of foreign currencies, publicly declared or deliberately obscured. Each combination implies its own trade-off of risks and rewards for the individual government involved.

In the contemporary era such choices have been legally available only since amendment of the International Monetary Fund's charter in 1976. Previously, under the rules written in 1944 at the Bretton Woods monetary conference establishing the IMF, states had been formally obligated to maintain a stable par value for their currencies in terms of gold, either directly or indirectly through a peg to the U.S. dollar. For nearly thirty years, exchange rates were permitted to vary only within very narrow margins (except for the occasional devaluation).[21] Early in 1973, however, following months of turbulence in the exchange markets, the par-value system broke down when the major industrial countries all allowed their currencies to float. Since 1976 every government has been free to tailor its exchange-rate arrangements to suit itself.[22]

Many taxonomies of these choices are possible. Most sources rely on a standardized set of categories established by the IMF, as outlined in Table 3.1.[23] The richness of the menu is obvious. The principal options, between outright use of a foreign money or a currency board at one extreme and an independent float at the other, are as follows:

(1) *Peg: single currency.* This category includes countries that formally peg to a major currency with narrow margins and infrequent adjustments. Some establish a firm one-for-one parity with the anchor currency, as in Southern Africa where the currencies of Lesotho (loti), Namibia (Namibian dollar), and Swaziland (lilangeni) all exchange on a one-for-one basis with the South African rand. Other examples include the Bahamas, whose dollar circulates at par with its U.S. counterpart; Bhutan, linking its ngultrum at parity with the Indian rupee; and Luxembourg, whose franc is directly interchangeable with Belgium's in the context of a long-standing economic union. In most cases, however, the peg is at something other than par, reflecting historical circumstance and past adjustments.

(2) *Peg: currency composite.* A currency composite is essentially a weighted average of two or more foreign currencies. Home money is managed to maintain a stable value in terms of the composite—technically, to maintain a stable "effective" exchange rate. Composites may be a standardized unit such as the IMF's Special Drawing Right (SDR) or the European Union's ECU (European Currency Unit), or they may be designed by the country itself to include foreign currencies and weights more representative of its own particular conditions and experience.

(3) *Limited flexibility: a single currency.* The value of the national money is pegged to a single anchor but within wider margins. Adjustments are relatively infrequent.

(4) *Limited flexibility: cooperative arrangements.* Applying solely to members of the Exchange Rate Mechanism (ERM) of the European Monetary System (EMS), this arrangement of the European Union is discussed in greater detail in Chapter 4. This category combines a peg of individual EMS currencies to one another with a joint float vis-à-vis nonmembers.

(5) *Greater flexibility: adjusted to an indicator.* The currency is adjusted more frequently, and more or less automatically, in accord with a selected indicator. One commonly used indicator is a measure of the nominal exchange rate adjusted for the difference between home and foreign inflation, technically known as the "real" exchange rate. Another indicator is a preannounced change.

(6) *Greater flexibility: managed float.* The central monetary authority sets the rate for the currency but may alter it frequently according to a variety of indicators, including variations in the exchange rate of one or more anchor currencies. The indicators may or may not be publicly announced, and adjustments are broadly judgmental rather than automatic.

Table 3.1. Exchange arrangements as of April 30, 1997

Pegged					Flexibility Limited against a Single Currency or Group of Currencies		More flexible	
Single currency			Currency composite		Single currency (h)	Cooperative arrangements (i)	Other managed floating	Independently floating
U.S. dollar	French franc	Other	SDR	Other				
Angola	Benin	Bhutan (Indian rupee)	Libyan Arab Jamahiriya (a, b)	Bangladesh	Bahrain (j)	Austria	Algeria	Afghanistan, Islamic State of (b)
Antigua and Barbuda	Burkina Faso	Bosnia & Herzegovina (Deutsche-mark)	Myanmar (b)	Botswana (b)	Qatar (j)	Belgium	Belarus	Albania
Argentina	Cameroon	Brunei Darussalam (Singapore dollar)		Burundi	Saudi Arabia (j)	Denmark	Brazil (b)	Armenia
Bahamas, The (b)	Central African Republic	Estonia (Deutsche-mark)		Cape Verde (c)	United Arab Emirates (j)	Finland	Cambodia (b)	Australia
Barbados	Chad	Kiribati (d) (Australian dollar)		Cyprus (c)		France	Chile (b)	Azerbaijan
Belize	Comoros	Lesotho (South African rand)		Czech Republic (e)		Germany	China	Bolivia
Djibouti	Congo	Namibia (South Africa rand)		Fiji		Ireland	Colombia (l)	Bulgaria
Dominica	Cote d'Ivoire	San Marino (d) (Italian lira)		Iceland (f)		Italy	Costa Rica	Canada
Grenada	Equatorial Guinea	Swaziland (South African rand)		Jordan		Luxembourg	Croatia	Ethiopia
Iraq (b)	Gabon			Kuwait		Netherlands	Dominician Republic (b)	Gambia, The
Liberia	Guinea-Bissau			Malta		Portugal	Ecuador (b)	Ghana
Lithuania	Mali			Morocco (g)		Spain	Egypt (b)	Guatemala
Marshall Islands (d)	Niger			Nepal			El Salvador	Guinea
Micronesia, Federated States of (d)	Senegal			Seychelles			Eritrea (b)	Guyana
Nigeria (b)	Togo			Slovak Republic (g)			Georgia	Haiti
Oman				Solomon Islands			Greece	India
Panama (d)				Thailand			Honduras (b)	Jamaica
St. Kitts and Nevis				Tonga			Hungary (k)	Japan
St. Lucia				Vanuatu			Indonesia	Kazakhstan
St. Vincent and the Grenadines				Western Samoa			Iran, Islamic Republic of	Kenya
Syrian Arab Republic (b)							Israel (l)	Lebanon
							Kyrgyz Republic (l)	Madagascar
							Korea	Malawi
							Lao People's Democratic Republic	Mauritania
							Latvia	Mexico
								Paraguay
								Peru
								Philippines
								Romania
								Rwanda
								Sao Tome and Principe (b)
								Sierra Leone
								Somalia (b)
								South Africa
								Sweden
								Switzerland
								Tajikistan
								Tanzania
								Trinidad and Tobago
								Uganda
								United Kingdom
								United States
								Yemen (b)
								Zaire (b)
								Zambia (b)
								Zimbabwe

Moldova
Mongolia
Mozambique
New Zealand
Papua New
Guinea

Macedonia,
Former
Yugoslav
Republic of
Malaysia
Maldives
Mauritius
Nicaragua

Norway
Pakistan (b)
Poland (l)
Russia
Singapore

Slovenia
Sri Lanka
Sudan
Suriname
Tunisia

Turkey
Turkmenistan (b)
Ukraine
Uruguay
Uzbekistan (b)

Venezuela (e)
Vietnam

Source: International Monetary Fund, *Annual Report*, 1997.

Notes: (a) The exchange rate is maintained within margins of + / − 47 percent.
(b) Member maintains exchange arrangements involving more than one exchange market. The arrangement shown is that maintained in the major market.
(c) The exchange rate, which is pegged to the European currency unit (ECU), is maintained within margins of + / − 2.25 percent.
(d) Country uses peg currency as legal tender.
(e) The exchange rate is maintained within margins of + / − 7.5 percent.
(f) The exchange rate is maintained within margins of + / − 6 percent.
(g) The exchange rate is maintained within margins of + / − 3 percent.
(h) In all countries listed in this column, the U.S. dollar was the currency against which exchange rates showed limited flexibility.
(i) This category consists of countries participating in the exchange rate mechanism (ERM) of the European Monetary System (EMS). In each case, the exchange rate is maintained within a margin of + / − 15 percent around the bilateral central rates against other participating currencies, with the exception of Germany, and the Netherlands, in which case the exchange rate is maintained within a margin of + / − 2.5 percent.
(j) Exchange rates are determined on the basis of a fixed relationship to the SDR, within margins of up to + / − 7.25 percent. However, because of the maintenance of a relatively stable relationship with the U.S. dollar, these margins are not always observed.
(k) The exchange rate is maintained within margins of + / − 2.25 percent with regard to the currency basket.
(l) The exchange rate is maintained within margins of + / − 7 percent with regard to the currency basket.

Monetary blocs

The number of countries availing themselves of one or another of these different exchange-rate options is very large. The number of moneys that serve the role of anchor currency, on the other hand, is quite small, just the U.S. dollar and a tiny handful of others. The monetary blocs created by such hierarchical linkages may at times be large, but they are hardly profuse. In practice, currency hegemony is a privilege of the few.[24]

Some monetary blocs are quite formal. Most prominent is the French franc zone in Africa, some fourteen countries, all but one (Equatorial Guinea) a former colony of France. Except for the Comoros, which has its own separate money, all are part of a single currency area, the CFA Franc Zone, that is tied firmly to France's franc. Another is the Common Monetary Area (CMA) linking Lesotho, Namibia, and Swaziland to South Africa through a common set of institutions. Both are described in more detail in Chapter 4.

Today's two biggest groupings, however, are those that have grown up around the dollar and its principal rival, the German mark, now generally recognized as the world's second most important international currency. Both the dollar and DM blocs are relatively more informal than the CFA Franc Zone or CMA, encompassing both official single-currency pegs and less obvious exchange-rate linkages. In contrast to nearly two dozen countries still formally aligned with the dollar, only two countries, Estonia and Bosnia & Herzegovina, officially peg to the DM. But in the opinion of many experts, all the members of the European Union should also be viewed as part of a de facto DM zone, because of Germany's disproportionate monetary influence in the area.[25] And in addition many other currencies tend to be loosely linked to either the dollar or the DM through their exchange rates, even where governments have ostensibly opted for more flexible monetary rules. The anchor roles of dollar and DM are in fact quite extensive, though difficult to measure precisely because of the diversity and, frequently, the obscurity of many of the arrangements involved.

Some indicators of the broader anchor use of the dollar and DM are provided in Table 3.2, based on separate studies by two French economists, Agnès Bénassy-Quéré and Pierre Deusy-Fournier (1994), and by two Americans, Jeffrey Frankel and Shang-Jin Wei (1993, 1994, 1995a).[26] Both studies compare, for varying samples of countries, the statistical influence of the world's three most widely circulated currencies—the Japanese yen as well as the dollar and DM—on the observed values of various lesser moneys, excluding formal pegs. To permit direct comparisons, Table 3.2 includes only countries covered by both studies. In the three lefthand columns, taken from the French study, the relationship is inverse: the lower the figure shown for an individual country, the greater the correlation between movements of its money and the anchor currency. In the righthand columns, taken from the U.S. study, the relationship is direct: the lower the figure,

Table 3.2. Relative influence of the U.S. dollar, German mark and Japanese yen on selected currencies, 1987–1993

	Bénassy-Quéré and Deusy-Fournier (a)			Frankel and Wei (b)		
	dollar	mark	yen	dollar	mark	yen
	(inverse relationship)			(direct relationship)		
Europe						
Austria	0.50	0.02	0.44	0.01	1.00	0.01
Belgium	0.45	0.09	0.46	0.02	0.94	0.04
Denmark	0.44	0.12	0.44	0.05	0.95	0.00
Finland	0.36	0.25	0.37	0.27	0.71	0.01
France	0.46	0.08	0.46	0.05	0.93	0.02
Greece	0.44	0.12	0.40	0.08	0.86	0.05
Iceland	0.40	0.22	0.37	0.31	0.57	0.11
Ireland	0.41	0.15	0.44	0.08	0.86	0.05
Italy	0.38	0.21	0.41	0.12	0.82	0.06
Netherlands	0.50	0.02	0.48	0.00	1.00	0.01
Norway	0.43	0.13	0.40	0.35	0.54	0.10
Portugal	0.41	0.16	0.43	0.18	0.77	0.04
Spain (a)	0.39	0.18	0.43	0.58	0.42	0.02
Sweden	0.38	0.23	0.38	0.35	0.59	0.06
Switzerland	0.44	0.16	0.36	0.03	0.85	0.11
Western Hemisphere						
Argentina	0.33	0.34	0.33	0.35	0.10	0.54
Canada	0.14	0.44	0.42	0.63	0.02	0.35
Chile	0.18	0.44	0.38	0.83	0.02	0.16
Colombia	0.09	0.50	0.41	0.95	0.05	0.01
Mexico	0.09	0.42	0.49	0.67	0.27	0.07
Asia						
China	0.24	0.42	0.34	0.68	0.25	0.06
Indonesia	0.04	0.51	0.45	0.92	0.05	0.06
Korea	0.08	0.49	0.43	0.99	0.02	0.00
Malaysia	0.13	0.46	0.41	0.88	0.09	0.04
Philippines	0.19	0.41	0.40	0.85	0.07	0.07
Singapore	0.18	0.43	0.39	0.78	0.10	0.13
Thailand	0.09	0.49	0.42	0.83	0.13	0.03

Sources: Bénassy-Quéré and Deusy-Fournier (1994); Frankel and Wei (1993, 1994, 1995a).
a. 1989–1993 for all countries, except Spain (1988–1992).
b. 1987–1990 for Europe and Western Hemisphere, 1989–1990 for Asia.

the lower the correlation. For both studies, the weights assigned to each anchor currency have been adjusted to sum (apart from rounding) to one.

The separate studies cover slightly different time periods, but their results are remarkably similar. In Europe, most currencies give heavy weight to the DM, with a correspondingly smaller role for the dollar. The degree of subordination to Germany's currency varies considerably, however, from very tight linkage for Austria, the Benelux, and France to looser ties for Norway, Spain, and Sweden.

According to the Frankel-Wei study, for instance, the DM accounts for virtually all of the movement of the Austrian and Dutch currencies and more than 90 percent of that of the Belgian and French francs, whereas Germany's weight is less than 60 percent for Norway and Sweden and barely more than 40 percent for Spain. Comparable disparities, in mirror image, are evident in the French study.

Elsewhere, the dollar is clearly dominant, not only in the Western Hemisphere, as we might expect, but even in much of East Asia, where the yen might have been thought to play a larger role. In fact, the yen appears to lack any significant bloc of its own. As Bénassy-Quéré and Deusy-Fournier (1994:138) say: "The yen zone is reduced to Japan."

Also conspicuous by its absence is Britain's pound sterling, once the proud leader of the broadest monetary bloc in history—the fabled sterling area—today not even a pale shadow of its former self. The roots of the sterling area go back to the nineteenth century, when the pound bestrode the financial world like a colossus (B. Cohen 1971a). As a formal entity the sterling bloc first emerged after 1931, following breakdown of the global gold standard, when nations with close economic ties to Britain voluntarily chose to peg their currencies to the pound and to maintain the bulk of their monetary reserves in London. After 1939 sterling-area membership involved an additional feature: a system of joint exchange controls. Individual states retained discretionary control over their respective currency values and monetary policies, but full freedom of capital movements within the group was maintained behind a wall of common restrictions vis-à-vis nonmembers. For overseas participants, the constraint on national policy autonomy that resulted from these arrangements was outweighed by the benefits of exchange-rate stability and access to the financial resources of the City of London. Following World War II, however, these advantages began to erode as a result of Britain's financial and political decline, and membership gradually lost its appeal. In time, more and more countries dropped out, culminating in a final rush for the exits after the advent of currency floating in 1973. The sterling area was formally terminated in 1979 (B. Cohen 1992b).

Monetary blocs, whether formal or informal, have always been recognized as a variation of the conventional Westphalian model, *pace* the One Nation/One Money myth. Depending on circumstances, governments may find it convenient to subordinate or surrender their monetary sovereignty in one way or another; moreover, the ways to do so are many. The question that remains is: How do states select from such a rich menu of options?

Making Choices

The economics literature generally addresses the question of choice among exchange-rate rules as an optimization problem, but one limited exclusively to issues of either public finance or macroeconomic performance. It pays little attention to the value of political symbolism or insulation from foreign influence.

In a minority strand of the literature, some economists focus on the seigniorage privilege and worry about the potential impact of exchange-rate choices on a government's ability to raise revenue.[27] The more firmly a currency is pegged, the less room policymakers have to resort to inflationary money creation to augment public spending—once again, the stringent logic of the Unholy Trinity is at work. Credibility of monetary policy is gained, but at a loss of fiscal flexibility. As one commentator puts it: "The monetary authorities, in determining the inflation rate, face a trade-off between revenue collection and exchange rate stability" (Grilli 1989a:585). Choices among currency rules are thus assumed to reflect the exigencies of public finance.

The bulk of the relevant literature, however, focuses not on government operations but on the well-being of the economy as a whole. Policymakers are assumed to concern themselves with maximizing output and minimizing inflation in the context of an open economy subject to internal or external shocks. Choices, it is assumed, reflect considerations of general economic welfare rather than the state's own fiscal requirements. At the level of formal theory, the issue is thus cast as one of "optimal exchange-rate management"—selecting the best possible currency regime from the point of view of macroeconomic performance.[28] At the empirical level, diverse variables representing economic characteristics of individual countries are tested for their influence on the choice among alternative degrees of exchange-rate flexibility, including everything from a currency board to an independent float.[29]

Not unexpectedly, because they use such a limited perspective on what matters to governments, econometric results tend by and large to be relatively inconclusive. It does seem fairly clear that currency boards and single-currency pegs are mostly employed by small open economies, particularly those with a high degree of geographical or commodity concentration of trade, whereas states with more diversified foreign economic relations tend to prefer composites. It also seems evident that looser forms of pegging are often associated with more advanced financial development and more sophisticated economic management. But beyond such broad generalizations, this approach provides little explanatory power for the observed pattern of currency arrangements. Concedes one recent study: "Overall the country characteristics do not help very much to explain the countries' choice of exchange rate regime. It might be that the choices are based on some other factors, economical or political" (Honkapohja and Pikkarainen 1994:47–48). Indeed—why should we be surprised that politics might also enter such a critical decision?

In fact, political factors enter in two ways. First, the policy calculus is obviously affected by domestic politics: the tug and pull of organized interest groups of every kind. As Jeffry Frieden has emphasized, "domestic distributional considerations are also central to the choice of exchange rate regimes" (1993a:140).[30] The critical issue is familiar: Who wins and who loses? The material interests of specific constituencies are systematically influenced by what a government decides to do with its currency. Producers of tradable goods, for example, as well as internationally active investors, are all apt to be favored by a currency rule that maximizes the predictability of exchange rates. Currency volatility, for such groups, is anathema. Domestically oriented sectors, by contrast, are more likely to benefit from stability at home and thus to attach priority to preserving as much national policy autonomy as possible. Such groups stand to lose most from a fixed rate, insofar as such a regime reduces the flexibility of monetary policy. Government choices are bound to be sensitive to the interplay among such domestic political forces.

Second, the calculus includes much more than macroeconomic performance alone. Plainly, political goals—symbolism, seigniorage, insulation—also figure in government choices. As a practical matter, what matters most to public officials is their discretion to pursue a broad and diverse range of policy objectives in the event of adverse developments, up to and including war. No government wishes to give up its "revenue of last resort" if it can help it; in an insecure world, most states logically minimize their vulnerability to any chance that their monetary dependence might be exploited. Policy flexibility, in short, is a defense against uncertainty. Many governments prefer to hold back from firm exchange-rate commitments rather than risk having to renege because of an unexpected change of circumstance (Cukierman, Kiguel, and Liviatan 1992).

The degree of importance attached to such noneconomic considerations also varies systematically. The inflation tax, for instance, as we noted in Chapter 2, tends to attract governments plagued by unstable or divided polities, where tax collection is difficult. But the ability to extract seigniorage depends on maintaining an effective monetary monopoly, which is easiest when the exchange rate is allowed to float. Not surprisingly, therefore, the available evidence suggests that resistance to pegging tends to be greatest in countries with a high degree of political instability (Edwards 1996).

Few students of politics would be startled by the fact that, with rare exceptions, no country of any size or capacity has voluntarily accepted for long the discipline of a currency board or a truly tight exchange-rate peg.[31] Nor is it particularly astonishing to find that over time states have drifted toward less demanding forms of monetary commitment, as can be seen clearly in Table 3.3. Two decades ago, when experience with currency flexibility was still limited, nearly two-thirds of all nonindustrial countries in the IMF maintained a single-currency peg, and some one-quarter used composites. By 1996, the comparable proportions had fallen to one-third and one-sixth. The proportion of developing or transition economies availing themselves of more flexible arrangements, in the meantime, had risen from less than one-sixth to more than one-half.[32]

Table 3.3. Exchange arrangements, 1980–1997
(numbers of countries)

Classification status	1980	1981	1982	1983	1984	1985	1986	1987	1988	1989	1990	1991	1992	1993	1994	1995	1996	1997
Currency pegged to																		
U.S. dollar	39	38	38	33	34	31	32	38	36	32	25	24	24	21	23	23	21	21
French franc	14	14	13	13	13	14	14	14	14	14	14	14	14	14	14	14	14	15
Other currency peg	4	5	5	5	5	5	5	5	5	5	5	4	12(a)	8	8	7	9	9
SDR	15	15	15	12	11	12	10	8	7	7	6	6	5	4	3	3	3	2
Other currency composite	22	21	23	27	31	32	30	27	31	35	35	33	29	26	21	20	19	20
Cooperative exchange arrangements	8	8	8	8	8	8	8	8	8	9	9	10	9	9	10	10	10	12
Limited flexibility (b)	⎱ 38 ⎰	41	15	14	13	10	11	9	9	9	7	9	7	8	7	7	6	4
Managed floating			20	25	20	21	21	23	22	21	23	27	23	29	33	39	44	47
Independently floating			8	8	12	15	19	18	17	20	25	29	44	56	58	56	55	51
Total	140	143	146	146	148	149	151	151	151	152	154	156	167	175	178	179	181	181

Sources: International Monetary Fund, *Annual Report*, various years.

a. This number includes, for one year, six currencies officially pegged to the Russian ruble.

b. Includes both currencies with limited flexibility against a single currency and currencies adjusted in accord with a selected indicator.

The real key to each country's selection is its ability to expand its scope for discretionary action without losing credibility—a matter that has much more to do with state institutions, domestic politics, foreign threats, and historical policy behavior than with any range of current economic characteristics. Governments that have coped successfully with the Unholy Trinity in the past are likely to find even the loosest sort of exchange-rate rule reasonably easy to manage in the present. A case in point today is Chile which, after a massive retrenchment starting in the 1970s, is now able to live comfortably with quite a high degree of external currency flexibility. Other countries, by contrast, with less impressive records of accomplishment to call upon, may discover—as Argentina did in 1995—that not even an arrangement as rigid as a currency board is enough to protect against capital flight. Even with its parity to the dollar enshrined in domestic law, the new Argentine peso fell victim to the ravages of the tequila effect.

On its face, such an outcome might seem paradoxical. A currency board, after all, formally institutionalizes a state's commitment to an exchange-rate regime, raising barriers to exit. We know from the recent theoretical literature on transactions costs that organizational design can play a key role in promoting credible commitments (North 1990). From this perspective, the legal mandate involved in a currency board should instill more confidence than do less formal currency rules. It should not be easy to reverse a solemn act of parliament.

In fact, however, such details appear to play remarkably little part in sustaining compliance with monetary commitments, as I have noted elsewhere (B. Cohen 1993a). High barriers to exit or not, vows can always be broken. In the words of one recent commentary:

> Arguments [for a currency board] may sound convincing, but they presume that once a currency board system is in place, a country will adhere to it forever. This assumption is as unrealistic and naive as the belief that a wedding ring guarantees an everlasting marriage. . . . A currency board does not magically restore the credibility of a country's economic policies.[33]

In brief, nothing may be taken for granted. As in a good marriage so with monetary commitments, constant effort is required to sustain an adequate level of trust.

∿

The bottom line is simple. Not all states can avoid some degree of subordination of their monetary sovereignty. The options available to them, however, are best defined not by formal design but by each government's own calculation of the advantages and disadvantages of compliance with a monetary rule of any kind. In practice, a loose exchange-rate peg or managed float may constrain monetary authority more, despite appearances, than even the purest form of orthodox currency board; conversely, room for discretionary action may be considerable despite a formally rigid currency link. The issue, ultimately, is a government's own credibility. By definition, the Westphalian model of political geography assumes that, in extremis, no state is bound by any prior commitment (not even a commitment to use another country's money in lieu of its own). Everything is reversible—in currency relations no less than in any other area of foreign affairs. In the end, therefore, the decision of how much monetary sovereignty to surrender or subordinate will depend on how high a price a state is willing to pay to sustain trust in its word.

Sharing Monetary
Sovereignty

"Most independent nations—except for a few that belong to currency unions—continue to issue their own currencies and use them within their borders."

Ellen Hoffman, "One World, One Currency?" 1991

Exchange-rate rules and other arrangements that *subordinate* a country's monetary sovereignty (our first S) are of course not the only unorthodox species to be found as we roam money's imaginary landscape. As the journalist Ellen Hoffman reminds us, sovereignties may also be effectively *shared,* in a currency union or equivalent configuration (our second S). Here too, however, variations on the Westphalian model are conventionally—and conveniently—assumed to be creatures of state choice rather than of market forces. The bond between nation and money may be loosened, but the spotlight remains sharply focused on the central role of government and its calculus of costs and benefits. In lieu of One Nation/One Money, we have Several Nations/One Money. States are still seen as the principal determinants of monetary geography.

Formal monetary alliances come in two basic forms: either participating governments retain some degree of separate control or they do not. Although terminology is not standardized, at one extreme is the full *monetary union* or *currency union,* where all monetary authority is formally centralized in a single supranational agency and separate national moneys are all replaced by a single common currency; at the other extreme, a simple *exchange-rate union,* ostensibly freezing mutual currency values but otherwise leaving monetary management largely to the discretion of individual governments. As with the hierarchical configurations discussed in Chapter 3, actual practices are located along a continuum between these two alternatives. And like those earlier choices, each option has its own trade-offs between potential gains and losses.

Historical Experience

History provides diverse examples of both kinds of monetary alliance, going back to the nineteenth century and the start of the era of territorial money. No sooner had the movement to consolidate territorial currencies gotten under way than a variety of exchange-rate unions began to be discussed. Two—the Latin Monetary Union and the Scandinavian Monetary Union—actually lasted well into the twentieth century. Currency mergers have also occurred more recently; four of them—the Belgium-Luxembourg Economic Union, CFA Franc Zone, East Caribbean Currency Area, and Common Monetary Area (in southern Africa)—still exist and operate effectively. And of course in our own times yet another very prominent example will be provided if the European Union succeeds in its attempt to create a common currency for its members.

History also provides many examples of monetary alliances that have eroded or failed, most notably the dramatic breakup of the ruble zone following the collapse of the Soviet Union in December 1991. In principle currency unions, like marriage, are irrevocable. Indeed, permanence is ostensibly one of the key features thought to distinguish such arrangements from the less absolute currency commitments discussed in Chapter 3: pegged-rate arrangements of various kinds are the equivalent of amorous cohabitation, and a noted economist once jokingly described them as no more than "pseudo-exchange-rate unions" (Corden 1972). In practice, however, nothing can be taken for granted. Many marriages end in divorce, and many independent states have taken back their share of monetary sovereignty when they saw fit. Monetary sovereignty may be subordinated, but nothing can be regarded as truly irreversible.

Nineteenth century

Perhaps the most ambitious monetary alliance considered during the nineteeth century was a projected "universal currency" to be based on equivalent gold coins issued by the three biggest financial powers: Britain, France, and the United States.[1] By chance, the gold content of French coins at the time was such that a 25-franc piece—not then in existence but easily mintable—would have contained 112.008 grains of gold, very close to both the English sovereign (113.001 grains) and the American half-eagle, equal to five dollars (116.1 grains). Why not, then, standardize coinage among the three countries, to achieve in effect one single money? That was the proposal of a monetary conference sponsored by the French government to coincide with an international exposition in Paris in 1867. Delegates from some twenty countries, with the critical exception of Britain's two representatives, enthusiastically supported creation of a universal currency based on a 25-franc piece and called for appropriate reductions in the gold content of the sovereign and half-eagle. In the end, however, no action was taken in either London or Washington. For lack of sustained political support the idea just faded away.[2]

Two years before the 1867 conference, however, the French government did succeed in gaining agreement for a more limited currency initiative—the Latin Monetary Union (LMU). Joining Belgium, Italy, and Switzerland with France, the LMU was intended to standardize the existing gold and silver coinages of all four countries. Greece subsequently adhered to the terms of the LMU in 1868, though it did not become a formal member until 1876.[3]

In practical terms, a monetary alliance among these countries had begun earlier, as Belgium, Greece, Italy, and Switzerland independently decided to model their currency systems on that of France. Here is yet another example of the flattery of imitation in monetary relations. Each state chose to adopt a basic unit equal in value to the French franc—actually called a franc in Belgium and Switzerland— with equivalent subsidiary units defined according to the French-inspired decimal system. Starting in the 1850s, however, serious Gresham's Law–type problems developed as a result of differences in the weight and fineness of silver coins circulating in each country. The LMU established uniform standards for national coinages and, by making each member's money legal tender throughout the union, created a wider area for the circulation of a harmonized supply of specie coins. In substance a formal exchange-rate union was created; responsibility for the management of participating currencies remained with each separate government.

Group members were distinguished from other countries by the reciprocal obligation of their central banks to accept one another's currencies at par and without limit. Soon after its founding, however, and beginning in the late 1860s, the LMU was subjected to considerable strain by a global glut of silver. The resulting depreciation of silver eventually led to a suspension of silver coinage by all the partners, effectively transforming the LMU from a bimetallic standard into what came to be called a "limping gold standard." Even so, the alliance managed to hold together until the general breakdown of global monetary relations during World War I. Switzerland's decision to withdraw in 1926 provoked formal dissolution of the LMU in the following year.

The Scandinavian Monetary Union (SMU) too was an exchange-rate alliance designed to standardize existing coinages, although it was from the start based on a monometallic gold standard. Formed in 1873 by Sweden and Denmark, and joined by Norway two years later, the union established the krone (crown) as a uniform unit of account. National currencies were permitted full circulation as legal tender in all three countries.

As in the LMU, members of the SMU were distinguished from outsiders by a reciprocal obligation to accept one another's currencies at par and without limit; likewise mutual acceptability was initially limited to coins only. In 1885, however, the three members went further, agreeing to accept one another's banknotes and drafts as well, thus facilitating free intercirculation of all paper currency and resulting eventually in the total disappearance of exchange-rate quotations among the three moneys. By the turn of the century the SMU had come to function as a single unit for all payments purposes, and it did so until relations were disrupted by the suspension of convertibility and the floating of individual currencies at the start of World War I. Despite subsequent efforts to restore at least some elements of the union, particularly following the members' return to the gold standard in the mid-1920s, the agreement was finally abandoned following the global financial crisis of 1931.[4]

Repeated efforts to standardize coinages were made by various German states prior to Germany's political union, but with rather less success. Early accords, following the start of the Zollverein (the German region's customs union) in 1834, ostensibly established a German Monetary Union—technically, like the LMU and SMU, also an exchange-rate union—but in fact divided the area into two distinct currency alliances: one encompassing most northern states, using the thaler as its basic monetary unit; another including states in the south, based on the florin (also known as the guilder or gulden).[5] Free intercirculation of coins was guaranteed in both groups, but not at par: the exchange rate between the two unit of accounts was fixed at one thaler to 1.75 florins (formally, 14:24.5) rather than one-for-one. Moreover, states remained free to mint nonstandardized coins in addition to their basic units, and many important German states (e.g., Bremen, Hamburg, and Schleswig-Holstein) chose to stay outside the agreement altogether. Nor were matters helped much by the short-lived Vienna Coinage Treaty signed with Austria in 1857, which added to the mix yet a third currency, Austria's own florin, with a value slightly higher than that of the south German unit. The Austro-German Monetary Union was dissolved less than a decade later, following Austria's defeat in the 1866 Austro-Prussian War. Full merger of all the currencies of the German states did not finally arrive until modern Germany was consolidated, under Prussian leadership, in 1871.[6]

Twentieth century

The twentieth century, to date, has seen five major formal monetary alliances established among sovereign states. Four are still in existence. First was the Belgium-Luxembourg Economic Union (BLEU), founded in 1922. Its traditional ties with the German Zollverein severed after World War I, tiny Luxembourg elected to link itself commercially and financially with Belgium, agreeing to a comprehensive economic union. A key feature of the BLEU was a merger of the partners' separate money systems.[7]

Formally, like its nineteenth-century predecessors, the BLEU was an exchange-rate union between nominally sovereign currencies. Inevitably, though, given the considerable disparities in size between the two countries,[8] the arrangement embodied a fairly high degree of hierarchy, making it more like a currency board than a true alliance of equals. Under the BLEU, Belgian francs form the largest part of the money stock of Luxembourg as well as Belgium and alone enjoy full legal-tender status in both countries. Only Belgium, moreover, has a full-scale central bank. The Luxembourg franc is issued by a more modest institution, the Luxembourg Monetary Institute, serves as legal tender only within Luxembourg itself, and can be issued only in exchange for Belgian francs. Nonetheless, the union is not pure subordination, for both governments participate in joint policy-making bodies, decisions are taken by mutual consent (with a veto reserved for Luxembourg in some instances), and Luxembourg is separately represented at most international monetary meetings. Luxembourg may be small, but it is no Monaco or San Marino.

The four remaining cases all involve developing countries and have their origins in earlier colonial arrangements. In francophone Africa, the roots of today's CFA Franc Zone go back to 1945, when the French government decided to consolidate the diverse currencies of its various African dependencies into one money, "le franc des Colonies Françaises d'Afrique" (CFA francs). In the early 1960s, as independence came to France's African empire, the old colonial franc was replaced by two new regional currencies, each cleverly named to preserve the CFA franc appelation: for the seven members of the West African Monetary Union,[9] "le franc de la Communauté Financière d'Afrique," issued by the Central Bank of West African States; and for the six members of the Customs and Economic Union of Central Africa, "le franc de la Coopération Financière en Afrique Centrale," issued by the Bank of Central African States.[10] Together, the two groups comprise the "Communauté Financière Africaine" (African Financial Community). Each of the two currencies is legal tender only within its own region, but the CFA Zone is much more than a simple exchange-rate union, since the two moneys are equivalently defined and jointly managed under the aegis of the French Ministry of Finance as integral parts of a single entity (Boughton 1992, 1993a, 1993b).

The roots of two other examples, both involving former British dependencies, go back to Britain's use of currency boards to manage its colonial financial affairs. In the Caribbean Britain's monetary legacy has proved remarkably successful, as the British Caribbean Currency Board, first created in 1950, evolved first into the East Caribbean Currency Authority in 1965 and then the East Caribbean Central Bank in 1983, issuing one currency, the East Caribbean dollar, to serve as legal tender for all seven participating states.[11] Embedded in a broadening network of related agreements among the same governments (the East Caribbean Common Market, the Organization of Eastern Caribbean States), the East Caribbean Currency Area has functioned as a true monetary union without serious difficulty since its establishment in 1965 (McClean 1975; Nascimento 1994).

In East Africa, on the other hand, Britain's colonial legacy ultimately failed, despite creation of the East African Currency Board as early as 1919 to administer a single money, the East African shilling, for the territories of Kenya, Tanganyika (later part of Tanzania), and Uganda. The three colonies also had a customs union dating from 1923, as well as a variety of other common services for railways, harbors, air transport, and the like. Yet once independence arrived in the region (Tanganyika in 1961, Uganda in 1962, and Kenya in 1963), joint institutions quickly began to break apart. By the middle of the decade all three countries had decided to install central banks and national moneys of their own.

In 1967 a fresh attempt was made to preserve some semblance of the former currency union in the context of the newly established East African Community and Common Market, which specifically provided for free exchange between separate national currencies at par. Although the EAC for the first time provided a formal legal basis for the integration of the three economies, regional cooperation continued to disintegrate; and by the mid-1970s all vestiges of the economic community had completely disappeared. The final nail in the coffin was hammered home in 1977, when all three governments extended existing exchange controls to each other's currencies (Letiche 1974; Ravenhill 1979).

The last example is the so-called Common Monetary Area combining the Republic of South Africa—a sovereign state for decades—with two former British colonies, Lesotho and Swaziland, and South Africa's own former dependency, Namibia (formerly the UN Trust Territory of South West Africa). The origins of the CMA go back to the 1920s when South Africa's currency, now known as the rand,[12] became the sole legal tender in three of Britain's nearby possessions, Bechuanaland (later Botswana), British Basutoland (later Lesotho), and Swaziland, as well as in South West Africa, a German colony until 1918. In effect, therefore, a sort of monetary alliance existed even before independence came to the region in the late 1960s, albeit an alliance that like the Belgium-Luxembourg Economic Union initially involved a large measure of hierarchy.

Since decolonization the alliance in southern Africa has been formalized, first in 1974 as the Rand Monetary Area, later in 1986 as the CMA (though without the participation of diamond-rich Botswana, which has promoted its own national money, the pula). With the passage of time, however, the degree of hierarchy has diminished considerably, as the three remaining junior partners have asserted their growing sense of national identity. What began as a monetary union based on the rand has gradually been transformed into a looser exchange-rate union as each of South Africa's partners has introduced its own distinct national currency; one of them, Swaziland, has even gone so far as to withdraw the rand's legal-tender status within its own borders. Moreover, though all three continue to peg their moneys to the rand at par, they are no longer bound by currency board–like provisions on money creation and may now in principle vary their exchange rates at will. The CMA may still be a far cry from a true alliance of equals, but it is hardly the simple monetary hegemony that it once was.

European Union

The best-known example of an attempted monetary alliance in the twentieth century is of course the European Union's EMU (Economic and Monetary Union), in the works for years but still not formally realized. Interestingly, currency merger was not even on the agenda of the EU when it first came into existence in 1958. Originally called the European Economic Community or Common Market, later simply the European Community (EC), the EU started as a pure customs union, freeing trade in manufactures among its six founding partners[13] and unifying their commercial policies vis-à-vis outsiders. Indeed its founding document, the Treaty of Rome of 1957, contains no mention of any kind of common currency policy.[14] Nonetheless, consideration of a more formal monetary alliance began almost immediately. Over the four decades of the EU's development, even as its membership has grown from a half-dozen to fifteen, four distinct efforts have been made to promote true monetary union. The current effort to create the new Euro is only the latest and most ambitious.[15]

The first initiative, short-lived and now long forgotten, came in 1962 in the form of a "program of action" proposed by the European Commission, the Common Market's executive body based in Brussels, outlining a comprehensive set of reforms intended to lead to full monetary union by the end of the decade. Members, it was hoped, would as a first step gradually move to freeze mutual exchange rates (an exchange-rate union) while creating a "federal-type banking system" with a council of central-bank governors as its "central organ" to manage an eventual common currency. Nothing ever came of the plan because of the adamant opposition of President Charles De Gaulle of France, an avowed monetary nationalist. For the next seven years, until De Gaulle's sudden resignation in 1969, the subject of monetary union was in effect proscribed in European policy circles.

After De Gaulle's departure, however, the idea suddenly reemerged—ironically, at the prompting of none other than De Gaulle's successor at the Élysée Palace, Georges Pompidou, together with Germany's chancellor Willy Brandt. At a summit of EC heads of government at The Hague in late 1969, both leaders called for a renewed effort to "deepen" the EC, stressing the goal of currency integration in particular. Two years later, after a series of studies directed by Raymond Barre, a French member of the European Commission (and later prime minister of France), and by Pierre Werner, then prime minister of Luxembourg, broad agreement was reached on a three-stage transition to full Economic and Monetary Union (the first time the EMU label was used).

Under the 1971 accord, monetary merger was to begin with an experimental narrowing of the margins of fluctuations among the partners' currencies—the famous "snake in the tunnel." The image of the snake referred to the narrow band within which EC currencies would move relative to one another, with currency values linked through a matrix of bilateral cross-rates, the so-called parity grid. The tunnel was the wider range within which they would be permitted to vary jointly vis-à-vis outside currencies under the terms of the old Bretton Woods par-value system. All EC partners were expected to join in the project, including the group's three prospective new members, Britain, Denmark, and Ireland.

Because of global monetary disturbances, however, triggered in particular by suspension of the dollar's gold convertibility in August 1971, the new scheme was not put into effect until April 1972—and almost immediately ran into trouble. Balance-of-payments pressures forced five of the nine participants—Britain, Denmark, France, Ireland, and Italy—to withdraw from the arrangement (Denmark later rejoined, and France briefly tried to do so but failed), and the tunnel itself disappeared in 1973 when the par-value system was abandoned. The experiment clearly had not worked. All that remained, in effect, was a "minisnake"—a regional bloc centered on Germany's DM and including smaller EC members as well as such nonmembers as Austria, Norway, Sweden, and Switzerland, all pegged formally or informally to the DM. In the words of one observer, EMU "became the biggest non-event of the 1970s" (Tsoukalis 1991:165).

Yet the idea would not die, and in 1978 a third attempt was launched as a result of a dramatic public initiative by German chancellor Helmut Schmidt, Brandt's successor. In the spring Schmidt unexpectedly put forth a radical new plan for a "zone of monetary stability" in Europe.[16] The proposed European Monetary System, building on the remnants of the earlier experiment, was formally endorsed at an EC summit meeting at Bremen in June 1978 and, after remarkably swift negotiations, came formally into being nine months later. At the heart of the EMS was the Exchange Rate Mechanism (ERM), designed to create in effect a new "supersnake" for Europe. Currencies that had dropped out of the earlier arrangement were to be brought back within the narrow margins of fluctuations (+ / − 2.25 percent) set by the joint float of the DM and its monetary satellites, starting with France, Ireland, and Italy and subsequently including Britain and most of the group's newer participants as well. By 1992 only Greece, of the EU's fifteen members, remained wholly outside the ERM.[17]

Viewed in terms of the ERM alone, the EMS was a considerable success. Not only did the new supersnake eventually grow to encompass virtually every EC country. It also reduced the degree of exchange-rate variability within the group, enabling participants to cope more effectively with the challenge of the Unholy Trinity. Credibility was balanced with flexibility partly by means of periodic small realignments of exchange rates, partly through residual capital controls in France and Italy, and partly by surrendering some degree of policy autonomy to the dominant influence of Germany's Bundesbank. In effect, Schmidt's goal, a zone of monetary stability, was very quickly realized.

Viewed in terms of the broader idea of monetary union, however, the EMS was already by the mid-1980s something of a disappointment. Formally the restored joint float, like the snake in the tunnel before it, was no more than the first step of a three-stage transition to full currency merger. The second stage, according to the EMS agreement, was to begin "not later than two years after the start of the scheme"; that is, not later than March 1981. In practice, though, the original timetable was soon conveniently forgotten as the EC fell into a long period of stagnation, what many Europeans sadly labeled "Eurosclerosis." Once again, a major initiative appeared to turn into a nonevent.

But then came a new wave of enthusiasm for EC integration triggered by the Single European Act of February 1986, which called for final elimination of all remaining economic barriers within the Community. The goal, now, was a genuinely unified European market, in the act's words: "an area without internal frontiers in which the free movement of goods, persons, services and capital is ensured." Liberalization came through harmonization of national rules and regulations in as many as 300 separate areas of policy—the famous "300 directives" (really only 279). Since the deadline was December 31, 1992 (or as soon thereafter as possible), the whole endeavor became known as Project 1992 or, simply, EC92. Sclerotic Europe seemed to be rejuvenated.

In turn EC92 led to renewed interest in a single money, or something like it, to complement the single market. In 1987 central banks participating in the ERM took a key first step in that direction by a significant reform of operating procedures in the management of their joint float. Henceforth, they declared, they would rely less on either periodic realignments (which were practically banished in subsequent years) or residual capital controls (which in any event were to be eliminated by EC92) to cope with potential payments disturbances. Rather, in the words of the so-called Basle-Nyborg Agreement, all would rely principally on "interest-rate differentials to defend the stability of the EMS parity grid"—in effect, committing adherents to a virtual freeze of existing rates of exchange. The era of the new or "hard" EMS, as some commentators describe it, had begun.[18]

The really big step, however, came five years later, in February 1992, with the signing of the Maastricht Treaty. The new agreement, in addition to rechristening the European Community as the European Union, undertook a variety of reforms and laid down yet another three-stage timetable for full currency merger—once again, as in the 1970s, under the label Economic and Monetary Union. Stage One, by now largely complete, eliminated remaining capital controls and incorporated all EC currencies into the ERM. Stage Two began in 1994 with creation of the European Monetary Institute (EMI) to prepare the way for an eventual European Central Bank (ECB). Stage Three, scheduled to start no later than January 1,

1999, is supposed to permanently freeze exchange rates and soon thereafter introduce the new common money, the Euro, which will then gradually replace existing national currencies. Exchange rates are to be irrevocably locked, and the ECB is to take over all responsibility for EU monetary policy.

In principle, of course, every EC member is expected eventually to adopt the Euro as its own—but not necessarily right away. In practice, as the Maastricht Treaty makes clear, only a limited subgroup was ever thought likely to fulfill all the conditions required for EMU participation from the start. A final decision on eligibility was anticipated in the spring of 1998. Four so-called convergence criteria are specified[19]:

(1) "Achievement of a high degree of price stability," as evidenced by an average rate of inflation no more than 1.5 percentage points above that of the three "best performing" member states;

(2) "Sustainability of the government financial position," defined to mean both a fiscal deficit no higher than 3 percent of GDP and a level of public debt no higher than 60 percent of GDP;

(3) "Observance of the normal fluctuation margins provided for by the ERM," meaning no "severe tensions" and no devaluation for at least two years; and

(4) "Durability of convergence . . . in long-term interest rate levels," interpreted as an average rate over one year that is no more than 2 percentage points above that of the three "best performing" member states.

These are not easy conditions to fulfill. Nor have they been made any less challenging by subsequent developments: major crises of the ERM in late 1992 and again in 1993 drove both Britain and Italy out of the joint float altogether and ultimately led to a widening of exchange margins for most remaining partici- pants from + / − 2.25 percent to 15 percent in either direction.[20] In early 1998, it was still not clear which EU countries, if any, would be able to meet all the specified criteria. One way or another, most observers expected the hard core of Germany, France, the Benelux countries, and Austria to be among the initial "ins," together most probably with Finland and Ireland. The status of the "Club Med" countries—Italy, Spain, and Portugal—remained uncertain, however, while Britain, Denmark, and Sweden will almost surely opt to remain outside for some time to come. (Greece is not thought likely to qualify for years.) "Outs" are expected to join as circumstances permit.

But this scenario assumes that the project will not be delayed or as in the past allowed to languish indefinitely, because of unforeseen difficulties, in a state of suspended animation. The failure of three previous attempts does not give an abundance of reasons for confidence. Europe continues to profess its determina- tion to share monetary sovereignty. At time of writing, however, the jury remains out and we have no final verdict.

Monetary disintegration

The example of EMU shows how difficult it can be to achieve a true currency union among sovereign states. Other past cases like the LMU, SMU, and East African Community demonstrate that it may be even more difficult, if not impossible, to keep a formal monetary alliance together once its constituent parts decide to go their separate ways. In the twentieth century we have seen several unified monetary areas break up into individual national currencies, usually as a by-product of political dissent or dissolution. A celebrated instance occurred after World War I when the Austro-Hungarian Empire was dismembered by the Treaty of Versailles. Almost immediately, in an abrupt and quite chaotic manner, new currencies were introduced by each successor state—Czechoslovakia, Hungary, Yugoslavia, and ultimately even shrunken Austria itself—to replace the old imperial Austrian crown (Dornbusch 1992, 1994; Garber and Spencer 1994). Comparable examples have also followed the more recent fragmentation along ethnic lines of both the Czechoslovak and Yugoslav federations.[21]

No case has been more spectacular, however, than the collapse of the ruble zone following disintegration of the seven-decade-old Soviet Union in late 1991. Out of the rubble of the ruble no fewer than a dozen new currencies have ultimately emerged to take their places on the world stage.[22]

Breakup of the ruble zone was not an immediate objective of most of the fifteen Soviet "republics" [23] that found themselves suddenly transformed into sovereign states. The only exceptions were the three Baltic nations—Estonia, Latvia, and Lithuania—which for historical reasons were determined to go their own way, monetarily and otherwise, as soon as possible.[24] For the rest, given the general uncertainty of the political environment, the safest option at first was to preserve the status quo. Most foreign advisers, including most prominently the International Monetary Fund, concurred. Successor states, it was argued, were highly integrated economically and institutionally, and retaining a single money would help to minimize commercial and financial dislocations.

At the heart of the ancien régime's monetary system was the State Bank (Gosbank), with responsibilities comparable to those of a central bank elsewhere. In effect the ruble zone functioned as an adjunct of the central-planning system, with the Gosbank mandated to allocate credits to government, enterprises, and households according to a detailed financial plan. Loans, financed by budgetary transfers, were issued to enterprises to support authorized production and investment; enterprise profits, where they existed, were transferred back to the government to underwrite fiscal outlays; and the Gosbank itself provided any additional credits needed by enterprises that might face revenue shortfalls. Workers, meanwhile, received wage payments in cash, which meant in effect that the Soviet Union had not one but two currencies in circulation—on the one hand, a cash ruble used by households; on the other, a bank-deposit (noncash) ruble employed by enterprises and government.

As each republic after independence converted its local Gosbank branch into a national monetary authority, centralized management of the ruble zone broke down. Issue of cash rubles remained the monopoly of the new Central Bank of Russia (CBR), since all the presses for printing banknotes happened to be located within the Russian federation. (In mid-1992, the Soviet ruble was renamed the Russian ruble.) Each of the other central banks, however, retained the privilege of issuing noncash loans denominated in the same common unit—a sure recipe for instability, since every republic was technically free to turn to its own central bank to help finance public spending virtually without limit.

In principle, governments might still have managed the ruble collectively, through coordination of monetary policies.[25] In practice, the temptation to exploit the system for individual advantage—to free ride, issuing credits at the expense of others—was overwhelming. Disintegration of the Soviet Union had cut off customary budgetary transfers from Moscow, local economies were in chaos, and tax receipts were down. The republics were desperate to find revenue anywhere they could. Hence the currency alliance quickly degenerated into a runaway competition for seigniorage, resulting in rampant inflation and a rapid erosion of monetary control. The ruble zone, Patrick Conway has written, "became a battleground for securing seigniorage resources" (1995:40).[26]

Most concerned by these developments was the Russian central bank, the agency ultimately responsible for management of the ruble. Most of the republics ran structural deficits with Russia, because they depended on Russia for supplies of energy and raw materials. As a result, noncash rubles issued by local central banks were ending up inside Russia, to be either respent or converted into cash rubles by exporting enterprises. In effect, therefore, real resources were being appropriated by the successor states with credits financed indirectly by money creation in Moscow. Not only did this make Russia the big loser in the race to employ the inflation tax. It also undermined any effort by the CBR to exert effective authority over aggregate monetary conditions.

Very soon, accordingly, the CBR struck back. It began in 1992 and 1993 with measures intended to tighten control over the use of noncash ruble credits inside Russia by the successor states. Limits were gradually imposed on growth and transferability of the correspondent accounts that, following breakup of the Gosbank, local central banks maintained at the CBR. These accounts served as the main vehicle for financing expenditures on Russian exports. And then in mid-1993 came a further initiative aimed at constraining the use of cash rubles. In response to earlier restrictions many of the republics had begun to issue "coupons," a kind of parallel currency usable for local wage and consumption payments, which effectively freed some of their ruble liquidity to be spent on purchases from Russia. As a countermeasure, in July 1993, the CBR introduced a new ruble banknote to replace the old Soviet-era currency still in circulation. As the new banknotes were available only inside Russia (and old banknotes were no longer acceptable), the republics were deprived of a usable means of payment for Russian products.

The purpose of these reforms, quite plainly, was to compel all the sucessor states to make a clear choice—accept the authority of the CBR over the entire ruble zone, or leave. The IMF had earlier advocated some form of compromise between these drastic alternatives, based on a shared responsibility for monetary management (Hernandez–Cata 1995), and agreement might still have been possible had Moscow been willing. As late as September 1993 the Russians signed a multilateral agreement with Armenia, Belarus, Kazakhstan, Tajikistan, and Uzbekistan calling for a "Ruble Zone of a New Type" with unified monetary and fiscal policies. But when Moscow demanded that the others deposit all their gold and hard-currency reserves with the CBR, it became clear that the Russians were more interested in control than in cooperation. In Conway's delicate phrasing: "The CBR's actions indicate[d] a desire to maintain the ruble area, but on terms favorable to Russia (1995:34)."[27] After a year and a half of bitter experience, a true monetary alliance no longer seemed politically feasible.

The issue was forced. Republics now had to choose between subordinating their monetary sovereignty to Russia or replicating the Westphalian model by creating their own territorial currency. Within months, every successor state other than Belarus and Tajikistan moved decisively to adopt the latter option. The first to follow the Baltic nations was Kirghizia, which with IMF assistance had already introduced a new national money, the som, in May 1993. The last was Ukraine, which replaced a temporary coupon money with the hryvnia in September 1996.

In less than five years the ruble zone shrank from fifteen constituent members to three: Russia and the sad cases of Belarus and Tajikistan, both still using the Russian currency alongside their own "interim" versions. With only eleven million people, an economy overwhelmingly dependent on Russian oil, and an uncertain sense of its own nationhood, Belarus has signed repeated agreements handing over control of monetary and credit policies to the CBR, though none has yet been fully implemented. The government of Tajikistan, threatened by an Islamic insurgency supported from Afghanistan, receives two-thirds of its state budget from Moscow and relies on the Russian military for survival. The country is, in effect, a Russian protectorate. Neither Belarus nor Tajikistan has much real sovereignty to share.

Creating a Monetary Alliance

The diversity of these historical experiences raises two interesting and related questions. First, what motivates governments, ever jealous of their independence, even to consider the possibility of sharing monetary sovereignty? Second, what determines whether a monetary alliance, once formed, will long survive or fail? The former question, discussed in this section, has to do with the decision to *create* a currency merger of some kind; the latter, to be addressed in the following section, pertains to the ability of states to *sustain* their mutual commitments over time. At each stage, not surprisingly, politics as well as economics plays an important role in the calculation of gains and losses.

Gains and losses

The decision to join a currency alliance dilutes all four of the unique boons associated with a national monetary monopoly: a symbol of state identity, seigniorage, macroeconomic control, and political insulation. These are real losses. No longer can each government frame policies with its own interests uppermost in mind. Now powers must be shared, and compromises are often required. What compensating benefits might make the sacrifice of autonomy seem worthwhile?

One gain, frequently cited in the current EMU debate, is the creation of an important symbol for eventual merger at the political level. From its beginnings the EU has, in the words of the Maastricht Treaty, made "an ever closer union among the peoples of Europe" its principal and overarching objective. In this context the projected Euro can help promote the imagined community of Europe just as separate national currencies did in the process of state-building in the nineteenth century. The repeated efforts, halting though they were, of Zollverein members to construct a workable German monetary union in the last century may well have had the same effect.

Another gain, also political in nature, may be an improved power position in relation to the outside world. Inside a currency alliance, members are less insulated from one another. But for the group as a whole, exposure to foreign influence or constraint can be significantly reduced. Benjamin Franklin, at the signing of America's Declaration of Independence in 1776, exhorted his colleagues with the famous words: "We must indeed all hang together or, most assuredly, we shall all hang separately." More recently, albeit less colorfully, the same thought has been expressed by a student of economic integration: "Relatively small countries have an incentive to integrate in the monetary field in order to avoid the monetary domination of larger countries" (Jovanovic 1992:123). A desire for some measure of mutual security has undoubtedly been an adhesive binding together both the CFA Franc Zone and the East Caribbean Currency Area, each comprised of small and not particularly puissant former colonies. Quite noticeably, it has motivated even the European Union during its recurrent attempts to attain a common currency.

For the Europeans a key issue, going back to the origins of the Euro-currency market, has always been their inordinate dependence on the dollar, which leaves them vulnerable to financial disruption and even policy coercion from Washington. Insulation from an increasingly troubled dollar was quite plainly a motivation for both the original snake-in-the-tunnel experiment and the later EMS. When Helmut Schmidt spoke in 1978 of a zone of monetary stability in Europe, everyone knew that the *in*stability of America's greenback—whose steep depreciation in preceding months had wrought havoc in European financial markets—was uppermost in his mind. As I wrote shortly after the EMS got under way: "A principal attraction of the EMS for Community members was that it would help shield them from similar instabilities of the dollar in the future" (B. Cohen 1981:11). Europeans have long seen EMU as a necessary condition for reducing U.S. monetary hegemony in their part of the world. A unified currency, they argue, would both compete more effectively with the dollar in private markets and enhance Europe's bargaining strength in intergovernmental monetary negotiations.[28]

On the economic side, a variety of benefits are often mentioned, in particular improvements in the usefulness of money in each of its principal functions: as a medium of exchange (transactions costs diminish as the number of required currency conversions decreases), store of value (exchange risk goes down as the number of currencies decreases), and unit of account (information saving accompanies a decrease in the number of required price quotations). Additional benefits may also accrue: international reserves may be saved due to an internalization through credit of what would otherwise be external trade and payments; and a broadening of the foreign-exchange market vis-à-vis third countries may decrease currency volatility (Mundell 1973).

Evaluating costs and benefits

How do states evaluate the potential costs and benefits of sharing sovereignty? The formal economics literature addresses this decision, like the choice among exchange-rate rules discussed in Chapter 3, as an optimization problem—but one limited exclusively to issues of public finance or macroeconomic performance. Here too little attention is paid to domestic distributional concerns or to the value of political symbolism or insulation from foreign influence.

For economists who focus on seigniorage, the main question is fiscal: how can a single money or equivalent be reconciled with divergent state revenue requirements?[29] Differences in fiscal structures may justify fairly substantial differences in optimal seigniorage rates. Joining a currency alliance thus may cause problems if it means giving up a critical instrument of taxation. As the economist Rudiger Dornbusch has written:

> Public finance imposes an important constraint on the possibility of monetary unions. Countries for whom the efficient tax structure implies the use of an inflation

tax—because the marginal cost of an extra dollar of resources raised this way is significantly less than that of raising (say) social security tax rates—should not merge with others for whom zero inflation is the policy objective. (1988:26)

Here too, however, the bulk of analysis focuses not on government operations but on the economy as a whole: not the state's fiscal requirements but general economic welfare, as reflected in standard measures of macroeconomic performance. This is the familiar theory of "optimum currency areas" (OCAs), which was in fact the progenitor of the more recent studies of optimal exchange-rate management I mentioned in Chapter 3. The country characteristics that are considered for their influence on the choice among degrees of exchange-rate flexibility first made their appearance in OCA theory, dating back to a pioneering article by Robert Mundell in 1961.[30] The two branches of theory are closely related, even though one is concerned with subordination of monetary sovereignty whereas the other poses the possibility that currency authority might be shared.

In its first incarnation, OCA theory was strikingly apolitical. Following Mundell's lead, most early contributors concentrated on a search for the most appropriate domain of a currency irrespective of existing national frontiers. The globe was treated as in effect a tabula rasa. The central issue was to find the best criterion for the organization of monetary space. But as the practical limitations of the so-called "criteria approach" (Tavlas 1994:213) became clear, an alternative— and, in political terms, less naïve—approach eventually prevailed, focusing instead on material gains and losses, as seen from a single country's point of view, from participation in a common currency area or its equivalent. Against the advantages of a more useful money, governments are assumed to compare the disadvantages of the corresponding surrender of monetary autonomy: the potential cost of having to adjust to domestic or external disturbances without the option of changing either the money supply or the exchange rate. As the noted economist Paul Krugman summarizes the calculus, it "is a matter of trading off macroeconomic flexibility against microeconomic efficiency" (1993:4).

The OCA literature stresses a diverse range of variables, including: wage and price flexibility, labor and capital mobility, commodity diversification, geographic trade patterns, size and openness of economies, levels of development, inflation trends, and the nature, source, and timing of potential payments disturbances. Each variable arguably affects the magnitude of losses at the macroeconomic level by influencing either the severity of potential shocks or the ease of consequent adjustment. The explanatory power of OCA theory, however, appears to be no greater than that of optimal exchange-rate management models. There are simply too many permutations possible among the many factors cited. As one source puts it, quite bluntly, "theoretical ambiguities abound" (Argy and De Grauwe 1990:2). Not all of an economy's characteristics point in the same direction, making forecasts difficult; nor are the variables necessarily mutually independent or easy to measure or compare for relative importance. Concludes Charles Goodhart: "The evidence . . . suggests that the theory of optimum currency areas has relatively little predictive value" (1995:452).

In fact, it is plain that as in the selection of currency regimes discussed in Chapter 3, political factors must weigh at least as heavily as economic issues in the calculations of governments. Certainly, we may assume that states are sensitive to the balance between macro flexibility and micro efficiency. But in considering whether to share their monetary sovereignty, they are hardly likely to limit their thinking to that one trade-off alone. Here too there must be a strong political incentive, driven by either domestic politics or foreign policy, to persuade governments to make the firm commitment that is demanded.

And that certainly appears to be the lesson of history, as the economist Paul De Grauwe has observed: "Not a single monetary union in the past came about because of a recognition of economic benefits of the union. In all cases the integration was driven by political objectives" (1993:656). For all the diverse experiences noted in this chapter, it is impossible to find an example of a monetary alliance motivated exclusively, or even predominantly, by the concerns highlighted in OCA theory. In the nineteenth century, Keynesian-style monetary management was not yet a priority. Of the five unions established earlier in the twentieth century, one (BLEU) clearly grew out of the security needs of a small and vulnerable quasi-state; the other four, from arrangements initially imposed by colonial powers. In Europe today, after decades of debate, it has become abundantly clear that the purely economic case for EMU is inconclusive at best. The real issues, most observers concur, are undoubtedly political, relating first and foremost to the Maastricht Treaty's declared goal of an "ever closer union." To its enemies as well as to its friends, the single currency is a harbinger of eventual political integration. In the words of one careful survey:

> Although there are surely economic benefits to be expected from a monetary union, the main driving force for [EMU's] resurgence remains the quest for the political integration of Europe. . . . The main objections to monetary union have also been largely political. (Fratianni et al. 1992:1–2)[31]

In brief: economics may matter, but politics matters more.

Sustaining a Monetary Alliance

But what politics? The diverse origins of our historical cases, each of which seems *sui generis*, allow little room for generalization about the specifics of the trade-offs involved. We can gain more insight by looking at what happens to monetary alliances *after* they come into existence. Some unions have successfully survived for decades; others have eroded or failed almost immediately. Much can be learned by exploring the conditions that determine the sustainability of mutual state commitments of this kind.[32]

Manifestly, the historical record is diverse. Only four past unions (BLEU, CFA, ECCA, and CMA) may fairly be described as successful, having been sustained for decades. Others, including EAC as well as the Soviet Union's ruble zone and other former federations, have disintegrated almost as soon as their members gained political independence and can only be judged failures. And the nineteenth century's two major examples, the LMU and SMU, elicit a mixed verdict. Each functioned more or less effectively until World War I (a not inconsiderable achievement) yet ultimately proved unsustainable. What explains these striking contrasts in experience?

Economics and organizational design

Economic variables offer little assistance. As I have noted elsewhere (B. Cohen 1993a), for every one of the characteristics conventionally stressed in the OCA literature, there are contradictory examples—some cases that conform to the expectations of theory and others that do not. None seems sufficient to explain all observed outcomes. I do not suggest that economic factors are therefore unimportant—clearly they do matter insofar as they tend, through their impact on adjustment costs, to ease or exacerbate the challenge of a monetary alliance. But it is just as clear that more has gone on in each case than such variables can account for alone.

Nor is much help offered by an analysis of organizational design: legal provisions concerning the issuing of currency and the management of monetary policy. Such formalities have differed sharply in various cases. Only in three instances have members voluntarily relied exclusively on a common currency—in the East Caribbean and, more briefly, in East and southern Africa. In all the others, including EAC after 1967 and CMA after 1974, arrangements have featured national or regional currencies that were officially linked to some extent or another. And in parallel fashion monetary institutions have also varied greatly, ranging from a single central authority in two cases (ECCA and, before the mid-1960s, EAC) to two regional authorities in one case (CFA), and separate national agencies in all the others (including the ruble zone and other such federations after their breakup). No systematic relationship is evident, however, between these organizational differences and the success or failure of various alliances.

In principle, such differences might be thought to matter insofar as they affect the net costs of compliance or defection by individual states. The recent theoretical literature on transactions costs emphasizes the key role that organizational design can play in promoting credible commitments, by structuring arrangements to match anticipated incentive problems (North 1990). From this perspective,

creation of a single currency looks superior to a formal linking of national currencies because of the higher barriers to exit: reintroducing an independent money
and monetary authority will be much more costly.[33]

That is also the conclusion of recent policy discussions of EMU, which have
directly addressed the relative merits of full monetary union versus simple
exchange-rate union (Gros and Thygesen 1992:230–233; von Hagen and Fratianni 1993). Most analysts doubt that a system which retains existing moneys and
central banks, no matter how solemn the political commitments involved, will be
as credible as a genuine joint currency, precisely because the risk of reversibility
will presumably be greater. Compliance mechanisms are likely to be weaker to the
extent that governments continue to exercise any control over either the price or
the quantity of their currency. Thus one might expect to find a direct historical
correlation between the degree of centralization of a monetary alliance and its
practical sustainability over time.

Indeed, one economic historian, Mark Griffiths (1992), suggests that is precisely the reason why the Latin Monetary Union ultimately collapsed. Much of
the strain experienced by the LMU in the decades before World War I is directly
attributable to its decentralized structure, which permitted each national central
bank to pursue its own domestic policy objectives. Once global depreciation of
silver began in the late 1860s, several members (in particular, Italy) succumbed to
the temptation to increase the amount and circulation of their silver coinage, in
effect seeking to extract additional seigniorage gains at the expense of their partners (especially France, where many of the silver coins ended up). To hold the
union together, members first restricted and in 1878 suspended all silver coinage
other than token money (the limping gold standard); and subsequently, from
1885, added a liquidation clause at the behest of France requiring any state
wishing to leave the group to redeem its silver held by other member-governments
in gold or convertible paper. Even before the financial disruptions of World War I,
the only sense of common interest remaining among union members was a mutual
desire to avoid a potentially costly dissolution. In Griffiths's words: "This
demonstrates the rather obvious point that a monetary union based on independent central banks is potentially unstable" (1992:88).[34] A similar free-rider problem was of course also manifest in the disintegration of the ruble zone after 1991
as well as in the earlier break-up of the Austro-Hungarian Empire.

But what then of the Scandinavian Monetary Union, which was also based on
independent central banks yet managed to function far more smoothly than the
LMU in the decades before World War I? Or the Belgium-Luxembourg Economic Union, CFA Franc Zone, and Common Monetary Area, all of which are
still sustained successfully even though they lack either a joint currency or a single
central institution? Or the East African Community, where neither a common
currency nor a central authority in the end could stop disintegration? Once again,
contradictory examples abound.

In fact, the same lesson seems to apply here as in the choice among exchange-rate rules discussed in Chapter 3. Clearly, the degree of centralization must matter, insofar as it influences the potential cost of exit. But here too, however high the barriers to exit, vows can be—and, indeed, frequently have been—broken when governments decide it is in their interest to do so. Organizational design is probably no less important than economic characteristics. But it is equally clear that something else is at work here that overshadows them both. That something, of course, is politics.

Political factors

From a political perspective, two characteristics stand out as crucial for the fate of monetary alliances. One is suggested by traditional realist approaches to international relations: the presence or absence of a dominant state willing to keep such an arrangement functioning effectively on terms agreeable to all. The other is suggested by institutional approaches: the presence or absence of a broad constellation of related ties and commitments sufficient to make the loss of policy autonomy, whatever the magnitude of prospective adjustment costs, basically acceptable to each partner. The first implies a subordination as well as a sharing of monetary sovereignty. It calls for a local hegemon and is a direct reflection of the distribution of interstate power. The second calls for a well-developed set of institutional linkages and reflects, more amorphously, the degree to which a genuine sense of solidarity—of *community*—exists among the countries involved. Judging from the historical record, one or the other factor is necessary to sustain monetary alliances among sovereign states. Where both are present, they are a sufficient condition for success. Where neither is present, unions erode or fail.[35]

Consider, for example, the Belgium-Luxembourg Economic Union, by far the most durable alliance still in existence. Both of these necessary political characteristics have long been evident in BLEU. Belgium from the beginning has been the acknowledged dominant partner, making all the most important monetary decisions for both countries.[36] In part, the success of the arrangement reflects Belgium's willingness and ability to shoulder the main responsibility for managing the partners' joint affairs. And in part it reflects a broader constellation of reciprocal ties, in BLEU itself as well as in related regional groupings such as Benelux and the European Union. Between these states is a web of institutional linkages and a sense of common interest sufficient to make a permanent commitment to monetary cooperation attractive, or at least not intolerable.

At the opposite extreme is the East African Community, one of the least durable among recent cases. Here neither of the necessary political characteristics was to be found. Certainly there seems to have been little feeling of solidarity among the three countries, despite their legacy of common colonial services and institutions. Much more influential was a pervasive sensitivity to any threat to newly won national sovereignty. Once independent, each of the three new governments eagerly concentrated on building state identity rather than on preserving regional unity. A hardening of national priorities and interests, compounded by sharp divergences in ideology and political style, quickly eroded any commitment to continued economic cooperation (Rothchild, 1974).

Nor was any locally dominant power in the EAC willing and able to use its influence to counteract these forces. Kenya was most advanced in terms of industrial development but still too poor to act the role of hegemon. Instead of using its leading position in intraregional trade to promote community ties, Kenya was understandably tempted to exploit its position for its own ends, thus aggravating rather than moderating strains and tensions among the members (Mugomba 1978; Mbogoro 1985). Beyond the EAC, Britain as former colonial master might have continued support for regional institutions but, burdened by its own economic difficulties, chose instead to distance itself from its former dependencies. The sterling area was dismantled in the early 1970s, and so removed the last barrier to pursuit of independent currency policies by each government. These inauspicious political circumstances make it hardly surprising that the EAC failed totally.

The importance of a local hegemon is also demonstrated by the two successful African cases, both clearly dominated by a single core country (Honohan 1992). In the Common Monetary Area South Africa is the leader: it not only stands as lender of last resort for its junior partners but even compensates two of them, Lesotho and Namibia, for the seigniorage they forego in using the rand as legal tender. (Compensation is based on an estimate of the income that would accrue to them if they had reserves of equivalent amount invested in rand-denominated assets.) In the CFA Franc Zone leadership is provided by France, the former colonial power. The durability of the CFA, most sources agree, is directly attributable to the pivotal role played by the French Ministry of Finance in underwriting—in effect, subsidizing—francophone Africa's monetary alliance.

Although not formally a member of the CFA Zone, France exercises decisive influence through the so-called operations accounts maintained by the group's two regional central banks at the French Treasury, into which each is obliged to deposit some two-thirds of its foreign-exchange reserves. In return, France enhances the credibility of the CFA franc by guaranteeing its convertibility at a fixed price. Monetary discipline is implemented through rules that affect access to credit from the Treasury as well as through the firm peg of the CFA franc to the French franc, a ratio of 50:1 for more than four decades before a 50-percent devaluation (to 100:1) in 1994 (Clement 1994, 1995). CFA countries also share some sense of community, of course; a common language and colonial experience, and a constellation of related regional agreements. But for better or worse,[37] the role of France is paramount.

French hegemony was also decisive in the Latin Monetary Union, albeit in rather less benign form. In this case, the dominant state used its power in a much more narrowly self-interested fashion, first to promote France's monetary leadership and later to prevent a costly dissolution. As Griffiths (1992:141) has written: "Throughout [the LMU's] evolution the influence of France remained ever-present, extracting concessions from its fellow members. Although only one country out of four [*sic*], France remained dominant, reflecting the realities of its economic and political power."

Even before LMU was formally established, France's influence, mainly based on its dominating position in regional trade, was evident in the willing adaptation to its currency system by its smaller trading partners. French hegemony was further evident in the bloc's initial decision to base LMU on a bimatellic standard even though France's partners would all have preferred a monometallic gold standard (Bartel 1974:695–696). And it was certainly evident after the LMU was transformed into a limping gold standard, when France resorted to a threat of penalties—formalized in the liquidation clause added at its behest in 1885—to discourage member withdrawals that would have left the French with large holdings of unredeemable silver coins. But for this pressure from France, the LMU might have broken up well before the financial disruptions of World War I.

The importance of an institutionalized sense of community is amply demonstrated, in a negative way, by the speed with which the ruble zone and similar failed federations (the Austro–Hungarian Empire, Czechoslovakia, Yugoslavia) fell apart once competing nationalisms gained political ascendancy. Disintegration of the ruble zone, in particular, was obviously hastened by the unwillingness of successor states to place group cohesion above their separate desires for seigniorage revenue. Breakup became unavoidable after Russia, the acknowledged senior partner, made it clear that it would bear the responsibilities of leadership only on its own terms.

In a more positive manner, the importance of community is demonstrated by two long-lived alliances, the East Caribbean Currency Area and the Scandinavian Monetary Union, neither of which could be described as in any way hegemonic systems. In the ECCA the partners are all island microstates, comparably small and poor, and they have been left more or less on their own by their former colonial master. In the SMU Sweden may have been first among equals, but it exercised nothing like the power that France enjoyed in the LMU. Yet both unions functioned reasonably well for decades—the SMU until 1914, the ECCA to the present day. The explanation for their longevity seems directly related to the genuine feelings of solidarity that have existed among their members.

In the East Caribbean, unlike in East Africa, there has never been much value placed on separate sovereignties: identities have always been defined more in regional than in national terms, institutionalized in a dense web of related economic and political agreements. The ECCA, as one observer has noted, is just one part of a much broader effort by which these seven governments "have pooled their resources in a symbolic, symbiotic and substantive way with the aim of furthering their development" (Jones-Hendrickson 1989:71). Likewise the Scandinavian nations, unlike the members of the LMU, had long shared a tradition of cooperation based on a common cultural and political background. As one source puts it: "Language, social life, administration, legislation, judiciary, poetry and literature, science, and many other aspects of life created bonds between these peoples who had been intimately linked for such a long and important period" (Wendt 1981:17). Given the depth of existing ties, a common currency system seemed not only natural but almost inevitable until it was fatally disrupted by World War I.

When it comes to sustaining a monetary alliance, in short, the issue is only secondarily whether members meet the traditional criteria identified in OCA theory or whether monetary management and currency issue happen to be centralized or decentralized. The primary question is whether a local hegemon or a fabric of related ties exists to neutralize the risks of free-riding or exit. Sovereign governments require incentives to stick to bargains that turn out to be inconvenient. The evidence from history suggests that these incentives may derive either from side-payments or from sanctions supplied by a single powerful state or from the constraints and opportunities posed by a broad network of institutional linkages. One or the other of these political factors, it appears, must be present to serve as an effective compliance mechanism.

Once again, the bottom line is simple. Monetary alliances between independent states are neither infrequent nor unmanageable. But nothing can be taken for granted in a world where everything governments do is potentially reversible. For Michael Mussa, the essence of a currency union is the irrevocable commitment: "For a monetary union, 'What the Lord hath joined together, let no man put asunder'" (Mussa 1997:218). In fact, though, as I stressed in Chapter 3, a wedding ring by no means guarantees an everlasting marriage. Divorce remains an option. Conditions must be right, therefore, for governments voluntarily to share—and then stick to their commitment to share—something as valuable as their national monetary sovereignty.

Nearly three decades ago, the economist Norman Mintz wrote:

> It has often been argued that the conditions under which monetary integration might reasonably be expected to succeed are very restrictive. In fact, these conditions appear no more restrictive than the conditions for the establishment of a successful common market. The major, and perhaps only, real condition for the institution of either is the *political will* to integrate on the part of prospective members. (1970:33, emphasis added)

At one level, this conclusion may appear naive—yet another example of the economist's propensity to compress all the complexities of political process into the simple notion "political will." But Mintz shows profound insight if we understand "political will" to refer either to the motivations of a local hegemon or to the value attached to a common endeavor. In fact, these *are* the main conditions necessary for success of such variants on the Westphalian model.

Currency Competition
and Hierarchy

"**Y**ou are an old man who thinks in terms of nations and peoples. There are no nations, there are no peoples, there are no Russians, there are no Arabs, there are no Third Worlds, there is no West. There is only one holistic system of systems, one vast and immense interwoven, interacting, multivariate, multinational dominion of dollars, petro–dollars, electro–dollars, multi–dollars, Reichsmarks, rubles, pounds, and shekels. It is the international system of currency which determines the totality of life on this planet. That is the natural order of things today. That is the atomic, and subatomic, and galactic structure of things today."

Arthur Jensen to Howard Beale in the movie *Network*, 1976

Imagine the setting: an elegant corporate boardroom, a bewildered TV news anchorman, and the agitated chairman of the network loudly proclaiming that the age of territorial money is over. In the film *Network*, some two decades ago, these words were meant as the ravings of a lunatic. In the real world today, Arthur Jensen's harangue now seems prophetic.

The reason, of course, is the rapid acceleration of cross-border currency competition, which has transformed the spatial organization of global monetary relations. National currency domains are more interpenetrated today than at any time since the dawn of the era of territorial money. Less and less is money's imaginary landscape accurately represented by the outdated myth of One Nation/One Money. More and more the state-centric Westphalian model, with all its diverse variations, is revealed for what it is: a very special case. Today, monetary geography is best understood in functional rather than physical terms—currency spaces that are flow-based rather than bound to place. We may not yet have arrived at the "holistic system of systems" envisioned by the movie character Jensen, so reminiscent of the market-driven world of denationalized money advocated by Nobel laureate Friedrich Hayek. But the monetary universe has certainly become far more interwoven and multinational than a strictly territorial imagery would imply.

Can the dimensions of this new "galactic structure" be precisely measured? The answer, unfortunately, is No. We lack the comprehensive, consistent data on global currency use that we need to fully identify the authoritative domain of each individual money. A flow-based model of currency spaces, accurately embodying hierarchical links as well as transactional networks, is not easy to operationalize for empirical purposes. Partial indicators, however, are available from a variety of published and unpublished sources, and we can usefully employ them to gauge at least the rough outlines of our new "virtual" geography. The aim of this chapter is to piece together a large sample of relevant financial statistics. The picture that emerges from this survey is one of intense competition as well as distinct hierarchy among the world's many currencies.

Cross-Border Use

Moneys are employed outside their country of origin in one of two broad ways—transactions either across national borders or within foreign states. The former is usually referred to as international currency use (or currency internationalization); the latter is typically described as currency substitution and will be referred to as foreign-domestic use. For short we may use the abbreviations CI and CS, respectively. CI alters money's imaginary landscape by accentuating the hierarchical relationship among currencies, expanding the authoritative domains of a few popular moneys well beyond the jurisdictions of the countries that issue them. CS is a direct invasion of traditional territorial domains, diminishing the use and influence of less popular currencies. Both types of cross-border activity undermine our standard images of monetary geography, accentuating the value of a flow-based rather than a state-centric model of monetary geography.

Past treatments

Monetary specialists are familiar with both CI and CS and often discuss them in the technical economics literature,[1] but they address the analytical implications for the organization of currency space only infrequently and rarely in other than conventional terms.

Currency internationalization can occur at two levels of operation: at the private level, as a medium of exchange (a "vehicle") for foreign trade, as a unit of account for commercial invoicing, and as store of value for international investments; and at the official level, as a reserve and intervention medium and as a peg for exchange rates.[2] Use at either level clearly may affect the authoritative domains of individual currencies, by altering transactional networks or power relationships. In standard discussions, however, such impacts tend to receive little systematic attention. Inasmuch as the ramifications for monetary geography are addressed at all, they are generally presented in terms of orthodox variations on the traditional Westphalian model.

Take, for example, the role that CI may play in subordinating monetary sovereignty, which Jonathan Kirshner recently described as "a neglected area of study" (1995:3). That role has of course come up in historical and institutional studies of the nineteenth-century gold standard as well as of the Bretton Woods system after World War II.[3] It figures too in more contemporary accounts of dominance-dependence relations among national currencies;[4] and, not surprisingly, it is also integral to Kirshner's own detailed treatise on international monetary power. But of all the effects examined, most tend to be limited to relations between nominally sovereign governments—reflecting the analytical norms of conventional political geography.

Likewise CI is obviously crucial to studies of the anchor role of international currencies. But as we saw in Chapter 3, the monetary blocs ostensibly created by exchange-rate pegs remain firmly rooted in a territorial imagery based solely on states. Implications of CI for the sharing of monetary sovereignty have only very recently begun to receive serious scholarly treatment (Thygesen et al. 1995).

The same limitations are also evident in the literature on currency substitution. Two key variants of CS are generally distinguished. One is the more or less symmetrical interchangeability of money or monetary assets characteristic of financial relations among industrial countries.[5] CS in this sense, which encompasses activity in the Euro-currency market as well as in national financial markets, compromises the exclusive territoriality of currencies by permitting substitution of foreign for domestic money as a vehicle for saving, borrowing, or investment. Symmetrical CS may be viewed as integral to the process of global portfolio diversification and might more appropriately be regarded as part of the phenomenon of currency internationalization—cross-border use of money as a store of value. It is what economists normally have in mind when they talk of "capital mobility." Authoritative domains are reciprocally extended.

The other variant of CS, often labeled "dollarization," refers to the asymmetrical situation of many developing countries and transition economies where home demand for a desirable foreign currency (e.g., the U.S. dollar) is not matched by a counterpart demand from abroad for the domestic money.[6] Here, the authoritative domain of the foreign money effectively extends to encompass much of the local economy, and that of the domestic currency is correspondingly eclipsed. Though technically also a form of capital mobility, this CS is better described as "capital flight." Not only is monetary preference unreciprocated. It is also often (though not always) difficult to reverse, subject to what specialists call strong hysteresis or ratchet effects.[7] Once people develop a taste for an appetizing foreign currency, it is not easy to persuade them to give it up.[8]

The first variant of CS, once widely discussed by monetary theorists,[9] has been formally related to the spatial organization of currency relations almost exclusively in the context of the European Union (EU), as part of ongoing debates over EMU. Early on, the main question was the extent to which currency substitution, widely seen as contributing to exchange-rate volatility in Europe, might provide a decisive incentive for formal monetary unification.[10] Later the issue was turned on its head by advocates of less politicized money, taking their lead from Friedrich Hayek. A common currency, various sources argued, might better be attained not by government fiat—the Maastricht strategy—but through a direct competition of moneys in the marketplace.[11] To date, however, only a few sketchy attempts have been made to systematically analyze the effects of this variant of CS on a monetary alliance. Results are inconclusive.[12] Otherwise its possible relevance to the sharing of monetary sovereignty is mentioned, if at all, only in passing.

CS in the second sense, which may be for any or all of the usual monetary purposes, has to my knowledge never been explicitly related to the spatial organization of currency relations.

Motivations

Both types of cross-border currency use, international and foreign-domestic, emerge from a broad and intense process of market competition. Each reflects the same demand-driven, Darwinian struggle that characterized global practice throughout most of money's history prior to the nineteenth century.[13] Neither is at all irrational as a form of behavior. On the contrary, each may be regarded as a quite natural response to prevailing market structures and incentives.

Analytically, the motivations for each type are easily appreciated. Internationalization (including the symmetrical variant of CS)[14] derives from the economies of scale, or reduced transactions costs, to be gained from concentrating cross-border activities in just one or at most a few currencies with broad transactional networks—the network externalities stressed in Chapter 1. To do business in each country in a separate money is analogous to barter and clearly inefficient. Just as monetary exchange rather than barter reduces the expenses associated with search and bargaining within a single national economy, so costs of transactions between states are narrowed by making use of one or just a few currencies rather than many. In the words of one recent discussion: "The necessity of 'double coincidence of wants' in a decentralized foreign exchange market may be overcome by using indirect exchange, through a generally acceptable medium of exchange instead of direct exchange of currencies."[15] The greater the volume of transactions that can be done via a single vehicle currency, the smaller are the costs of gathering information and converting from one money to another.

In fact, the advantages of internationalization are really much the same as the economic benefits claimed for a formal interstate monetary alliance, as outlined in Chapter 4. Like currency unification, CI improves the usefulness of money in each of its principal functions. A vehicle role enhances a currency's value both as a commercial medium of exchange and as a unit of account for invoicing; and these effects in turn broaden its appeal as a store of value, by facilitating accumulation of wealth in assets of more universal purchasing power. At a minimum, it will pay transactors to hold some working balances in a popular international currency. Depending on cross-border variations of interest rates and exchange-rate expectations, it will often pay them to use it for longer-term investment purposes too. And of course once a money comes to be widely used at the private level, it is more likely to be employed at the official level as well, as a reserve and intervention medium. Governments too can benefit from the economies of scale offered by a broad transactional network.[16]

The typical motivation for asymmetrical CS is a high or accelerating inflation rate, which reduces a currency's purchasing power both at home and, through exchange depreciation, for transactions abroad. Residents, accordingly, have an incentive to turn to some more stable foreign money as a preferred store of value—an inflation hedge for their savings—and perhaps even as a unit of account and medium of exchange. Foreign money, in effect, becomes the public's financial refuge, a convenient defense against abuse of the seigniorage privilege by government. As one source has explained, using a medical metaphor:

> Few national currencies survive the destructive power of high inflation. Like a crippling disease that leaves no part of the organism untouched, high inflation severely hinders the ability of a currency to perform its basic functions. . . . [But] unlike an organism that is unique and cannot be replaced, substitutes for a sick currency are easy to come by. . . . Not surprisingly, then, the public turns to a foreign money in its quest for a healthy currency (Calvo and Vegh 1993:34).

Who would not choose inoculation against a crippling disease if a cure is so easy to find?

Choices

Which currencies are likely to prevail in the Darwinian struggle? The principal qualities required for competitive success are familiar to specialists and hardly controversial.[17] Demand is shaped by three essential attributes.

First, at least during the initial stages of a currency's cross-border use, is widespread confidence in a money's future value backed by political stability in the country of origin. The historian Carlo Cipolla, in his early discussion of the "dollars of the Middle Ages" (1967: chap. 2), laid particular emphasis on "high unitary value and intrinsic stability" as essential conditions for the emergence of a dominant international money. More recently, economists such as George Tavlas (1996b) have made much the same point in emphasizing the importance of a proven track record of relatively low inflation and low inflation variability. High and fluctuating inflation rates increase the cost of acquiring information and performing price calculations. No currency will be willingly adopted for cross-border purposes if its purchasing power cannot be forecast with some degree of assurance.

Second are two qualities that I have elsewhere referred to as "exchange convenience" and "capital certainty" (B. Cohen 1971a)—a high degree of transactional liquidity and a reasonable predictability of asset value. The key to both is a set of well-developed financial markets, sufficiently open to ensure full access to non-residents. Markets must not be encumbered by high transactions costs or formal or informal barriers to entry. They must also be broad, with a large assortment of instruments available for temporary or longer-term forms of investment. And they must be deep and resilient, with fully operating secondary markets for most if not all financial claims.

Finally, and most important of all, a money must promise a broad transactional network, since nothing enhances a currency's acceptability more than the prospect of acceptability by others. Historically, this factor has usually meant an economy that is large in absolute size and well integrated into world markets. A large economy creates a naturally ample constituency for a currency; economies of scale are further enhanced if the issuing country is also a major player in world commerce. As Jeffrey Frankel has suggested: "The currency of a country that has a large share of international output, trade and finance has a natural advantage" (1995a:4). No money has ever risen to a position of international preeminence which was not initially backed by a leading national economy. The greater the volume of transactions conducted in or with a country, the greater are the potential network externalities to be derived from use of its money.

None of these attributes is a constant, however, as history amply demonstrates. Quite the contrary, in fact. Every one of a currency's attractions is subject to erosion with time, particularly if an issuing government imprudently abuses its monetary privilege.[18] Hence the shape of demand, which determines the outcome of the competitive process, is also likely to change substantially from one period to the next. Shakespeare's words are as apt for money as they are for monarchs: "Uneasy lies the head that wears the crown." No currency has ever enjoyed permanent dominance for either international or foreign-domestic use.

Empirical Evidence

Available data, as I have indicated, are insufficient to document fully either type of cross-border currency use. But enough statistics can be mobilized to provide at least rough orders of magnitude for both. Taken together, these diverse indicators—however uneven or incomplete they may be—offer a composite map of money's flow-based geography that is strikingly at variance with the conventional imagery of strictly territorial currencies.

Currency internationalization

The phenomenon of currency internationalization is far better documented than is that of currency substitution. Regularly published data are available from the major multilateral financial institutions, including especially the International Monetary Fund and the Bank for International Settlements (BIS), and they outline in considerable detail the currency composition of central-bank reserves (Tables 5.1 and 5.2) as well as outstanding stocks of claims in world financial markets (Table 5.3). These sources provide a reasonably satisfactory indication of the store-of-value use of various moneys at both the official and the private levels of international transactions. Rather more spotty data can also be found for the currency denomination of merchandise trade flows (Tables 5.4–5.9) and gross turnover in the global foreign-exchange market (Table 5.10) to offer some measure of the extent of private use for unit-of-account and medium-of-exchange purposes. Trade-invoicing statistics may be regarded as indicative of currency use for "retail" commercial purposes; exchange-market statistics, for activity at the "wholesale" level. And while, as a rule, central banks keep data on their own operations secret,[19] enough information on the currency distribution of reserve purchases and sales has been released recently (Table 5.11) to give a hint about the use of national moneys as official intervention media, too.

Overall, two messages stand out in the available statistics. First is the enormous magnitude of international currency use, which continues to grow at a phenomenal pace. The clearest signal is sent by the foreign-exchange market, as shown in Table 5.10, where average daily turnover has accelerated from $620 billion in 1989 (the first year for which data are available) to close to $1.3 trillion six years later—a rate of increase of nearly 30 percent per annum. A parallel story is evident in Table 5.3, which records changes in cross-border holdings of private financial assets. Elsewhere (B. Cohen 1986) I have described the first years of the Euro-currency market as the Incredible Quarter Century: a span during which foreign bank loans grew from less than $1 billion in the late 1950s to something close to $1.3 trillion dollars by the early 1980s. Table 5.3 shows that the period since has been barely less incredible, as the aggregate stock of international claims—what Thygesen et al. (1995) call "global financial wealth," defined to include bond issues and foreign-currency deposits as well as bank loans—has continued to mushroom exponentially, from less than $1 trillion before 1985 to more than $4.5 trillion a decade later. Table 5.1 shows that official currency reserves also more than doubled over the same ten-year period.

The second message is that CI, while substantial in magnitude, is highly concentrated. Just a small handful of moneys account for the great bulk of use at both the private and the official levels. The U.S. dollar, though diminished somewhat, is still dominant in central-bank reserves and interventions, commercial banking claims and bond issues, and wholesale foreign-exchange market activity. Vying distantly for second place is the DM, especially important in official reserves and exchange markets; and third is Japan's yen, notable mainly in bank deposits and foreign securities. Together the dollar, DM, and yen are the Big Three of international currencies. The only other moneys of any note are the pound sterling and French and Swiss francs, and beyond them the Dutch guilder, Belgian franc, Italian lira, and Canadian dollar.

The dollar's preeminence is particularly evident at the official level, where it remains the clear favorite of most governments for all monetary uses. Certainly this seems to be the implication of recent trends in official reserve holdings, as shown in Tables 5.1 and 5.2. After declining gradually in the 1970s, following the breakdown of the Bretton Woods par-value system, the greenback's share of foreign-exchange reserves stabilized throughout the 1980s and has even increased modestly since then. Admittedly, some part of that performance has been a reflection of weakness, not strength, as the central banks of Europe and Japan have sought, through dollar purchases, to keep America's currency from depreciating relative to their own. But much of it undoubtedly pays eloquent testimony to the dollar's enduring usefulness as a store of value and intervention medium.

Indeed, if anything, tables 5.1 and 5.2 systematically understate the dollar's staying power, for two reasons. First is the separate inclusion in Table 5.1 of the European Currency Unit, even though ECUs are really no more than dollars by another name. Technically a composite reserve unit, the ECU is created by members of the European Monetary System through a complex set of revolving swaps designed to pool a proportion of their outstanding dollar holdings. In effect, ECUs are simply the label applied to each central bank's claim on the dollar pool and might well be included in the global total of dollar reserves, as they are in the final column of Table 5.1 and in all of Table 5.2. Second is the fact that during the period covered by the two tables, both the dollar's principal rivals, the DM and the yen, appreciated greatly against the greenback—in nominal terms, between 1980 and 1995, by 27 percent and 141 percent respectively. Without such valuation effects, which bias the data against a weakening currency, the dollar's share would appear even larger.

Significantly, the biggest drop in the dollar's reserve role has been in Europe— a natural concomitant of the emergence of the DM bloc since the snake experiment started in the early 1970s. Yet even among EU countries the dollar outranks Germany's money by a ratio of 3:1. Elsewhere the greenback remains the overwhelming preference of most central banks, in Latin America and even in Asia, confirming impressions gained from the studies of anchor currencies cited in Chapter 3. Though the number of moneys formally pegged to the dollar has been cut by more than half since 1979 (as we saw in Table 3.3), informal links to the greenback obviously survive. As I suggested earlier, the DM's influence at this level is still confined primarily to the European region.

This differential pattern is also indicated by the limited data on foreign-

Table 5.1. Currency composition of official foreign-exchange reserves, end of year, 1985–1996ª (percentages)

	1985	1986	1987	1988	1989	1990	1991	1992	1993	1994	1995	1996	Memorandum ECU-dollar swaps included with dollars (c) 1996
Total ($ billion)	348.3	363.8	455.8	494.2	545.0	593.8	625.4	646.6	717.6	775.6	890.6	1,301.5	...
All countries													
U.S. dollar	55.3	56.4	56.0	55.3	51.9	50.3	50.9	55.1	56.2	55.9	56.4	58.9	63.7
Deutschemark	13.9	13.2	13.4	14.5	18.0	17.4	15.7	13.5	14.1	14.3	13.7	13.6	14.0
Japanese yen	7.3	7.1	7.0	7.1	7.3	8.2	8.7	7.8	8.0	8.2	7.1	6.0	6.2
Pound sterling	2.7	2.3	2.2	2.5	2.6	3.2	3.4	3.2	3.1	3.5	3.4	3.4	3.5
French franc	0.8	0.7	0.8	1.0	1.4	2.3	2.8	2.4	2.2	2.1	1.8	1.6	1.6
Swiss franc	2.1	1.9	1.8	1.8	1.4	1.3	1.2	1.1	1.2	1.0	0.9	0.7	0.8
Netherlands guilder	0.9	1.0	1.2	1.0	1.1	1.0	1.1	0.6	0.6	0.5	0.4	0.3	0.4
ECU (European Currency Unit)	11.6	12.5	14.2	11.7	10.5	9.6	10.0	10.1	8.3	7.8	6.5	5.9	...
Unspecified currencies (b)	5.4	4.8	3.4	5.1	5.7	6.7	6.2	6.1	6.2	6.6	9.7	9.5	9.8
Industrial countries													
U.S. dollar	50.1	54.2	54.8	54.5	48.4	45.7	43.8	49.0	50.5	51.2	52.8	55.5	64.9
Deutschemark	16.7	14.6	14.1	15.5	20.6	19.8	18.3	15.0	16.4	16.4	15.7	16.4	17.5
Japanese yen	7.6	7.2	6.3	6.4	7.5	8.8	9.7	7.6	7.9	8.3	6.9	5.9	6.2
Pound sterling	1.6	1.1	1.0	1.3	1.2	1.7	1.8	2.3	2.2	2.3	2.1	2.0	2.1

French franc	0.1	..	0.3	0.7	1.1	2.3	3.0	2.7	2.5	2.1	2.1	1.6	1.7
Swiss franc	1.8	1.5	1.5	1.5	1.1	0.9	0.8	0.4	0.3	0.2	0.1	0.1	0.1
Netherlands guilder	0.9	0.9	1.1	1.0	1.1	1.1	1.1	0.4	0.4	0.2	0.2	0.2	0.2
ECU (European Currency Unit)	20.1	19.2	19.9	16.2	15.0	13.8	15.8	16.5	14.7	14.1	12.3	11.5	..
Unspecified currencies (b)	1.2	1.2	1.0	3.0	4.0	5.8	5.7	6.1	5.2	5.3	7.8	7.3	6.8
Developing countries													
U.S. dollar	62.5	60.4	59.1	57.5	60.5	60.6	63.3	64.6	63.8	61.8	60.5	62.5	62.5
Deutschemark	9.8	10.7	11.5	11.9	11.7	11.9	11.0	11.2	11.1	11.8	11.4	10.6	10.6
Japanese yen	6.8	7.0	8.6	8.9	6.9	6.9	7.0	8.3	8.1	8.2	7.3	6.2	6.2
Pound sterling	4.3	4.6	5.4	5.7	5.8	6.6	6.2	4.6	4.4	4.9	4.9	4.9	4.9
French franc	1.9	2.0	2.0	2.0	2.1	2.3	2.3	1.9	1.8	2.1	1.5	1.5	1.5
Swiss franc	2.6	2.5	2.7	2.4	2.2	2.1	2.1	2.2	2.4	2.0	1.8	1.4	1.4
Netherlands guilder	0.9	1.1	1.3	1.1	1.0	0.9	1.0	1.0	1.0	0.9	0.8	0.5	0.5
ECU (European Currency Unit)	..	..	..	..	..	..	..	..	..	..	..	..	..
Unspecified currencies (b)	11.3	11.6	9.5	10.5	9.9	8.8	7.1	6.3	7.6	8.3	11.8	12.3	12.2

Source: International Monetary Fund, *Annual Reports*, various issues.

Note: Components may not sum to totals because of rounding.

a. Data provided are as of the end of the respective years.

b. The residual is equal to the difference between total foreign reserves of Fund member countries and the sum of the reserves held in the currencies listed in the table. Calculations for developing countries rely to a greater extent on Fund staff estimates than do those provided for the group of industrial countries.

c. This column is for comparison and indicates the currency composition of reserves when ECUs issued against dollars are assumed to be dollars and all other ECUs are ignored.

Table 5.2. Currency composition of official foreign-exchange reserves by region, 1980–1994[a] (percentages)

	1980	1982	1984	1986	1988	1990	1992	1994
Selected EU countries								
U.S. dollar	80.2	80.9	72.9	71.3	63.7	58.6	66.5	64.2
Deutschemark	12.0	10.3	16.6	14.9	20.3	22.1	17.6	19.5
Japanese yen	2.0	3.5	4.7	6.2	6.7	5.2	4.1	5.9
Pound sterling	1.0	0.8	1.4	1.7	1.3	0.7	1.6	1.3
French franc	0.8	0.2	0.1	0.1	1.4	2.3	2.1	1.5
Swiss franc	1.0	1.6	1.8	2.1	2.2	1.9	1.4	1.3
Netherlands guilder	1.0	1.0	0.8	1.1	1.0	1.0	0.5	0.4
Unspecified currencies	2.0	1.8	1.8	2.8	3.4	8.2	6.2	5.9
Selected Asian countries								
U.S. dollar	48.6	53.2	58.2	50.6	54.6	56.3	55.8	57.8
Deutschemark	20.6	17.6	14.6	16.7	16.6	16.6	16.3	15.0
Japanese yen	13.9	17.6	16.3	20.2	16.6	12.2	14.2	13.7
Pound sterling	3.0	2.7	3.5	4.1	5.9	8.1	6.3	6.0
French franc	0.6	0.7	0.6	1.1	0.8	0.9	1.0	1.2
Swiss franc	10.6	5.6	4.9	5.1	4.5	1.0	5.0	5.1
Netherlands guilder	2.8	2.6	1.9	2.2	1.2	5.0	1.2	1.3
Unspecified currencies (b)	. . .	. . .	. . .	. . .	. . .	1.2	. . .	. . .
Selected Latin American countries								
U.S. dollar	54.6	58.7	75.7	79.8	73.2	77.1	76.9	71.9
Deutschemark	10.5	10.0	4.0	2.7	3.0	3.2	3.9	5.8
Japanese yen	3.4	3.4	2.4	4.3	5.2	4.2	4.9	5.3
Pound sterling	1.5	1.0	0.8	0.7	1.0	1.3	0.9	0.9
French franc	0.7	0.3	0.3	0.3	0.2	0.7	0.8	1.0
Swiss franc	2.6	1.0	0.7	0.3	0.7	0.9	0.6	0.2
Netherlands guilder	1.1	0.6	0.3	0.1	0.1	0.1	0.3	0.1
Unspecified currencies	25.6	25.0	15.9	11.9	16.6	12.4	11.8	14.7

Source: Tavlas (1996b), from Tavlas and Ozeki (1992), and IMF staff estimates.
a. Data provided are as of the end of the respective years.
b. The holdings of unspecified currencies by the selected Asian countries have been negligible.

exchange interventions by EMS members reproduced in Table 5.11, which show a dramatic switch from dollars to the DM since the supersnake was born. The yen remains a distant third among official users, even in Asia. Its sizable share in U.S. exchange interventions reflects the special character of the bilateral Japanese-American trading relationship rather than any broader international role.

At the private level too the dollar is the most important of all currencies, despite intensifying competition. In the global foreign-exchange market, Table 5.10 shows, use of the dollar in recent years is down a bit from 1989 but still more than twice the corresponding rate for the DM and triple that of the yen.[20] In 1995 the greenback was involved on one side or the other of more than 80 percent of all transactions. The share of the DM has risen substantially over the same period, again confirming its central role in European monetary affairs. But use of the yen

Table 5.3. Currency composition of international financial claims, 1982–1995 (percentages)

	1982–84 Average	1985–87 Average	1988	1989	1990	1991	1992	1993	1994	1995
Bank loans (a)										
U.S. dollar	80.4	65.5	64.2	70.0	58.9	84.5	75.4	81.0	80.7	76.8
Deutschemark	1.7	2.4	2.8	3.5	6.7	2.1	1.8	3.2	1.1	4.1
Japanese yen	7.6	15.2	6.1	5.3	1.7	1.1	1.4	0.7	0.2	0.2
Pound sterling	3.8	7.7	17.4	11.3	17.5	4.2	1.9	2.2	8.6	11.7
Swiss franc	0.8	1.9	0.3	0.4	0.1	0.6	0.3	0.4	0.1	0.1
ECU	1.3	3.9	3.3	4.9	8.7	3.9	15.0	6.4	3.9	3.8
Other	4.5	3.4	5.9	4.6	6.4	3.6	4.2	6.1	5.4	3.3
Bond issues (a)										
U.S. dollar	62.1	48.6	35.4	45.9	33.3	28.5	36.9	35.9	37.5	39.5
Deutschemark	6.9	8.3	11.6	7.5	8.3	7.1	10.4	11.8	7.8	15.5
Japanese yen	5.5	11.1	8.7	8.7	13.5	12.9	11.2	9.6	13.3	12.6
Pound sterling	3.8	5.5	10.8	8.4	9.5	9.1	7.6	10.8	8.8	5.9
Swiss franc	14.6	11.7	12.4	8.7	10.5	7.3	5.8	6.1	4.8	5.6
ECU	2.1	4.2	5.4	5.6	8.1	11.1	6.8	1.6	2.0	1.7
Other	4.9	10.5	15.6	15.2	16.8	24.0	21.3	24.2	25.8	19.2
Foreign currency deposits										
	1986	1987								
U.S. dollar	63.5	58.2	60.0	59.7	51.9	50.5	50.4	47.6	46.7	44.3
Deutschemark	12.8	14.2	13.3	13.9	16.2	15.7	16.4	17.4	17.4	16.6
Japanese yen	4.5	5.8	5.5	5.5	5.0	4.9	4.5	4.8	5.3	5.9
Pound sterling	2.1	2.8	3.4	3.1	4.2	3.8	3.6	3.4	3.5	3.2
Swiss franc	7.2	7.7	5.4	4.9	5.6	5.1	4.7	4.3	4.3	4.3
ECU	2.6	2.8	3.0	3.2	4.5	5.5	5.2	4.9	4.2	3.4
Other	7.2	8.4	9.4	9.7	12.6	14.6	15.0	17.5	18.7	22.2
All international claims (b)										
Total ($ billion)	747.3	1421.2	1949.5	2460.7	2986.9	3185.5	3250.8	3453.2	4030.7	4600.1
U.S. dollar	67.1	55.7	47.6	50.0	45.0	43.2	44.0	42.4	39.3	37.9
Deutschemark	8.9	9.8	10.1	11.4	12.2	12.6	14.3	14.8	14.9	15.5
Japanese yen	3.7	6.6	8.0	6.9	7.8	7.9	7.7	9.0	11.5	12.4

Source: Henning (1997), Frenkel and Goldstein (1997), and official sources.

a. 1982–84 and 1985–87 averages are based on end-year 1983 and 1986 exchange rates respectively. The remaining years are based on 1990 exchange rates.

b. International claims includes international bonds, cross-border bank liabilities to non-banks, foreign currency liabilities to domestic non-banks (from 1984) and foreign currency notes (from 1989).

in the meantime has actually declined marginally, as has activity in the pound and Swiss franc. The dollar is still plainly the most favored vehicle for wholesale currency trading. Similarly in global financial markets (Table 5.3), the dollar's role is down somewhat from earlier years, especially for international bonds, but still greater by a considerable margin than that of any other single currency. Here too the mark and yen seem firmly planted in second and third place.

The only real exception lies in the area of trade invoicing, where a noticeably less asymmetrical pattern of use tends to prevail. The pioneering empirical work

Table 5.4. Currency denomination of exports of selected industrial countries, 1980–1996 (percentages)

	Dollar	Dmark	Yen	Pound	Fr. franc	It. lira	N. guilder	B. franc	F. markka	Other
					1980 (a)					
United States	97.0	1.0	—	1.0	1.0	—	—	—	—	—
Germany	7.2	82.3	—	1.4	2.8	1.3	1.2	—	—	3.6
Japan	65.7	1.9	29.4	1.1 (b)	0.6 (b)	0.1 (b)	0.6 (b)	—	—	0.6
United Kingdom	17.0	3.0	0.1	76.0	2.0	0.5 (b)	1.0 (b)	—	—	0.4
France	13.2	9.4	—	3.2	62.5	—	—	—	—	11.7
Italy	30.0	14.0	—	—	8.0	36.0	—	—	—	12.0
Netherlands	16.5	21.5	—	4.2	5.4	0.9 (b)	43.5	—	—	8.0
Belgium–Luxembourg	12.9	17.0	—	2.9	13.6	—	7.3	41.2	—	5.1
Finland	26.1	8.0	—	7.3	2.9	—	—	—	10.4	45.3
					1992–1996 (c)					
United States	98.0	0.4	0.4	0.3	—	—	—	—	—	0.9 (d)
Germany	9.8	76.4	0.6	2.4	2.8	—	—	—	—	8.0
Japan	52.7	—	35.7	—	—	—	—	—	—	11.6
United Kingdom	22.0	5.0	0.7	62.0	3.5	1.7	2.3	—	—	2.8
France	18.6	10.6	1.0	4.2	51.7	3.1	1.5	2.6	—	6.7
Italy	23.0	18.0	—	—	7.0	40.0	—	—	—	13.0
Netherlands	20.7	18.5	0.7	4.1	4.5	1.5	43.3	2.9	—	3.3
Belgium–Luxembourg	18.0	18.6	0.7	4.2	13.6	2.4	7.3	28.6	—	6.6
Finland	24.0	15.6	1.2	9.4	4.7	2.0	2.8	1.5	18.3	21.7

Source: Tavlas (1996b), from Page (1981), Thygesen et al. (1995), and official sources.

a. Data for 1980 for all countries except Belgium-Luxembourg and Finland are from Page (1981). For Belgium-Luxembourg and Finland the 1980 data have been obtained from official sources.

b. Estimates made by Page (1981).

c. Data for the United Kingdom pertain to 1992 and are from Thygesen et al. (1995). Data for Germany, Finland, and Italy are for 1994 and were obtained from official sources. Data for France, Japan, Belgium-Luxembourg, and the Netherlands pertain to 1995 and were obtained from official sources. Data for the United States are for March 1996 and were provided by the U.S. Bureau of Labor Statistics.

d. Comprised mainly of Canadian dollars.

Table 5.5. Currency denomination of imports of selected industrial countries, 1980–1996 (percentages)

	Dollar	Dmark	Yen	Pound	Fr. franc	It. lira	N. guilder	B. franc	F. markka	Other
					1980 (a)					
United States	85.0	4.1	1.0	1.5	1.0	1.0	0.2	—	—	6.7
Germany	33.1	42.8	1.5 (b)	3.1	3.3	2.4	2.0	—	—	11.8
Japan	93.1	1.4	2.4	0.9	0.9 (b)	0.2 (b)	0.1 (b)	—	—	1.0
United Kingdom	29.0	9.0	1.3	38.0	5.0	1.7 (b)	2.8 (b)	—	—	13.2
France	33.1	12.8	0.1	3.8	34.1	3.0 (b)	1.8 (b)	—	—	11.3
Italy	45.0	14.0	0.5	3.2	9.0	18.0	1.7	—	—	8.6
Netherlands	29.4	22.9	0.8 (b)	4.7	4.4	1.1 (b)	25.1	—	—	11.0
Belgium–Luxembourg	26.1	16.9	—	4.4	10.6	—	8.3	27.5	—	6.2
Finland	41.9	12.5	—	5.9	2.2	—	—	—	9.2	28.3
					1992–1996 (c)					
United States	88.8	3.2	3.1	—	—	—	—	—	—	4.9 (d)
Germany	18.1	53.3	1.5	1.9	4.4	—	—	—	—	20.8
Japan	70.4	2.8	22.5	—	—	—	—	—	—	4.3
United Kingdom	22.0	11.9	2.4	51.7	5.3	2.2	3.2	—	—	1.3
France	23.1	10.1	1.0	2.9	48.4	3.7	1.4	2.2	—	7.2
Italy	28.0	13.0	—	—	8.0	37.0	—	—	—	14.0
Netherlands	25.5	17.4	1.3	3.4	0.8	0.7	42.8	2.6	—	3.5
Belgium–Luxembourg	20.4	20.9	1.7	3.3	10.0	2.5	7.9	28.7	0.1	4.5
Finland	28.4	18.2	2.6	4.5	2.4	2.3	2.6	0.8	22.5	15.7

Source: Tavlas (1996b), from Page (1981), Thygesen et al. (1995), and official sources.

a. Data for 1980 for all countries except Belgium–Luxembourg and Finland are from Page (1981). For Belgium–Luxembourg and Finland the 1980 data have been obtained from official sources.

b. Estimates made by Page (1981).

c. Data for the United Kingdom pertain to 1992 and are from Thygesen et al. (1995). Data for Germany, Finland, and Italy are for 1994 and were obtained from official sources. Data for France, Japan, Belgium–Luxembourg, and the Netherlands pertain to 1995 and were obtained from official sources. Data for the United States are for March 1996 and were provided by the U.S. Bureau of Labor Statistics.

d. Comprised mainly of Canadian dollars.

Table 5.6. Currency denomination of German foreign trade, 1980–1993 (percentages)

	1980	1985	1988	1989	1990	1991	1992	1993
Exports								
U.S. dollar	7.2	9.5	8.0	7.5	6.5	7.8	7.3	10.4
Deutschemark	82.5	79.5	79.2	79.2	77.0	77.2	77.0	74.1
Japanese yen	—	0.4	0.4	0.4	0.4	0.4	0.6	0.8
Pound sterling	1.4	1.8	2.0	2.6	2.7	2.5	3.2	2.6
French franc	2.8	2.7	3.2	3.4	3.9	3.3	3.4	3.2
Italian lira	1.3	1.5	1.8	1.8	2.2	2.0	2.2	2.0
Others	—	4.6	5.4	5.1	7.3	6.8	6.3	6.9
Imports								
U.S. dollar	32.3	28.1	21.3	22.3	20.9	20.4	18.4	18.5
Deutschemark	43.0	47.8	52.6	52.6	54.3	55.4	55.8	54.3
Japanese yen	—	1.8	2.5	2.0	1.8	1.9	1.7	2.1
Pound sterling	3.4	3.0	2.4	2.6	2.5	2.3	2.2	2.2
French franc	3.3	3.8	3.6	4.1	3.6	3.0	3.0	3.0
Italian lira	2.4	1.5	1.6	1.8	1.9	1.8	1.7	1.4
Others	—	14.0	16.0	14.6	15.0	15.2	17.2	18.5

Source: Deutsche Bundesbank, *Monthly Report,* November 1991, and press release, May 10, 1994.
Note: The data on imports up to mid-1990 relate exclusively to western Germany. From July 1990, the import data also include the imports of the new Länder. The data on exports relate exclusively to western Germany.

Table 5.7. Currency denomination of Japanese foreign trade, 1970–1991 (percentages)

	1970	1975	1980	1985	1986	1987	1988	1989	1990	1991
Exports										
Japanese yen	0.9	17.5	28.9	39.3	36.5	33.4	34.3	34.7	37.5	39.4
Other	90.4	82.5	71.1	60.7	63.5	66.6	65.7	65.3	62.5	60.6
Of which: U.S. $	90.1	78.0	66.3	52.2	53.5	55.2	53.2	52.4	48.8	46.7
Imports										
Japanese yen	0.3	0.9	2.4	7.3	9.7	10.6	13.3	14.1	14.5	15.6
Other	99.7	99.1	97.6	92.7	90.3	89.4	86.7	85.9	85.5	84.4
Of which: U.S. $	80.0	89.9	93.1	n.a.	n.a.	81.7	78.5	77.3	75.5	75.4

Source: Ito (1993), from official sources.

of Swedish economist Sven Grassman (1973a, 1973b, 1976) established that the most favored vehicle for trade among industrial countries, particularly involving manufactures, tends to be the exporter's own currency, regardless of the significance (or nonsignificance) of the national money for other international purposes.[21] In Ronald McKinnon's terms, home currency is the "preferred monetary habitat" (1979). This pattern has been variously labeled the symmetry theorem,

Table 5.8. Currency denomination of French foreign trade, 1980–1994 (percentages)

	1980	1984	1988	1989	1990	1991	1992	1993	1994
Exports									
U.S. dollars	13.2	17.0	16.0	17.2	15.5	16.2	16.5	19.1	19.1
Deutschemark	9.4	9.0	8.8	9.3	9.9	10.8	10.4	10.3	9.3
Japanese yen	. . .	. . .	0.7	0.7	0.8	0.8	0.9	1.0	0.9
French franc	62.4	61.2	58.1	57.9	57.4	54.6	54.6	52.9	51.9
ECU	. . .	. . .	0.3	0.4	0.5	0.6	0.7	0.7	0.6
Imports									
U.S. dollar	33.1	30.7	21.7	23.6	22.3	23.5	23.1	24.6	24.1
Deutschemark	12.8	11.7	12.7	11.4	11.8	11.5	11.7	11.2	10.6
Japanese yen	. . .	. . .	1.5	1.3	1.2	1.4	1.3	1.4	1.1
French franc	34.1	39.8	48.3	47.9	47.9	46.2	46.7	46.1	47.1
ECU	. . .	. . .	0.4	0.6	0.7	0.7	0.8	0.7	0.7

Source: Banque de France, staff estimates.

Table 5.9. Currency denomination of U.S. imports from selected countries, 1985 and 1996 (percentages)

Imports from:	U.S. dollar	Local Currency	Other
	1985 (a)		
Canada	90.5	9.5	—
France	73.0	25.8	1.2
Germany	42.7	57.1	0.2
Japan	78.8	21.2	—
Switzerland	42.8	56.6	0.6
United Kingdom	63.9	36.1	—
Brazil	100.0	—	—
Korea	99.6	—	0.4
Mexico	98.7	1.3	—
Taiwan	99.6	0.2	0.2
	1996 (a)		
Canada	86.2	3.8	10.0
France	84.8	11.0	4.2
Germany	59.4	38.9	1.7
Japan	83.1	16.9	—
Switzerland	46.7	53.3	—
United Kingdom	75.5	23.4	1.1
Brazil	100.0	—	—
Korea	100.0	—	—
Mexico	100.0	—	—
Taiwan	98.2	1.8	—

Source: Tavlas (1996b), from U.S. Bureau of Labor Statistics
a. March data; based on data used to construct U.S. import price indicators.

Table 5.10. Currency composition of gross turnover in global foreign-exchange markets, 1989–1995 (percentages)

	April 1989	April 1992	April 1995
U.S. dollar	90	82	83
Deutschemark (b)	27	40	37
Japanese yen	27	23	24
Pound sterling	15	14	10
French franc	2	4	8
Swiss franc	10	9	7
Canadian dollar	1	3	3
ECU (European Currency Unit)	1	3	2
Australian dollar	2	2	3
Other EMS Currencies	3	9	13
Currencies of other reporting countries	3	3	2
Other currencies	19	8	8
All currencies	200	200	200
Average daily turnover ($ billion)	620	880	1,260

Source: Bank for International Settlements (1996).

Note: Because two currencies are involved in each transaction, the sum of transactions in individual currencies comes to twice total reported turnover.

a. Number of reporting countries in 1989: 21; and in both 1992 and 1995: 26. Data for 1989 and data for Finland in 1992 include options and futures. Data for 1989 cover local currency trade only except for U.S. dollar, Deutschemark, Japanese yen, pound sterling, Swiss franc, and ECU.

b. Data for April 1989 exclude domestic trading involving the Deutschemark in Germany.

Table 5.11. Currency distribution of foreign-exchange interventions, 1979–1992 (percentages)

	Intervention by members of the European Monetary System		
	1979–82	1983–85	1986–87
U.S. dollars	71.5	53.7	26.3
EMS currencies	27.2	43.5	71.7
(Deutschemark)	(23.7)	(39.4)	(59.0)
Others	1.3	2.8	2.0

	U.S. Federal Reserve and Treasury Intervention				
	1979–82	1983–85	1986–87	1988–89	1990–92
Deutschemark	89.7	67.9	57.5	56.4	64.1
Yen	10.3	32.1	42.5	43.6	35.9

Sources: Tavlas (1991), and official sources.

Grassman's Law, and Grassman's rule. A noticeable home-currency preference has long persisted in both the United States and Europe, and to a limited degree is becoming prevalent in Japan, which earlier in the post–World War II period had mainly used the dollar for its overseas trade.[22] Since 1970 the greenback's exceptional role in Japanese export invoicing has been cut nearly in half, though the dollar remains more popular than Japan's own yen. Except for Japan, Grassman's rule is clearly evident both in the larger sample of industrial countries shown in Tables 5.4 and 5.5 and in the more detailed data available for the Big Three and France shown in Tables 5.6–5.9.

Yet even for this purpose some currencies clearly are far more prominent than others. In bilateral trade between developed and developing economies, for example, the currencies of the industrial countries predominate whatever the national identity of the exporter. Even within the industrial world, the importance of home money in export invoicing tends to vary quite sharply with the issuing country's relative weight in global commerce: the smaller the country (e.g., Belgium, Finland), the smaller is the share of exports denominated in local currency. And in the vast area of trade in primary products—including, especially, oil—the dollar plainly remains the vehicle of choice.

Taking all of these facts into account, Thygesen et al. (1995) calculate that despite Grassman's rule, the dollar actually accounts for nearly half of all world trade—more than double America's share of world exports.[23] The DM share is 15 percent, virtually all accounted for by German exports or imports. The yen's share, at 5 percent, is actually lower than that of either the pound or the French franc (6 percent each). Thus the selection of moneys for retail purposes may be less asymmetrical than in the wholesale exchange market or global financial markets, but international use still remains highly concentrated in just a small handful of major currencies.

Currency substitution

A complementary pattern of asymmetry emerges from available data on currency substitution. Although not as well documented as currency internationalization, the phenomenon of foreign-domestic use is clearly substantial in magnitude and growth but quite concentrated in terms of numbers. Only the most familiar and trusted moneys circulate at all widely outside their country of origin, unless the privilege of legal-tender status is involved. As the popular synonym "dollarization" implies, the most frequent instances of CS involve the dollar, though significant use is made of the DM and yen as well, and even occasionally other, lower-profile currencies.[24] On the other hand, CS occurs in a very broad range of states, encompassing many of the economies of the developing world, particularly in Latin America and the Middle East, as well as of the former Soviet bloc. The sample of popular currencies whose reach extends beyond their national frontiers may be small; the universe of currencies whose territorial domains are correspondingly penetrated certainly is not.

Currency substitution takes two principal forms: physical movements of cash and denomination of banking deposits. Of the two, far less is known about the former because of the obvious difficulties involved in tracking the ownership of circulating notes and coins.[25] In fact, only a few governments even attempt to keep direct records of cross-border cash flows. Apart from various anecdotal reports, the only systematic data available consist of a few imaginative estimates—guesstimates, really—for the dollar and DM and some tantalizing hints from the Bank of Japan regarding the yen.

For the dollar, alternative sources suggest that anywhere from one-third to more than four-fifths of the supply of U.S. banknotes now circulates abroad.[26] Most authoritative is a study by two Federal Reserve economists (Porter and Judson 1996), comparing no fewer than ten alternative estimating techniques, which puts the figure at between 55 and 70 percent of the total, equivalent to perhaps $250 billion in 1995. The same study also reckons that as much as three-quarters of the annual increase of Federal Reserve Notes in recent years has gone directly abroad, up from less than one-half in the 1980s and under one-third in the 1970s. Appetite for the greenback is obviously growing.[27]

Dollar circulation abroad is remarkably widespread, as any American tourist can testify. According to a deputy assistant Treasury secretary, quoted in 1995, "Greenbacks are in demand in South America, Central America, Asia, the Middle East, Eastern Europe, Russia, and Africa" (Mutch 1995:10). The "global green-back," *Business Week* calls it.[28] In Argentina alone, another Federal Reserve study suggests, the sum of dollars at end-1992 could have been as great as $26 billion, equal to roughly 11 percent of the Argentine gross domestic product (Kamin and Ericsson 1993). Other estimates from within the U.S. government, based on fieldwork done in 1995, put dollar circulation at some $20 billion in Russia, $15 billion in India and Pakistan, $15 billion in several Gulf countries, and $5 billion in Turkey.

Such circulation is not necessarily permanent. In a handful of countries, such as Israel and a few of the transition economies, where dollarization had not gone on for long, the process has to a large extent been reversed by effective domestic stabilization programs. Hysteresis, it appears, needs time to take effect. More often than not, though, there does tend to be a strong ratchet effect, particularly where incentives are not quickly turned around by local policy measures. In many cases the greenback not only remains popular but has actually come to dominate the circulating supply of banknotes. Indeed, in some Latin American countries, such as Bolivia and Uruguay, the ratio of paper dollars to local money is said to be as high as three or four to one (Calvo and Vegh 1993).

Using a comparative approach similar to the Federal Reserve's, the Bundesbank has estimated Deutschemark circulation outside Germany at about 30 to 40 percent of the total, equivalent to some DM 65–90 billion ($45–65 billion) at end-1994 (Deutsche Bundesbank 1995; Seitz 1995, 1997). Consistent with the DM's regional role, more limited than the nearly universal reach of the dollar, most of this circulation appears to be concentrated nearby, in East-Central Europe and the Balkans. But wherever Germany's currency is used, demand seems to be at least as intense as it is for the dollar elsewhere. A prime example is provided by

Serbia where, *The Economist* (1996a) reports, "the D-mark has become Serbia's semi-official currency." In Bosnia & Herzogovina, the DM is formally accepted for private use as a parallel currency and circulates widely alongside the Bosnian dinar (Mutch 1995; Seitz 1997).

The Bank of Japan has recently taken cognizance of the expanding use of its banknotes in neighboring countries, especially in Southeast Asia and the Russian Far East (Bank of Japan 1994). Much of this increase is related to the generous spending of Japanese tourists, who often find it possible to pay for local goods and services in yen. An indirect indicator is provided by data on the repatriation of yen notes via foreign banks, which has swollen from as little as 1.6 billion yen in 1980 to more than one trillion yen (nearly $10 billion) per year in the 1990s.[29] Comments the Bank: "It is expected that the amount of Bank of Japan notes circulating abroad will continue to increase, although on a small scale compared to that of U.S. dollar notes" (1994:117). Privately, Bank officials reportedly believe that of the total supply of Japanese banknotes, some $370 billion at end-1993, as much as 10 percent may now be located outside Japan (Hale 1995:164).

Combining these diverse estimates, we get a minimum foreign circulation of the Big Three currencies of at least $300 billion—by no means an inconsiderable sum and, judging from available evidence, growing rapidly.[30] The evidence also validates the impression that a very wide range of countries is affected, even if the precise numbers involved remain something of a mystery. According to one authoritative source, foreign banknotes account for 20 percent or more of the local money stock in as many as three dozen nations boasting at least one-third of the world's population (Krueger and Ha 1996:60–61). The same source also suggests that, in total, as much as one-quarter to one-third of the world's circulating currency is presently located outside its country of issue (1996:76, n. 12).

Because of the paucity of reliable data on physical cash movements, most experts focus instead on banking deposits denominated in foreign currency, for which rather more information is publicly available (Dodsworth et al. 1987; Agenor and Khan 1992). Some developing and transition economies have allowed foreign-currency accounts—most often, interest-bearing time deposits—to be held directly in their domestic banking systems; many more permit (or have been unable to prevent) ownership by residents in banks abroad. Usually highly liquid, such balances serve as a handy proxy for the transactions function of foreign money as well as its store-of-value use.

The extent of currency substitution in this form is typically estimated by calculating the ratio of foreign-currency deposits to total money supply: the greater the ratio, the smaller the transactional domain of the home currency. The results of a sample of empirical studies for countries where disaggregated data are available for local holdings of foreign-currency accounts are presented in Table 5.12.[31] Though hardly comprehensive, the numbers clearly confirm both the broad scope and the considerable scale of CS through domestic banking systems. Countries from Argentina to Yemen have made extensive use of foreign money for

Table 5.12. Foreign-currency deposits in domestic banks: a sample, 1980–1993 (percentages of broad money)

	1980	1981	1982	1983	1984	1985	1986	1987	1988	1989	1990	1991	1992	1993
Argentina (a)	—	5.5	7.2	3.7	9.9	6.7	6.1	10.7	10.0	49.9	24.2	40.0	41.5	—
Bolivia (a)	11.7	10.9	0.9(1)	0.3(1)	0.2(1)	12.6	34.5	44.2	51.4	65.6	70.6	76.8	80.9	—
Chile (b)	3.6	6.3	—	—	—	—	—	—	—	—	—	—	—	—
Egypt (c)	25.0(2)	—	—	—	—	—	40.0(2)	—	—	—	—	—	—	—
Hong Kong (d)	11.6	17.1	41.5	46.1	45.1	50.1	54.1	54.1	56.9	58.8(3)	—	—	—	—
Israel (e)	69.0	70.0	70.0	69.0	76.0	65.0	41.0	27.0	22.0	—	—	—	—	—
Lebanon (f)	36.2	41.4	26.7	26.4	31.1	35.1	71.0	91.9	79.1	65.9	73.3	67.6	68.1	67.7
Mexico (g)	14.8	18.1	5.1(4)	2.5(4)	2.1(4)	3.9(4)	8.8(4)	—	—	—	—	—	—	—
Peru (g)	30.6	30.2	38.6	43.4	52.9	31.8(5)	11.8(5)	—	—	—	—	—	—	—
Poland (g)	—	—	—	—	19.0	25.0	31.0	46.0	65.0	69.0	31.0(6)	33.0	35.0	29.0
Russia (h)	—	—	—	—	—	—	—	—	—	—	—	16.9	42.2	45.8(7)
Uruguay (a)	18.3	24.9	52.3	42.7	44.6	37.3	42.3	48.4	46.5	58.6	66.0	60.5	57.1	—
Yemen (c)	5.0(2)	—	—	—	—	—	25.0(2)	—	—	—	—	—	—	—

Note: figures refer to the ratio of foreign-currency deposits in the domestic banking system to M2, defined as the sum of coins and currency in circulation, domestic-currency demand and time deposits, and foreign-currency deposits: for the end of each year unless otherwise indicated.

Sources: (a) Claassen and De La Cruz Martinez (1994).
(b) Ugo Fasano-Filho, *Currency Substitution and Liberalization* (Brookfield, Vt.: Gower, 1986).
(c) Mohamed El-Erian, "Currency Substitution in Egypt and the Yemen Arab Republic," *International Monetary Fund Staff Papers* 35, no. 1 (March 1988), 85–103.
(d) Jao and King (1990).
(e) Gil Bufman and Leonardo Leiderman, "Currency Substitution under Nonexpected Utility: Some Empirical Evidence," *Journal of Money, Credit, and Banking* 25, no. 3, (August 1993, Part I), 320–335.
(f) Sena Eken et al., *Economic Dislocation and Recovery in Lebanon*, Occasional Paper 120 (Washington: International Monetary Fund, 1995).
(g) Privately supplied from official sources.
(h) International Monetary Fund, *Russian Federation*, Economic Review no. 8 (Washington, June 1993).
1. Foreign-currency deposits were temporarily prohibited 1982–1985.
2. Figures refer to June of each year.
3. October.
4. Limitations imposed on foreign-currency deposits in domestic banks from 1982 onward.
5. Limitations imposed on foreign-currency deposits in domestic banks from 1985 onward.
6. From January 1990, enterprises were not allowed to increase foreign-currency deposits.
7. March.

Table 5.13. Cross-border bank deposits of nonbank residents of developing countries, 1987–1994 (billions of U.S. dollars; end of period)

	1987	1988	1989	1990	1991	1992	1993	1994
All developing countries	312.0	329.3	389.0	451.9	431.9	412.2	400.9	443.0
Africa	24.1	25.6	32.4	39.1	37.0	35.2	33.1	34.5
Asia	43.5	48.5	61.1	69.5	70.0	66.2	65.6	70.1
Hong Kong	(21.8)	(24.2)	(29.7)	(35.1)	(35.5)	(34.3)	(35.6)	(37.3)
Europe	6.1	6.8	9.2	12.4	13.6	15.6	18.2	20.3
Middle East	75.8	81.4	98.3	112.2	101.9	95.3	84.9	85.0
Kuwait	(8.4)	(9.0)	(9.5)	(12.0)	(9.0)	(9.2)	(7.2)	(7.3)
Saudi Arabia	(21.9)	(24.3)	(33.2)	(34.8)	(31.0)	(29.1)	(25.7)	(24.5)
United Arab Emirates	(13.3)	(14.9)	(17.6)	(21.1)	(20.9)	(18.8)	(17.4)	(18.0)
Western Hemisphere	162.5	167.0	187.9	218.7	209.5	199.8	199.0	232.4
Argentina	(9.7)	(11.1)	(14.5)	(17.0)	(17.0)	(15.0)	(12.3)	(13.5)
Bahamas	(7.2)	(7.9)	(7.3)	(8.4)	(8.1)	(8.4)	(10.0)	(10.4)
Bermuda	(10.6)	(11.2)	(12.0)	(13.5)	(13.7)	(14.0)	(15.9)	(15.1)
Brazil	(11.3)	(12.4)	(15.6)	(17.6)	(19.0)	(19.9)	(17.7)	(19.5)
Cayman Islands	(10.5)	(14.8)	(19.3)	(26.6)	(28.7)	(30.9)	(37.2)	(51.6)
Mexico	(19.6)	(20.0)	(20.5)	(19.5)	(18.0)	(16.0)	(15.0)	(17.7)
Netherlands Antilles	(18.6)	(15.5)	(13.5)	(17.8)	(17.0)	(17.1)	(17.9)	(23.7)
Panama	(35.2)	(32.2)	(39.7)	(46.0)	(38.6)	(35.2)	(30.0)	(32.3)
Venezuela	(13.8)	(14.6)	(15.7)	(16.2)	(17.4)	(15.5)	(14.8)	(16.7)

Source: International Monetary Fund, *International Financial Statistics,* various issues.

domestic purposes—in some cases, virtually to the exclusion of home currency. The pattern is also affirmed by separate statistics on foreign-currency deposits held abroad, which are provided on a regular basis by the IMF. Presented in Table 5.13, these figures make plain that CS through this channel too is both sizable in magnitude and, despite a pause in the early 1990s, growing rapidly.

The Currency Pyramid

The available data are obviously inadequate, providing at best only a dim outline of money's new "galactic structure"—much as the Hubble Space Telescope once did for astronomers, straining to glimpse the outer edges of the universe, before that satellite's lenses were repaired. Regrettably, we have no Hubble telescope. Yet for all their manifest imperfections, the numbers are compelling. The imaginary landscape they reveal, however imprecisely, is a far cry from the state-centric Westphalian model.

A new landscape

Two messages stand out in the statistics. First, the scale of cross-border currency use is extensive, reflecting both the scope and the intensity of market-driven competition. There is no longer any close correlation between the authoritative domains of individual moneys and their territorial domains. Strict autarky in monetary relations truly is a special case.

Second, the number of currencies employed for either international or foreign-domestic purposes tends to be rather small, but the number of those routinely facing rivalry at home from currencies abroad is quite large. There is no functional equivalence among moneys either. All currencies enjoy nominally equal status as a matter of international law, but in practice some—to paraphrase George Orwell—are far more equal than others. The population of the monetary universe is in fact distinctly stratified.

Add these two messages together, and a picture emerges that is strikingly at variance with the conventional "topological presuppositions" that have prevailed since the nineteenth century. In place of a flat, territorial organization of currency space, neatly divided into mutually exclusive "spatial packages," we find ourselves in a complex, multi-tiered landscape of far-reaching competition and hierarchy among the world's diverse moneys—much more like what existed before the era of territorial money. Individually, national currencies confront market forces that are increasingly indifferent to political frontiers. Authoritative domains coincide less and less with official territorial domains. The use and influence of some moneys, such as the dollar and the DM, now reach far beyond the legal jurisdiction of their issuing governments, spanning large parts of the globe in what I call currency regions.[32] The authoritative domains of many other moneys, meanwhile, have been sharply constricted, sometimes dramatically.

Even though we lack detail, therefore, it is clear that we need a new mental map of monetary geography: new topological presuppositions. The old Westphalian model, dating back to the 1800s, is no longer consistent with the facts. In reality, the spatial organization of monetary relations has been fundamentally transformed.

How can we best visualize this new landscape? Clearly, we must learn to think of currency space in functional rather than physical terms. The weakness of the Westphalian model is that it is a horizontal conceptualization, defined exclusively by the legal jurisdictions of sovereign governments. That territorial focus makes it a limiting case in a more general, flow-based model of currency relations. In its place, we now need to substitute a more representative vertical imagery, emphasizing competitive asymmetries and diverse authority relationships among separate currencies. In effect, the virtual geography of money must be "morphed" from a simple two-dimensional field of neatly divided spatial packages to something more like a vast, three-dimensional *pyramid:* narrow at the top, where a few popular currencies dominate; increasingly broad below, reflecting varying degrees of competitive inferiority. We may call it the Currency Pyramid. The image of the Currency Pyramid, based on flows rather than location, is the real key to understanding how currency spaces are organized today.

The image of a pyramid is hardly new. Hierarchy among the world's currencies has always existed, as I stressed in Chapter 2. In every epoch, one or a small number of full-bodied moneys—from the early Athenian drachma to the U.S. dollar today—has emerged from the Darwinian struggle to dominate currency relations. International currencies, such as sterling and the dollar, existed even at the height of the era of territorial money, providing a needed lubricant to grease the wheels of commerce between national economies. Moreover, the fact of hierarchy has frequently been acknowledged by monetary specialists, who speak variously of "key currencies,"[33] "master currencies," even "dream currencies"—the moneys that investors dream in (Brown 1978).

In a more profound sense, however, the image proposed here *is* new—at least in contrast to the old Westphalian model that still dominates most conventional thinking. Today currency internationalization has increased in scale far beyond anything attained by the pound or dollar; likewise, currency substitution has swollen to become a significant factor in literally dozens of countries around the globe. This accelerating cross-border use has not only stratified monetary relations dramatically. It has also *deterritorialized* them, harking back to the heteronomous model of monetary geography that preceded the so-called modern epoch—"back to the future," as it were.[34] That fact is not often acknowledged by specialists, most of whom, as already indicated, tend to restrict analysis largely to relations between governments and ignore the critical distinction between physical and functional notions of currency space. Hierarchy is recognized, but only within limits set by a traditional territorial imagery. Most specialists also tend to focus solely on international use rather than on the more invasive process of currency substitution; and so they are limited mainly to relatively crude distinctions among currencies at the peak of the pecking order, ignoring more subtle differences further down the scale.

Both facts are captured by the picture of a Currency Pyramid: the deterritorialization of currencies as well as their stratification by relative status, both driven by market forces as well as by government action. More general than the Westphalian model or Friedrich Hayek's denationalized counterpart, the Currency Pyramid offers insight into the complexities of today's monetary landscape. Certainly it appears to be the regime of representation most supported by the evidence. As a spatial image, it best expresses what we mean by a flow-based model of monetary geography.

An illustration

Can the Currency Pyramid be effectively employed for formal analytical purposes? Our aim, it will be recalled, is to gain a new understanding of structures of governance and the role of power in global monetary affairs. Toward that end, ideally, we want to relate each money's hierarchical rank precisely to the extent of its authoritative domain: the greater a currency's authoritative domain, the higher its place in the pyramid. With that information we could then proceed directly to a systematic analysis of the underlying politics of money. But of course our ability to do so is severely constrained by the inadequacies of existing statistics, which inhibit any kind of refined empirical measurement. Regrettably, only the roughest outline of money's new virtual geography can be perceived with any certainty. A rigorously quantitative approach is impossible.

A qualitative and comparative approach, on the other hand, is not impossible, as long as we remain aware of its many limitations. Even if we cannot quantify each currency's absolute status, we ought to be able to say something about *relative* positions, based on available information regarding use for various purposes at home or abroad. In turn, that should be more than enough to permit us to explore key implications for economic and political outcomes.

Serious discussion, in short, need not be ruled out by data limitations. Critical distinctions can still be made to enable analysis to proceed. To illustrate, I outline below a series of categories that might be useful in this context—not with any definitive map of money's imaginary landscape in mind, but simply to demonstrate what might be possible despite informational constraints. The taxonomy is frankly fanciful and not likely to be easily operationalized.

Seven categories are listed, each corresponding to a different hypothetical stratum in the Currency Pyramid. The number seems sufficient to convey the rich diversity of money's competitive links and authority relationships, while at the same time it does not exaggerate the degree of refinement that we can bring to the exercise. The labels for each stratum, though slightly tongue-in-cheek, accentuate the steeply vertical imagery appropriate to an accurate representation of monetary geography.

The seven categories are as follows:

1.   *Top Currency.* This rarefied rank[35] would be reserved only for the most esteemed of international currencies—those whose use dominates for most if not all types of cross-border purposes and whose popularity is more or less universal, not limited to any particular geographic region. During the modern era of political money, just two national currencies have qualified for this exalted status: sterling before World War I and the dollar since World War II. Although in principle more than one Top Currency might be in favor at one time, as were both pound and dollar during the interwar period, today the dollar alone occupies the highest stratum of the Currency Pyramid.

2.   *Patrician Currency.* Just below the top rank we find currencies whose use for various cross-border purposes, while substantial, is something less than dominant and/or whose popularity, while widespread, is something less than universal. Obviously included in this category today would be the Deutschemark and the yen, both of which are certainly patricians among the world's currencies. Neither, however, can

as yet claim an authoritative domain as extensive as the dollar's. Each remains second-ary to the dollar for most cross-border functions, and each has an influence that is largely limited to a single region or subset of cross-border transactions. Arguably, the French franc might also be included here, despite its relative lack of favor for most types of international transactions, owing to the central role it plays in the CFA Franc Zone. But no other currency even comes close.

3. *Elite Currency.* In this category would belong currencies sufficiently attractive to qualify for significant international use but of insufficient weight to carry much direct influence beyond their own national frontiers. Here we find the more peripheral of the international currencies, a list that today includes the British pound (no longer a Patrician Currency since termination of the sterling area), Dutch guilder, Belgian and Swiss francs, Italian lira, and Canadian dollar.

These moneys are part of a distinguished elite because of the enhanced reach of their transactional domain. Their authoritative domain, however, is more constrained than that of Patrician Currencies. At best, de facto authority may extend to perhaps one or two immediate neighbors (as, for instance, in the Belgium-Luxembourg Economic Union). But even for such moneys substantive control is likely to be effectively compromised, even at home, by the superior influence of their global and regional counterparts (as in Europe, where all the more peripheral international currencies are to some extent subordinate to the Deutschemark; or in North America, where Canada's dollar manifestly plays second fiddle to its U.S. namesake). Although insulated enough to exercise a fair degree of monetary sovereignty, Elite Currencies lack the clout to control their own destiny.

4. *Plebeian Currency.* One step further down from the elite category are Plebian Currencies—more modest moneys of limited international use whose substantive authority is even more seriously compromised from abroad. Here today we find the currencies of the smaller industrial states (e.g., Australia, Austria, Spain, and the Scandinavian nations) along with some middle-income developing countries (e.g., Singapore, South Korea, and Taiwan) and the wealthier oil-exporters (e.g., Kuwait, Saudi Arabia, and the United Arab Emirates).

Internally, Plebeian Currencies may retain a more or less exclusive claim to all the traditional functions of money; indeed, in the rare instances where an insulated territorial domain has been successfully combined with a floating exchange rate and/or exchange controls, as in apartheid-era South Africa, we come closest to the special case of pure monetary autarky. Externally, however, such moneys carry little weight (like the plebs, or common folk, of ancient Rome). Not only do they attract little cross-border use, except perhaps for a certain amount of trade invoicing. Even more critically their conditions of operation, at home as well as in neighboring countries, are most often dominated by more powerful foreign currencies. At best, the extent of their authoritative domain is defined in essentially domestic terms.

5. *Permeated Currency.* Included in this category are moneys whose authoritative domain is effectively compromised even at home, mainly through the market-driven

process of currency substitution. Although nominal monetary sovereignty continues to reside with the issuing government, foreign currency supplants the domestic alternative for at least some monetary purposes, accentuating the degree of functional inferiority. With a nod to Alan James's notion of the "permeated state," a term coined to describe potential challenges to sovereign statehood, these may be described as Permeated Currencies—moneys confronting what amounts to a competitive invasion from abroad.[36] Available evidence suggests that the range of Permeated Currencies today is quite broad, encompassing perhaps a majority of the economies of the developing world.

6.   *Quasi-Currency.* One step further down are currencies that are supplanted not only as a store of value but, to a significant extent, as a unit of account and medium of exchange as well. I have already mentioned Robert Jackson's use of the term quasi-state to describe countries whose political sovereignty is more juridical than empirical—in effect, governments that are legally constituted but incapable of effective governance. In similar fashion, the term Quasi-Currency characterizes moneys that retain nominal sovereignty but are largely rejected in practice for most purposes. Their authoritative domain too is more juridical than empirical. Anecdotal reports and other information suggest that some approximation of this intensified degree of inferiority has indeed been realized in less stable economies around the world, particularly in Latin America and the former Soviet bloc.

7.   *Pseudo-Currency.* Finally, we reach the bottom rank of the pyramid, where currencies exist in name only—Pseudo-Currencies. Included here are the effectively subordinated partners of relatively asymmetric monetary alliances, such as the Luxembourg franc or the subsidiary members of the Common Monetary Area; full-scale currency boards; or token moneys, like the Liberian dollar and Panamanian balboa, found in countries where a foreign currency (e.g., the dollar) remains the principal legal tender. Also included, if they existed, would be results of a genuinely exhaustive process of currency substitution—in effect, a Quasi-Currency taken to its extreme. Pseudo-Currencies have legal status but no significant economic impact.

~

The labels in this illustrative sketch of the Currency Pyramid may be fanciful, even whimsical, but the geography they describe is not. Money is serious business—too serious to be studied using an outmoded regime of representation. Currencies today are increasingly deterritorialized, not state-bound, and intricately linked in a complex hierarchy of diverse authority relationships. Our mental maps need to be adjusted accordingly, in order to explore the implications of this new spatial organization of monetary relations.

A New Structure of Power

"Toto, I've a feeling we're not in Kansas any more."
Judy Garland, as Dorothy, to her dog Toto in
the movie *The Wizard of Oz*, 1939

Like Dorothy, we find ourselves in a new landscape. But unlike that lost little girl, we have no yellow-brick road or good witch to guide us. We have to find our own way as we explore money's increasingly deterritorialized geography.

The most direct route takes us back to the same four elements of power that we first surveyed in Chapter 2. The monetary monopoly central to the Westphalian model privileges government through the boons of political symbolism, seigniorage, macroeconomic management, and insulation from external influence. Even when circumstances may require some subordination or sharing of monetary sovereignty—the Two Ss—the image remains state-centric, and gains and losses are strictly a matter of intergovernmental relations. But what happens to structures of power when currencies are no longer territorial? How are systems of governance altered once we enter the new galactic structure of accelerating cross-border use and competition? The first question is addressed in this chapter, the second in Chapter 7. The answers, we shall see, will carry us as far from the conventional One Nation/One Money myth as the tornado took Dorothy from her family farm in Kansas.

Political Symbolism

The break in the link between territorial and authoritative domains is bound to alter the distribution of resources and capabilities in monetary affairs. Only partly,

[119]

however, do effects directly involve the balance of power between states. At least as important are changes in the reciprocal interaction between states and markets—changes that can have a profound impact on the social spaces created by money's transactional networks.

Consider first the political symbolism of money. If a territorial currency cultivates a sense of national identity, deterritorialization might logically be expected to have the reverse effect. Eric Helleiner, for example, argues that deterritorialized currencies may "promote different senses of identity in both a symbolic and concrete fashion than the national identities that territorial currencies encouraged" (1996a:19). In fact, however, consequences for the state are rather less straightforward than they appear at first glance. In some cases, identification with the "imagined community" may actually be reinforced rather than reduced by the transformation of our currency landscape. Governments may gain as well as lose, depending not only on the outcome of the Darwinian struggle among currencies but also on how official policies interact with the preferences of market actors.

Deterritorialization clearly does dilute the magical qualities of money for governments with currencies near the bottom of the Currency Pyramid—moneys whose authority at home is significantly compromised by market-driven competition from abroad. The more a foreign currency is used domestically in lieu of national money, the less citizens will feel inherently connected to the state or part of the same social entity. The critical distinction between Us and Them is gradually eroded. Worse, an instrument intended to symbolize the power and nobility of the nation becomes instead a daily reminder of inadequacy and impotence—not sound currency but funny money. When extensive CS occurs, one source reminds us, domestic money "becomes a second-class citizen and commands little respect" (Sahay and Vegh 1995:36). Governments that issue such money are not apt to command much respect either.

A prime example is provided by Mexico—"so far from God, so close to the United States," as the former dictator Porfirio Díaz wryly said—where the dollar has for years overshadowed the country's own currency, the peso. Observers find remarkable "the extent to which the battered peso has been discarded by people who normally defend national symbols and reject any sign of American intervention on their native soil" (De Palma 1995:C1). Another example is Cuba, where Fidel Castro's government in 1993 in effect gave up on its own currency when it legalized the use of dollars—previously treated as the ultimate symbol of *Yanqui* imperialism. Perhaps most striking is the case of Vietnam where, despite a bitter war with the United States, the dollar long has circulated widely and effectively served as a second legal currency. More than two decades after the departure of American troops from Vietnamese soil, reports an authoritative source, "the greenback remains the currency of choice. . . . Vietnam's 72 million people are simply not ready to trust their government with their savings" (*Far Eastern Economic Review* 1995).

Looking to the top of the Currency Pyramid, on the other hand, it appears that deterritorialization is more likely to enhance than to dilute a money's magical qualities. A broader authoritative domain plainly enhances a state's overall reputation. For the government that issues a Top or Patrician Currency, extensive cross-border use becomes an important source of status and prestige—a highly visible sign of elevated rank in the community of nations. Certainly the general public cannot help but be impressed when a foreign money successfully penetrates the domestic financial system and gains widespread acceptability. "Great powers have great currencies," Robert Mundell has written (1993:10). What nation would not take pride in the esteem accorded one of its most tangible symbols?

Matters get more complicated, however, when governments intervene to modify or control market preferences. A weak currency, for instance, might become a source of strength when a government determines to do something—or at least, to appear to do something—about a competitive challenge from abroad. In effect, monetary policy may be transformed into an exercise in political symbolism. A market-driven invasion of foreign money can be treated as the equivalent of overt military aggression. Support of the national currency may be promoted as a glorious stand on behalf of the imagined community—the ultimate expression of *amor patriae*. In 1997, when the Indonesian rupiah came under speculative attack, Indonesia's government responded with public-service advertisements showing a currency trader wearing a terrorist mask made of U.S. $100 bills. "Defend the rupiah," the notices urged. "Defend Indonesia." Whether a gambit of this sort succeeds or fails, though, will depend in large part on how credible a government's maneuvers turn out to be.

Least successful are policies that run directly counter to market sentiment, as in some Latin American countries during the peak inflation years of the 1980s. Rather than rein in their appetite for seigniorage, several states tried instead to suppress dollarization by imposing exchange controls, forcibly converting foreign-currency accounts held at domestic banks into local currency. These nations included Bolivia and Mexico in 1982 and Peru in 1985. In all three cases the immediate response was a decisive vote of no confidence: a clandestine flight of capital into bank accounts abroad that undermined rather than reinforced respect for government authority. Studies indicate that in the aggregate, taking account of deposits held in foreign as well as domestic banks, currency substitution in these countries actually *increased* rather than decreased after exchange restrictions were instituted.[1] In all three, the measures failed and were ultimately abandoned.

Much more successful are policies that make significant concessions to market sentiment. Argentina's 1991 currency reform is a case in point. To outsiders, the government's decision to peg its "new" peso to the dollar through a currency board might have seemed a surrender to outside forces, a Pseudo-Currency at best. But for Argentinians, weary of hyperinflation and a humiliating succession of worthless moneys, the Convertibility Plan became a source of national pride. At long last, the country had a currency that could look the greenback squarely in the eye. Similarly, Estonians understood the link of their newly created kroon to Germany's mark not as an admission of weakness but as an assertion of social identity—not just borrowing credibility from a respected foreign central bank but more an act of faith in their resurrected state. The virtues of Estonia's currency board "are now so ingrained they're a religion," a foreign adviser has been reported to say. To change the peg "would be seen as an unpatriotic thing."[2]

Perhaps most instructive is the case of Brazil, which from 1980 to 1994 went through five separate currencies[3] and a cumulative inflation of no less than 146 *billion* percent. At that rate, a cup of coffee selling in 1980 for 15 cruzeiros, the monetary unit of the day, would without the subsequent currency changes have cost 22 billion cruzeiros a decade and a half later. Could Brazilians be blamed for treating their national money as something of a joke? When yet another currency, the "real," was introduced in mid-1994, it was laughingly likened to Elizabeth Taylor's latest marriage (Brooke 1994). But the new money was pegged firmly to the dollar and backed convincingly by a strong stabilization program. It proved more durable than any of its predecessors, inspiring new confidence in the government and especially in finance minister Fernando Henrique Cardoso, the official responsible for the reform. "Along with the real," reported *The Economist* (1994a), "hope, Brazil's most corroded currency, has begun to circulate again." Before the end of the year, former minister Cardoso had become the country's next elected president.

Conversely, a strong currency may become a source of weakness for a government, particularly if authorities attempt to preserve an international role for a money whose popularity has begun to fade. We know that no currency has ever enjoyed permanent dominance in cross-border use: all its attractions are subject to erosion with time. We also know that, once gained, the prestige of great-currency status may be understandably difficult to give up, even apart from any material benefits that may accrue. But just as a determined defense against an invading currency can inspire renewed confidence in a government, so fruitless efforts to revive a national money's fortunes abroad may have the reverse effect, encouraging skepticism and even ridicule.

Britain's global reputation, for example, was surely not helped by its protracted but ultimately futile effort after World War II to prevent dissolution of the once far-reaching sterling area. The pound may remain an Elite Currency, but it is certainly not what it used to be. In the bitingly satirical words of television celebrity David Frost: "It's a shame to see what has happened to sterling. Once, a note issued by the Bank of England proudly read: 'I promise to pay the bearer on demand the sum of one pound.' Now it simply reads: WATCH THIS SPACE."[4] France's government risks similar mockery today, with its highly publicized endeavors to sustain an overseas role for the French franc through the institutions of the CFA Franc Zone. But little real prestige can be gained from financial dominance, however decisive, that is limited to a baker's dozen of poverty-stricken ex-colonies.

Seigniorage

The impact of deterritorialization on the privilege of seigniorage too will vary with whether a money is near the bottom or the top of the Currency Pyramid, as well as with the interaction of official policies with market preferences.

Near the bottom of the pyramid, a government's capacity to appropriate resources via money creation is obviously compromised as convenient foreign substitutes for domestic currency become available. As one source has commented, "currency competition can provide a powerful check on inflationary propensities" (Willett and Banaian 1996:88). In effect the base for levying an inflation tax is shrunk, threatening two potentially serious consequences. First, quite directly, is a deceleration of fiscal revenue, which for countries with underdeveloped tax systems can be a particularly acute problem. Second, unless budgetary deficits are reduced, there may also be an acceleration of inflationary pressures, since to finance the same level of expenditures government now has to speed up the printing presses. The result might be "a vicious cycle of ever increasing inflation" (Brand 1993:46) that, in the end, can be reversed only by a severe curtailment of public spending. Either way, it is clear, state power to cope with unexpected contingencies is constrained.

But is state power correspondingly increased for countries near the top of the Currency Pyramid? At first glance, there seems no doubt. The larger a currency's authoritative domain, the easier it should be for its issuing government to exploit the fiscal benefits of seigniorage. Not only is the domestic monetary monopoly preserved. Now foreigners too are a source of revenue to the extent that they are willing to hold the money or use it outside its country of origin. Expanded cross-border circulation generates the equivalent of a subsidized or interest-free loan from abroad—an implicit transfer that is a real-resource gain for the state as a whole. Economists refer to this as international seigniorage, in order to distinguish it clearly from the more traditional domestic variety.[5] They recognize two components of international seigniorage. One, a current portion, consists of the direct, one-time augmentation of expenditures made possible by an increase in foreign holdings of the currency, somewhat akin to "living beyond one's means." The other, a capital portion, is the flow of net interest saved so long as the money continues to circulate abroad, in cash form or as interest-bearing claims, rather than return to be spent at home.[6]

International seigniorage can be quite considerable, as the historical experiences of both the pound sterling and the U.S. dollar amply demonstrate (B. Cohen

1971a; Bergsten 1975). For Britain, the greatest benefit of the pound's international preeminence came during World War II, when net sterling liabilities increased by some £3 billion ($12 billion), mostly to finance London's military efforts in the Middle East and Asia. In the words of one British economist: "The major economic support obtained in that conflict is probably the biggest gain Britain has derived from the sterling system" (Oppenheimer 1966:132).

For the United States, seigniorage gains still accrue from the use of dollars overseas. Consider just the foreign circulation of U.S. banknotes alone, which as we know has been conservatively estimated at some $250 billion in 1995. We can calculate an interest saving of some $11–15 billion a year (Frankel 1995a, 1995b; Blinder 1996)—equivalent to rather less than 1 percent of our economy's annual consumption, but hardly trivial. The benefit has been colorfully described by one journalist:

> The United States has an advantage few other countries enjoy: It prints green paper with George Washington's and Ben Franklin's and Thomas Jefferson's pictures on it. These pieces of green paper are called "dollars." Americans give this green paper to people around the world, and they give Americans in return automobiles, pasta, stereos, taxi rides, hotel rooms and all sorts of other goods and services. As long as these foreigners can be induced to hold those dollars, either in their mattresses, their banks or in their own circulation, Americans have exchanged green paper for hard goods. (T. Friedman 1994)

International seigniorage can be exploited, however, only so long as the currency in question retains its competitive superiority in the marketplace—an advantage that can never be permanently guaranteed. In practice, the seigniorage capacity of the issuing state in time decreases rather than increases.

Clearly the fiscal opportunity afforded by a popular currency will be greatest in the earliest stages of cross-border use, when the money is most in demand abroad. Later on, by contrast, the privilege is more likely to be eroded than augmented by the persistent accumulation of liquid liabilities in the hands of foreigners, increasing supply relative to demand. In Mundell's words: "Reserve currencies start off strong when they are scarce in world markets, but end up weak as they are expanded beyond the point of need" (1993:17). This is a lesson that both the British and the American governments eventually learned to their regret. For London, the disposition of sterling balances left over from World War II was a preoccupation for decades, until the sterling area finally was wound up in the 1970s. For Washington, a comparable "overhang" of dollar liabilities remains a chronic source of concern to the present day.

The problem can be simply stated. As overseas circulation grows, foreigners may legitimately worry more about the possibility of future devaluation or even restrictions on the usability of their holdings. Hence, over time, the issuing government will have to pay increasing attention to competition from other currencies and to curb its appetite for the inflation tax accordingly. Policy will almost certainly be inhibited by the need to discourage sudden or substantial conversions through the exchange market. At a minimum, interest rates may have to be raised significantly to maintain the money's financial attractiveness. Ultimately the capital portion of international seigniorage, on a net basis, may well be reduced to zero or even turn negative.[7]

In short, state power may be constrained for countries at the top as well as at the bottom of the Currency Pyramid. It depends on market sentiment, for in a world of accelerating cross-border use, no government can afford to ignore the preferences of market actors.

Macroeconomic management

Much the same can also be said about the third element of power derived from a territorial currency: a government's capacity for macroeconomic management. Here too state power is affected at all levels of the Currency Pyramid, and here too much depends on how official policies interact with market preferences.

In this connection, the main impact of deterritorialization is felt in the mechanism for balance-of-payments financing. Economists have long contrasted the relative ease of adjustment to interregional imbalances *within* countries with the frequently greater difficulties associated with payments adjustments *between* countries. Part of the difference may be attributed to the capacity of the state to transfer resources between internal regions, either via the government's own budget or through the operations of the central bank. But also of importance, as early sources pointed out (Scitovsky 1958; Ingram 1959), is a strictly market phenomenon: the greater scope for equilibrating capital flows within an individual country in the event of transitory disturbances, owing to the existence of a stock of generalized short-term financial claims that can be readily traded between surplus and deficit regions. The development of these generalized claims, in turn, is traditionally attributed to the existence of a single national currency, which of course removes exchange risk.

Such reasoning is obviously based on the conventional assumption of autarky in monetary relations. The same logic applies, however, even if that assumption is relaxed in recognition of the accelerating pace of cross-border currency use.[8] The wider the authoritative domain of a given money, the greater will be the effective range for equilibrating capital flows, taking the form of purchases and sales of generalized claims denominated in that single currency. Other things being equal, these flows should reduce the collective cost of adjustment to unanticipated payments shocks.

This result is not entirely surprising, since it largely replicates one of the key economic benefits of a common currency or equivalent suggested in Chapter 4: the savings that accrue from internalization through credit of what would otherwise be external transactions. But a crucial difference tends to be obscured in the context of the traditional Westphalian model. If, as that state-centric model insists, currency space is shaped predominantly if not exclusively by governments, it is not unfair to conclude that all participating countries are likely to share commensurately in this benefit of a monetary alliance. The same is less probable, however, when currency relations are shaped in larger part by market forces, which promote a hierarchy rather than a merger of national moneys. In that case, a state near the top of the pyramid gains disproportionately, to the extent that the functional domain within which its currency can be used to finance imbalances is enlarged. Its macroeconomic flexibility should be effectively enhanced. Countries further down the scale, by contrast, find themselves less able to rely on equilibrating capital flows in the adjustment process. If confidence in their moneys is lacking, their room for maneuver is correspondingly reduced.

Consequences for neither class of country are entirely unambiguous. For top-ranked states, increased use of a money abroad could, if total currency supply is inflexible, actually lead to losses of real income insofar as it causes a shortage of local currency at home. Moreover, domestic monetary policy could conceivably be pegged to a misleading target, since a large but indeterminate part of the money stock is in circulation abroad; or perhaps might even be destabilized periodically by unanticipated variations in foreign demand for the domestic currency. The gain in macroeconomic flexibility is by no means costless.

Likewise, for lower-ranked countries, implications depend on how governments respond to the reduction of their policy flexibility. Little economic control is gained, and much financial stability may be lost, if market actors do not regard efforts to preserve monetary autonomy as credible. Again the past strategies of some Latin American governments, which during the inflationary 1980s tried to suppress dollarization rather than reform their own behavior, are examples. On the other hand, a much healthier economic performance may be attained, with lower costs of adjustment, if governments in effect submit their nominal sovereignty, at least in part, to the strict discipline of the marketplace. It may not be necessary to denationalize money altogether, in the manner advocated by Friedrich Hayek, substituting freely competitive private currencies for official issue; nor hire a foreign currency in place of one's own, as James Meigs (1993) and others have recommended. It may not even be necessary to adopt a formal currency board or an equivalent exchange-rate rule, as discussed in Chapter 3. But it certainly is essential that such states take due account of market sentiment in framing macroeconomic policy—as an increasing number of developing and transition economies have elected to do in recent years.

Monetary Insulation

The story is much the same when we come to the fourth boon of a monetary monopoly: insulation from external influence. In this respect too, states near the top of the pyramid seem to gain disproportionately, insofar as expansion of a currency's authoritative domain offers a means to coerce others. Political power should be enhanced at the expense of lower-ranked countries that become more dependent on foreign money. But in this connection also, results are highly sensitive to the interplay of official policies and market preferences.

That hierarchy among currencies might influence the distribution of power between states has of course long been acknowledged by students of monetary relations. The very notion of hierarchy is political in nature and suggests varying degrees of reciprocal influence: differential impacts on the ability of governments to achieve goals at home or abroad. As we saw in Chapter 3, the possibility that monetary sovereignty might be subordinated to a dominant power, a hegemon, is accepted as a quite common variation on the traditional Westphalian theme. For many observers, the implications are obvious: hegemons win, others lose.

Some writers emphasize the political value of a currency's use for *international* purposes (currency internationalization). During the first decades after World War II, for instance, prior to the breakdown of the Bretton Woods par-value system, the dollar clearly dominated among governments as a reserve asset, intervention medium, and peg for exchange rates. At the official level of transactions, as at the private level, the greenback was acknowledged Top Currency. The United States was thus in a position to exercise influence over others through its control of access to dollar resources, either directly or through the decision-making processes of the IMF. Uncooperative states could be threatened with curtailment or even a cut-off of loans. Real resources could be gained through international seigniorage. And the structure of the system could be shaped to persuade other governments that they had a vital stake in continued adherence to existing rules. For numerous analysts, the gains for U.S. political leverage were self-evident. As Susan Strange once commented: "Of course, it is highly probable that any state economically strong enough to possess the international economy's Top Currency will also exert substantial power and influence. The really rich usually do."[9]

Others emphasize the value of a currency's *foreign-domestic* use (currency substitution). Writes another specialist, speaking of the dollar in Latin America:

> The process of dollarization has generated the functional equivalent of a dollar bloc
> . . . a dependency relation generated by the sheer political and economic power of the
> U.S. [which] has reduced the autonomy of domestic policy-makers and has added a
> new dimension to the countries' dependency. (Jameson 1990:532)

The dominance of the hegemon's currency is manifested, whether through CI or CS, in the sway it exercises over economic conditions elsewhere—specifically, through the various roles that the currency plays as a source of long-term capital or international reserves, as a vehicle for foreign trade or exchange interventions, or as a nominal anchor for exchange rates. All of these roles may be understood as indicators of the top-ranked money's expanded authoritative domain, and the dependence of others confers substantial political advantages on the issuing country, both internally and externally.

Domestically, the hegemon is better insulated from outside influence or coercion in formulating and implementing policy. Abroad, it is better able to pursue foreign objectives without constraint as well as to exercise a degree of influence or coercion over others. Reference has already been made to Jonathan Kirshner's list of ways in which such currency dependence might be exploited: (1) enforcement—manipulation of standing rules or threat of sanctions; (2) expulsion—suspension or termination of privileges; (3) extraction—use of the relationship to appropriate real resources; and (4) entrapment—transformation of the dependent state's interests. In effect, Kirshner's list distills the conventional wisdom on this subject.

Conventional views, however, are essentially state-centric, largely discounting the significance of the equally critical reciprocal interaction between government behavior and market preferences. Here too, plainly, leverage can be exploited only so long as the currency in question retains its competitive superiority in the marketplace.

Once rival moneys begin to emerge, the issuing country will find that its ability to manipulate the dependency of others may be compromised. Any attempt to limit borrowing by a client state, for example, could lead to increased loans from other sources. Threats of sanctions or exclusion could induce weaker governments to switch their allegiance to another hegemon. Prospective outcomes will depend on the reactions of market agents, which may either reinforce or nullify the impact of overtly coercive measures. Exercise of power thus will increasingly demand a systematic cultivation of favorable market sentiment via direct or indirect incentives of various kinds. The point is well summarized by Kirshner, in a brief allusion. The issue, he says, resorting to the familiar jargon of international-relations theory, "is whether the market will balance against or bandwagon with the currency manipulation. . . . The success of currency manipulation will increasingly be dependent on the ability of actors to skillfully manipulate market forces" (1995:37, 280). In other words hegemons may indeed win, but only if they avoid losing the markets.

Worse, once a significant overhang of liabilities develops, the country will find that its own insulation against outside influence has eroded. In principle, increased vulnerability could result from the actions of other governments, determined to weaken or even destroy the basis of the hegemon's power. Thomas Schelling (1980) has written of the advantages to be derived from "rocking the boat"—destabilizing behavior purposively designed to extract substantive concessions. Though they cannot offer their own money as a substitute for a Top Currency, smaller players can use the threat of liquidation or withdrawal to gain valuable bargaining leverage. Such tactics, labeled "systemic disruption" by

Kirshner, have been a specialty of France over the years, both during the interwar period, when its target was Britain's pound, and during the Bretton Woods era, when the dollar's "exorbitant privilege" was at issue.[10] In practice, however, apart from the French, instances of deliberate systemic disruption have been rare.

More to the point is the increased vulnerability that may result from market reactions to the hegemon's policies. Latitude for the issuing government is apt to be greatest, as already suggested, in the earliest stages of cross-border use, when its money is most popular. Later on, policy autonomy as well as material gains are more likely to be eroded by the accumulation of balances abroad. Equilibrating capital flows may continue to provide an extra degree of macroeconomic flexibility to deal with transitory payments shocks. Over time, however, policy will be increasingly constrained by the need to discourage sudden or substantial conversions into other currencies. Ultimately, effective political power may on balance be decreased rather than increased—precisely the reverse of the conventional wisdom regarding the political value of hegemony.

$\sim$

So where does our exploration of money's new deterritorialized landscape leave us? We find that a structure of power very different from the conventional Westphalian model is emerging on the horizon, "a new geography of power," to borrow the apt phrase of urbanologist Saskia Sassen (1996a: chap. 1). We see a world that no longer so clearly privileges government in relation to other social actors—a monetary world, to repeat, that takes us back to the future, to something more like what existed before the nineteenth century.

Some individual governments may benefit, of course, particularly those with moneys near the top of the Currency Pyramid. In relations between states, deterritorialization clearly implies a redistribution of power that favors those with the most widely circulated and accepted moneys. These happy few may anticipate material gains both from enhanced macroeconomic flexibility and, for a time, from the real-resource benefit of international seigniorage. Likewise, political gains will ensue from the status and prestige associated with a top-ranked currency as well as, more tangibly, from the opportunity afforded to exercise effective influence over others. But most other states appear to lose, economically as well as politically, insofar as they find themselves deprived of a large degree of policy autonomy. Only in circumstances where monetary stability needs to be created rather than preserved might the impact of cross-border currency competition be regarded as more an advantage to a state than a disadvantage.

On balance, however, the big winners are not governments at all, wherever their moneys stand in the Currency Pyramid. Rather the winners are a select set of private societal actors—specifically, those in the marketplace with the capacity and opportunity to choose among alternative transactional networks. In relations between states and society, it is plainly the latter that are favored by deterritorialization. Governments are privileged less, such elements of the private sector more.

In purely material terms, these societal actors attain a significant measure of efficiency gains: an improvement in the usefulness of money for all its principal functions, reflecting the rationality of the diverse motivations for cross-border use outlined in Chapter 4. Access to a currency with a broad authoritative domain generates substantial economies of scale, reducing transactions costs. It also provides an effective refuge against abuse of the seigniorage privilege by governments. Indeed, if freed entirely of elements of Westphalian monopoly, market forces might conceivably maximize microeconomic efficiency, thus achieving in practice what Robert Mundell and other early contributors to OCA theory set out to identify in principle—namely, the best criteria for the organization of monetary space irrespective of existing national frontiers.[11] Ironically, the acceleration of cross-border currency competition suggests that the first incarnation of OCA theory may not have been so naïve after all.

Politically, these societal actors achieve a measure of leverage over governments that would be unimaginable in the strictly state-centric Westphalian model. For the many governments with moneys lower down the Currency Pyramid, the discipline of the market is evident from the start. And even for the favored few near the top, policy autonomy—despite early gains—is likely to be eroded eventually by a growing overhang of foreign liabilities. Through the choices they make in the Darwinian struggle among currencies, private agents exercise a degree of influence over public policy that is unprecedented since the dawn of the era of territorial money, going well beyond what would normally be tolerated in direct state-to-state relations.

This shift in the structure of power generated by market competition is what one source meant when describing the impact of cross-border currency use as a "market-enforced monetary reform" (Melvin 1988a). James Meigs had the same idea in mind when, in addressing the financial problems of East-Central Europe and the former Soviet republics, he advocated hiring a widely accepted foreign currency such as the Euro-dollar (see Chapter 3). Such an approach, he argued, "would be market-driven [and] would provide an automatic, nonpolitical system for grading [policy] performance" (1993:717). Privileged societal actors not only help to shape currency space; they also exercise enormous influence over government behavior within the newly emergent galactic structure of money. We are indeed a long way from where we started.

SEVEN

Governance Transformed

"The nation state has become an unnatural, even dysfunctional, unit for organizing human activity and managing economic endeavor in a borderless world."

Kenichi Ohmae, "The Rise of the Region State," 1993

In some ways, of course, money's new "galactic structure" looks curiously familiar. We noted the growing disjuncture between a political system based on sovereign territory and a transnational economy that is worldwide in scope, in Chapter 1; and nowhere is the challenge to state sovereignty more evident than in the area of finance, where the globalization of markets has, as we know, provoked vigorous debate about whether the End of Geography is near (O'Brien 1992). The nature of the challenge to political authority, however, remains poorly understood. Contrary to the views of many, well represented by the dismissive comment of business consultant Kenichi Ohmae, governments have not necessarily become unnatural or dysfunctional. Societal actors have not taken over sole authority for monetary affairs. The shift in the structure of power generated by cross-border currency competition has not so much diminished as *transformed* the role of the state in money's newly deterritorialized geography. Governance is now uneasily shared between the public and private sectors.

The Role of the State

That the power of the state has diminished is obvious. Most observers focus on financial markets and the remarkable increase of capital mobility that has occurred in recent years.[1] Government authority has been seriously eroded as a result. But

[131]

how or *how much* government authority has eroded and, more important, what may or should public officials *do* about it?

The capital mobility hypothesis

The conventional view, what David Andrews (1994) calls the Capital Mobility Hypothesis, is that financial globalization has cost states their monetary auton-omy. As Andrews summarizes the proposition: "The degree of international capital mobility systematically constrains state behavior by rewarding some ac-tions and punishing others. . . . Consequently, the nature of the choice set avail-able to states . . . becomes more constricted" (1994:193, 204). But as Andrews cautions, this is only the beginning of the story, not the end.[2] In fact the Capital Mobility Hypothesis, for all its insight, borders on caricature, seriously misrep-resenting both the scope and the severity of the challenge to contemporary government.

There is nothing wrong with the logic of the proposition, which derives directly from the dilemma of the Unholy Trinity. Unless governments are willing to tolerate virtually unlimited currency instability, they must tailor their policies to avoid provoking massive or sudden capital movements. The challenge to state authority is indeed real, neither easy to withstand nor, typically, amenable to formal negotiation. The constraint imposed by globalized financial markets is not just a matter of individual constituencies with an axe to grind. Particularist pressures, exercised directly on government through lobbying or other "rent-seeking activities," have always been an integral part of the policy process in every national capital. What is different about financial globalization is the indirect role that markets can now play in inhibiting public policy—a discipline at once less tractable and more impersonal.

The key is the wider range of options that comes to more privileged elements of the private sector with the globalization of financial activity. For societal actors who can take advantage of the opportunities afforded by market integration, capital mobility means more degrees of freedom—more room for maneuver in response to the actual or potential decisions of government. Higher taxes or more regulation may be evaded by moving investment funds offshore; tighter monetary policies may be circumvented by accessing foreign sources of finance. And this latitude, in turn, means a significant increase of leverage in relation to political authority. Recalling the language of Albert Hirschman (1970), we can think of influence in the policy process as depending on the relative availability of three options: Exit, Voice, and Loyalty. The greater the ability of market actors to evade the preferences of public officials (Exit), the less will government be able to count on or command submissive Loyalty. "Investors vote with their feet," as Saskia Sassen (1996a:39) puts it. As a result, they gain more Voice to promote private priorities and objectives.[3]

In effect, therefore, financial globalization gives selected societal actors a de facto veto power, elusive but effective, over state behavior. It is elusive because it is exercised indirectly, through market processes rather than formal lobbying. Policy autonomy is threatened, but not in a purposive or hostile way. The veto is effective because it involves a menace, the risk of exit, that may never be implemented but is forever present. The pressure on government officials is endless. The imperative for governments is to avoid provoking exit, so above all they have to maintain the confidence and goodwill of the private sector. The full implications of this new "geography of power" have been aptly summarized, with approval, by a former finance minister of France:

> The world economy is increasingly dominated by financial markets, and we have to get used to accepting their verdicts, whether favorable to us or not. I think I understand their mind-set. They've become watchdogs who will promptly punish any country that lets inflation or public debt get out of control. But they reward good economic policies. A champion of free markets like me thinks that they provide good discipline.[4]

The Capital Mobility Hypothesis does correctly identify the nature of the challenge to governments. Its logic is impeccable. Public policy, more and more, is pressured to conform to what markets desire, whether or not this coincides with the preferences of elected officials. Less and less can governments ignore the signals of the financial marketplace. Yet in pursuing that logic, the proposition manages simultaneously both to *understate* and to *overstate* the constraints imposed on state behavior.

Constraints are understated because a focus on capital mobility, emphasizing financial-market integration, highlights only one function of money: its use for store-of-value purposes. In fact, of course, that is only one part of the story. Cross-border competition is really far more extensive, involving all the standard functions of currency for both international and foreign-domestic use—not just money's role as a private investment medium—and penetrating to the very core of what is meant by national political sovereignty. Our exploration has made it clear that much more is involved than just financial markets. It is, indeed, a matter of the basic effectiveness and legitimacy of government itself.

At the same time, constraints are overstated because the focus on capital mobility, stressing the preferences of currency users, highlights only one side of the market: the demand side. That too ignores an important part of the story—namely *supply*, which even in a deterritorialized world remains largely the privilege of the state. Governments are still the principal source of the currencies that now compete so vigorously across political frontiers. The Darwinian struggle may be intense, but it is a struggle that remains, for now at least, limited almost exclusively to state-issued moneys. They may face challenges, but governments still retain a considerable influence in relation to the private sector. The era of territorial money may be over, but that does not mean that states have become an anachronism in the governance of currency relations.

Competition on the supply side

Government dominance of the supply side is not absolute, of course. Even that remaining privilege may be eroded in time by competition from nonstate sources. "Denationalized" currencies already exist, both domestically and internationally, to rival the official issue of central banks. Until now, however, none has had an impact that might be described as anything more than marginal—though that too could change as money's galactic structure continues to evolve.

At the domestic level, some private moneys circulate in fairly sizable numbers. In the United States alone there are as many as 85 local currencies in 26 states, the best known being the system of "Ithaca Hours" based in Ithaca, New York (Frick 1996). In 1993 *The Economist* (1993c) reported the existence of some 45 local currencies in Britain—many with exotic, not to say eccentric, names such as beaks, bobbins, cockles, and kreds—and perhaps 300 worldwide. Such currencies, however, are really little different from systems of multilateral barter, and they remain deliberately local, circulating on a very restricted scale.[5] None trades across national frontiers.

At the international level, private substitutes for state-issued moneys have long existed in the form of what economists call "artificial currency units" (ACUs)—nonstate alternatives designed to perform one or more of the conventional roles of money. Traditionally, though, most ACUs have functioned as a unit of account or store of value—modern ghost moneys, in effect—rather than as a medium of exchange, thus posing little direct threat to government dominance of supply. Currently the only nonstate form of money used to any substantial degree internationally is a pool of privately issued assets denominated in ECUs, the European Union's old European Currency Unit that came into existence with the EMS in 1979.[6] But although it has attained a limited success in global financial markets, as we saw in Chapter 5 (Table 5.3), the ECU has never been widely accepted for private transactional purposes.[7]

In fact, the only real threat of competition on the supply side lies in the future—in the developing realm of cyberspace, the truly virtual geography of the internet and World Wide Web. Recall the first interpretation of Richard O'Brien's End of Geography thesis. As communications and information technologies continue to develop, it is not only physical location that becomes decreasingly important. So too does physical money, once digital entries in a computer can substitute easily for everyday cash and checking accounts. Around the world, entrepreneurs and institutions are racing to develop effective electronic means of payment: electronic cash or e-cash, as it is sometimes called. If and when they succeed, governments will face a competitive challenge like none they have experienced in living memory—full-bodied ACUs beyond their individual or collective control. Then their dominance of supply, not just demand, truly would be lost.[8]

That future, however, could be rather distant, if it arrives at all, given the difficulties of introducing any credible new form of money into the market. The key issue, as for all moneys, is trust: how to command confidence in the general acceptability of any sort of e-cash? Initially, at least, value is likely to be assured only by promising full and unrestricted convertibility into conventional legal tender. Later on, as *The Economist* has written, "it is possible to imagine the development of e-cash reaching [a] final evolutionary stage . . . in which convertibility into legal tender ceases to be a condition for electronic money; and electronic money will thereby become indistinguishable from—because it will be the same as—other, more traditional sorts of money" (1994b:23). But that day, surely, is still a long way off. Until then, officially sponsored moneys alone will continue to dominate the supply side for both international and foreign-domestic purposes. Governments, therefore, will continue to play a role that is anything but insignificant.

An indirect proof

Can the state's continuing relevance be demonstrated? Some proof may come from a brief thought experiment, comparing the special case of the standard, state-centric Westphalian model with its equally extreme alternative—the stark, market-driven world of denationalized money promoted by Friedrich Hayek and his followers (as well as the movie character Arthur Jensen). A Hayekian galactic structure, in which officially sponsored moneys play no role at all, is the limiting case at the opposite end of the spectrum of possible configurations defined by a flow-based model of currency space. The implications of such a laissez-faire system, ruled exclusively by private competitive forces, suggest that governments are by no means an anachronism, however much their power may seem diminished.

Governments have good reason to prefer the old Westphalian model, defining currency spaces in strictly territorial terms, coterminous with national boundaries whenever possible. If private-market actors had their way in a fully denationalized world, the number of separate moneys would be far smaller than governments prefer. In the absence of state authority, the Darwinian struggle would surely shrink the total number of currencies dramatically, to maximize the material benefits of money. We are nowhere near such an outcome, implying that governments must yet, in some way, exercise influence over the terms of cross-border competition.

How small might the number of moneys be in a truly denationalized world? Opinions differ. Most extreme is the view of the German economist Roland

Vaubel, an ardent exponent of free-currency competition.[9] For Vaubel, the number could turn out to be as small as one, owing to the overwhelming power of economies of scale. Unrestrained competition, he has argued, would lead eventually to a single, universal money—the ultimate expression of Gresham's Law in reverse. In his words:

> Ultimately, currency competition destroys itself because the use of money is subject to very sizable economies of scale. The money-industry must be viewed as a (permanently) declining-cost industry, i.e., as a "natural monopoly". . . . The only lasting result will be . . . the survival of the fittest currency." (1977:437, 440)

Vaubel's argument, however, is supported by neither historical evidence nor broader theory. Markets may prefer to reduce costs by driving out "bad" money. But a multiplicity of currencies, rather than one single money, seems the more probable outcome on both empirical and analytical grounds.

Historically, it is true, one money has often tended to predominate in international currency use, as I noted in Chapter 2. But dominance is not the same as annihilation. In practice, the Darwinian struggle has never tended to concentrate favor *exclusively* on any single money, even in the presence of competitive disparities as great as those, say, that existed between sterling and the dollar in the decades after World War I. As Paul Krugman has commented: "The impressive fact here is surely the inertia; sterling remained the first-ranked currency for half a century after Britain had ceased to be the first-ranked economic power" (1992:173). Similar inertia has been evident for millennia, in the prolonged use of such international moneys as the bezant and Mexican silver peso long after the decline of the imperial powers that first coined them; and they can still be seen today in the continued popularity of the dollar despite America's shrinking economic predominance. Such immobilism seems the rule, not the exception, in monetary relations.

In theoretical terms, Vaubel's argument relies deterministically, not to say simplistically, on a single critical variable: economies of scale. If scale economies were all that mattered, one universal money would indeed be inevitable; its absence, a paradox to be explained—the "paradox of the non-universality of money," one source labels it (Thygesen et al. 1995:41). But scale economies are by no means all that matter, as the recently developed economics of networks emphasizes. Of equal importance, this new literature stresses, are considerations of stability and credibility which suggest that the optimal number of moneys in a world of currency competition may in fact be considerably greater than one.

Network theory recognizes two distinct structures in the organization of spatial relations: the "infrastructure," which is the functional basis of a network; and the "infostructure," which provides needed management and control services. Economies of scale, by reducing transactions costs, obviously promote a consolidation of networks at the level of infrastructure, just as Vaubel argues. At the infostructure level, by contrast, the optimal configuration tends to be more decentralized and competitive, to maximize agent responsibility. Some finite number of rival networks will counter the negative effects of absolute monopoly, which frequently leads to weakened control by users and diluted incentives for suppliers. Hence a rational trade-off exists, an impulse for some degree of diversification, which is likely to result in an equilibrium outcome short of complete centralization—a smallish population of currencies rather than one universal money.

Inertia is also promoted by the existence of an already well-established transactional network. The same network externalities that are responsible for the scale economies Vaubel emphasizes are responsible as well for the hysteresis that is so often observed in currency substitution as well as in currency internationalization. In effect, prior use confers the natural advantage of incumbency. Switching from one currency to another involves expensive financial adaptation, as numerous authors have emphasized (Dornbusch et al. 1990; Guidotti and Rodriguez 1992). Considerable effort must be invested in creating and learning to use new instruments and institutions, with much riding on what other market agents may be expected to do at the same time. Hence however attractive a given money may seem, adoption will not prove cost-effective unless others make extensive use of it too. Conversely, once a switch does in fact occur, reversal will be resisted unless a sizable transactional network can be counted upon. In the words of economists Kevin Dowd and David Greenaway:

> Changing currencies is costly—we must learn to reckon in the new currency, we must change the units in which we quote prices, we might have to change our records, and so on. . . . [This] explains why agents are often reluctant to switch currencies, even when the currency they are using appears to be manifestly inferior to some other.[10]

Finally, immobilism is reinforced by the exceptionally high level of uncertainty inherent in any choice among alternative moneys. Uncertainty encourages a tendency toward what psychologists call "mimesis": the rational impulse of risk-averse actors, in conditions of contingency, to minimize anxiety by imitative behavior based on past experience. Once a currency gains a degree of acceptance, its use is apt to be perpetuated—even after the appearance of powerful new competitors—simply by regular repetition of previous practice. In effect, a conservative bias is inherent in the dynamics of the marketplace. As one source has argued, "imitation leads to the emergence of a convention [wherein] emphasis is placed on a certain 'conformism' or even hermeticism in financial circles" (Orléan 1989:81–83).

Three conclusions follow. One is that, a priori, no one currency configuration can be identified as optimal for every circumstance. In markets for money, as in other organized asset markets, outcomes are highly sensitive to the strategic interdependencies of decisionmaking. Much more likely is the possibility of multiple equilibria—an inference consistent with other recent approaches to the analysis of international money (Krugman 1992; Matsuyama et al. 1993; Hartmann 1994). As Barry Eichengreen has written: "As is so often the case when expectations are introduced, multiple equilibria are possible" (1996b:19).

The second conclusion is that the precise number of currencies cannot be predicted with any certainty, *pace* Vaubel. Hayek himself acknowledged as much even as he promoted the cause of denationalized money: "I believe that, once the system had fully established itself and competition had eliminated a number of unsuccessful ventures, there would remain in the free world several extensively used and very similar currencies" (1990:126). In similar fashion, the economist Benjamin Klein (1974) predicted that with unrestricted competition, the most likely outcome was "multiple moneys" linked by a common unit of account—not unlike the role played by early ghost moneys before the emergence of territorial currency. And even Vaubel, in his later writings (e.g., 1984), cast doubt on whether the supply of money is truly a natural monopoly. All that can be safely said is that the surviving population of currencies would almost certainly be greater than one.

The third conclusion is that whatever the precise number left in circulation, it would not be large—certainly nowhere near as large as the crowded menagerie we currently see. From the great number of currencies still in use today, it follows that governments must still play a role of some kind, albeit a diminished one, in the governance of monetary relations. Authority has not yet been transferred entirely into the hands of private agents.

The state as oligopolist

What, then, is the true relationship between states and societal actors in the shaping of currency space? In essence, the interaction has been transformed from *monopoly* to *oligopoly*. The monetary role of government has not been so much diminished as redefined. States, once largely supreme in their own territories, have now become something like competing firms in an oligopolistic industry.

The point is simple. Markets have two sides: supply and demand. Hence not one but two sets of actors are involved—not just the users of money but also its principal producers, who happen still to be governments. With deterritorialization states have lost the dominant authority they once enjoyed over demand: their local monopolies. Since some transactors now have an alternative, the happy option of Exit, government can no longer easily enforce Loyalty, an exclusive role for their own currency within established political frontiers. But states do still dominate the supply side of the industry, largely retaining control over the issuance of money. Thus they can still, like oligopolistic firms, exercise *influence* over demand insofar as they can successfully compete, inside or across borders, for the allegiance of market agents. Authority, accordingly, is retained to the extent that user preferences can be swayed. Like oligopolists, governments do what they can, consciously or unconsciously, to preserve or promote market share for their product.

Commercial rivalry between states is nothing new, of course. Governments have always contested for markets and resources as part of the great game of world politics. Nor is the idea that states now vie to attract diverse market agents any longer novel. More than a decade ago, Susan Strange was already noting how the spreading globalization of world markets was pushing governments into a new kind of geopolitical rivalry, "competing for world market shares as the surest means to greater wealth."[11] More recently, Philip Cerny crystallized the idea in his notion of the "competition state"—governments "driven by the imperatives of global competition to expand transnationalization."[12] The competition state, however, participates in markets only indirectly, mainly to alter incentives confronting agents on both demand and supply sides. What is unique about cross-border currency competition is that the state participates directly, as the dominant actor on the supply side. It is the government's own creation, its money, that must be marketed and promoted.

Furthermore, all states (excluding those few cited in Chapter 3 that have formally adopted another nation's money in lieu of their own) must be considered part of the oligopolistic struggle, no matter how competitive or uncompetitive their currencies may be. Rivalry is not limited merely to the small handful of moneys at the very top of the Currency Pyramid, as is sometimes suggested.[13] That would be true only if cross-border competition were restricted to international use alone: a few key currencies vying for shares of private investment portfolios or for use in trade invoicing. But deterritorialization extends to foreign-domestic use as well—CS as well CI—and hence involves all national currencies, to some degree, in direct competition with one another, the weak as well as the strong. Money's oligopoly is truly global.

Oligopoly provides a particularly apt analogy because of its two key structural characteristics: interdependence and uncertainty.[14] Both are inherent features of the traditional nation-state system as well. In an oligopolistic industry, as in the interstate system, actors are sufficiently few in number that the behavior of any one has an appreciable effect on at least some of its competitors; in turn, the actions and reactions of other actors cannot be predicted with certainty. The result is an interdependence of decisionmaking that compels each firm, like rival states, to be noticeably preoccupied with considerations of long-term strategy. In this respect, producers of currency are essentially no different from producers of cars, chemicals, or computers.

Like oligopolistic firms, moreover, governments have only a limited number of strategies available to defend their money's market position. These include:

(1) *Market leadership:* an aggressive policy intended to maximize cross-border use of the national currency, analogous to predatory price leadership in an oligopoly. In currency relations, this option is of course available only to the privileged few governments with moneys near the very top of the Currency Pyramid.

(2) *Market preservation:* a status-quo policy intended to maintain, rather than augment, a previously acquired market position. Such a strategy might be adopted by states with Patrician or Elite Currencies, anxious to preserve the enhanced authoritative domain of their money abroad. It might also be the choice of governments further down the scale determined to ward off invasion of their currency's territorial domain at home.

(3) *Market followership:* an acquiescent policy of subordinating monetary sovereignty to a stronger foreign currency (the first S), analogous to passive price followership in an oligopoly—a popular option among states in the bottom strata of the Currency Pyramid.

(4) *Market alliance:* a collusive policy of sharing monetary sovereignty (the second S), analogous to tacit or explicit cartels, which states at virtually any level of the Currency Pyramid may elect to follow.

(5) *Market neutrality:* a policy of maximum autarky in monetary affairs, most characteristic of Plebeian Currencies.

Finally, and also like oligopolistic firms, governments implement their strategies through efforts to manage the demand side of the market—in effect, to sell their product. Their targets are the users of money, at home and abroad. Their aim is to sustain or enhance their currency's transactional or authoritative domain. A few insightful analysts have noted the parallel between currencies, on the one hand, and goods sold under registered trademarks, on the other. As economist Robert Aliber has quipped, "the dollar and Coca-Cola are both brand names" (1987:153). Benjamin Klein (1974) has spoken of the role that "brand-name capital" plays in influencing market assessments of a money's value and reliability.[15] Similarly, commentator Judy Shelton has remarked on the imperative of producing "better products" in a world of currency competition: "To outperform rivals, a money producer would have to offer the public a better brand of money than the competitors" (1994:231). As Aliber summarizes: "Each national central bank produces its own brand of money . . . Each national money is a differentiated product . . . Each central bank has a marketing strategy to strengthen the demand for its particular brand of money" (1987:153, 156).

How can demand be strengthened? Two contrasting approaches are possible—*persuasion* and *coercion*. Though neither is foolproof, each may be highly effective in influencing a currency's overall attractiveness.

Persuasion is of course the standard approach of the private sector, where coercion is (presumably) illegal. In an industrial oligopoly, rival firms may enhance the appeal of their products via price cuts, quality improvements, aggressive advertising, and any number of similar marketing devices. In the international arena, states can try to do the same by investing in their money's reputation, acting to reinforce its attractiveness for any or all of the usual monetary purposes. The idea is to enhance confidence in the money's continued usefulness and reliability—unfortunately, not something that can be accomplished quickly, and certainly not without considerable cost and effort. As one source comments: "Monetary confidence cannot be created overnight [and] is not a free good" (Melvin 1988b:440). One might add that reputations are much easier to destroy than to build. Resources must be expended persistently to establish and sustain a successful brand name.

Several tactics are possible. Most narrowly, use of a money might be encouraged by higher interest rates, convertibility guarantees, or special tax advantages on selected liquid assets. More broadly, governments can try to promote acceptance by facilitating expansion of a money's transactional network—for example, by sponsoring development of debt markets denominated in their currency, in order to enhance its exchange convenience and capital certainty. Most fundamentally, a currency's reputation may be buttressed by a credible commitment to sound monetary management, promising the qualities of low inflation and low inflation variability that are so prized in the Darwinian struggle among moneys. Rational transactors are unlikely to be attracted to the currency of a government that cannot resist the temptation to willfully exploit the seigniorage privilege. States that wish to avoid a flight from their currency must, in effect, practice fiscal self-denial—a "patience for revenue," as one economist puts it (Ritter 1995:134)—voluntarily limiting issue of their own money.

One way to make such a commitment credible is a currency board or firm exchange-rate rule, in the manner of Menem's Argentina or Cardoso's Brazil. As many high-inflation states have discovered, in the former Soviet bloc as well as in the developing world, followership may be the only way to build or restore confidence in a feeble national currency. Alternatively, governments can seek to restore credibility, without direct subordination to a stronger foreign currency, by way of a convincing reform of macroeconomic policy at home—a strategy of neutrality instead of followership. Many states may prefer to submit to the discipline of the marketplace rather than to the dominion of another government.

Complementing all of this is the possibility of coercion—legally, the unique privilege of sovereign governments in a Westphalian world. True, oligopolistic actors in the private sector also resort at times to high-pressure tactics, such as compulsory tying arrangements or exclusive marketing schemes, but only insofar as the law allows and never backed by a legitimate threat of force. States, on the other hand, actually make the law and are the very embodiment of coercive authority. The principle of national sovereignty permits governments to rely on much more than just the art of persuasion to defend market position.

Indeed, coercion has long been a part of every government's arsenal in monetary affairs. The monopolization of monetary powers that began in the mid-nineteenth century would have been impossible had states not been free to limit the degree of competition between home and foreign currency, first by means of legal-tender laws and public receivability provisions, later by exchange and capital controls and other measures of financial repression. It may not be true that conventional territorial currencies would disappear completely in the absence of legal restrictions, as some economists have argued.[16] But it is evident that without such measures, the demand for many national moneys, particularly those toward the bottom of the Currency Pyramid, would be significantly reduced—for some, perhaps even to the vanishing point. One recent source commented wonderingly on the "remarkable resilience of bad currencies" around the world (Willett and Banaian 1996:79). In fact, that resilience is not at all difficult to explain once we take into account the coercive authority of national governments. Cross-border competition, no matter how intense, is unlikely to eliminate many currencies from circulation as long as the principle of absolute state sovereignty remains the core constitutive rule of international law.

In practice, of course, most governments make use of both approaches, persuasion as well as coercion, to promote the appeal of their currency. The two are not mutually exclusive. As long as the struggle for survival persists, no available policy instrument will be neglected for long.

The Role of the Market

In monetary matters, national governments have clearly lost much of their privileged status in relation to societal actors. They can no longer aspire to unilateral control of demand for their respective currencies. Yet private agents remain subject to enormous influence from the public sector too, through the state's still potent powers of persuasion and coercion. Governments, to repeat, have not become an anachronism. In that case, we are entitled to ask: who does in fact govern currency relations? Who makes the rules, how are they enforced, and where are outcomes determined? In brief, how is monetary authority actually exercised?

Authority or anarchy?

For some observers, the answer is simple: when power shifts to markets, *no one* governs.[17] Authority is replaced by anarchy. In fact, nothing could be more mistaken.

Representative is the view of Susan Strange, as expressed in a recent commentary aptly entitled *The Retreat of the State*.[18] Like many other scholars, Strange focuses on the challenge posed by economic globalization to the traditional Westphalian model of state sovereignty. Her starting point is conventional, as she readily concedes: "There is no great originality in the underlying assumption of this book—which is that the territorial boundaries of states no longer coincide with the extent or the limits of political authority over economy and society" (1996:ix). Nor is there anything particularly unusual in her observations about the increased "hollowness of state authority" (p. 6) caused by the growing influence of "impersonal forces of world markets" (p. 4). In her words: "The authority of the governments of all states, large and small, strong and weak, has been weakened as a result of technological and financial change and of the accelerated integration of national economies into one single global market economy (pp. 13–14)."

More dramatic, however, is the conclusion that she draws, which is that the system of governance itself is weakened. The erosion of state authority, she argues, has left no one in charge. Again in her words:

> Some of the fundamental responsibilities of the state in a market economy—responsibilities first recognised, described and discussed at considerable length by Adam Smith over 200 years ago—are not now being adequately discharged by anyone. At the heart of the international political economy, there is *a vacuum*. . . . What some have lost, others have not gained. The diffusion of authority away from national governments has left *a yawning hole of non-authority*, ungovernance it might be called. (p. 14, emphasis added)[19]

In a formal sense, of course, Strange is absolutely right. Aspects of governance that we all take for granted at the national level—what Adam Smith called the "magistracy" of the state, including protection of property rights, standardization of weights and measures, and provision of a general framework of law, order, and justice—are obviously diluted or absent at the global level, where no legal government exists. To that extent, ungovernance is a fair characterization. True, a wide range of substitutes for a single supranational authority, institutionalized in multilateral organizations and in regularized procedures for international cooperation, has been established over time to take on at least some of the responsibilities traditionally assumed by states. But without the powers that go with absolute sovereignty, such proxies remain pale imitations at best: less effective in providing outcomes that are efficient, stable, and equitable. In today's increasingly globalized marketplace, many functions of governance are indeed not being discharged in a way that might be described as adequate.

But does this mean that no one remains in charge—that we are left with nothing but a vacuum? Such a bold claim, though it is widely voiced,[20] is based on a serious misconception of the meaning of authority in social relations. In politics and law, authority is commonly understood as a capacity to enforce compliance.[21] Like its synonym, governance, it is an ability to exert influence over the behavior and decisions of actors. Authority is inseparable from power, which in its many guises is the sine qua non for effective control of outcomes. But it is indeed separable from the state, which is by no means the only agent capable of making and enforcing rules. Authority may be exercised under the banner of sovereignty—the Westphalian model—but it can also originate in a wide variety of other social institutions, some of which may be far less visible to the naked eye than the formal offices and explicit rules of governments or multilateral agencies. In other words, governance can also take more informal and implicit forms.

As a mode of organizing political space, authority falls somewhere between the contrasting modalities of coercion and persuasion. In the words of the philosopher Hannah Arendt: "If authority is to be defined at all, then, it must be in contradistinction to both coercion by force and persuasion through arguments" (1968:93). Hints of each may be implicit in the notion of authority, but by presumption only. Persuasion, for example, works its will through systematic argument and appeal—what is generally termed a "capacity for reasoned elaboration." Coercion, at the opposite extreme, rests on the naked use of force—a capacity for repressive violence. Both alternatives may lurk in the background of governance, as *possibilities* to be brought forward should deviant behavior occur. In certain circumstances, compliance may result from a belief that a capacity for either persuasion or coercion exists. But neither argument nor violence is a necessary condition for the effective exercise of authority.

The core issue is: Where does authority orginate, and how is it conveyed? Most scholars start with Max Weber's familiar typology, which lists no fewer than three distinct foundations for authority: law, tradition, and charisma. In Weber's own words (1925:328):

> There are three pure types of legitimate authority. The validity of their claims to legitimacy may be based on:
>
> 1. Rational grounds—resting on a belief in the 'legality' of patterns of normative rules and the right of those elevated to authority under such rules to issue commands (legal authority).
>
> 2. Traditional grounds—resting on an established belief in the sanctity of immemorial traditions and the legitimacy of the status of those exercising authority under them (traditional authority); or finally
>
> 3. Charismatic grounds—resting on devotion to the specific and exceptional sanctity, heroism or exemplary character of an individual person, and of the normative patterns or order revealed or ordained by him (charismatic authority).

It is easy to see that much more is involved here than governance by government alone. For Weber, of course, authority was directly associated with the state. His concern was with the sources of legitimacy for the traditional Westphalian model of governance. In fact, however, only one of his three categories, the de jure "rational-legal" mode of authority, is truly exclusive to formal government. Authority may indeed derive from juridical supremacy as embodied in the familiar institutions of sovereign states. But if Weber's two remaining categories are to be credited, that is clearly not the only possible provenance for authority. Neither tradition nor charisma is a monopoly of the state.

In fact, authority may be manifested through any number of de facto channels of control. Tradition and charisma are two of them; others include opinion, ideology, and even intellectual convention. By no means is it true, therefore, that we are left with a "yawning hole of non-authority" just because power in the world economy has shifted away from national governments. Market forces may be impersonal, but that does not make them any less capable of governance.

The key point is simple. Authority, ultimately, is *socially constructed*—like our representations of political space, a social episteme built up from our own ideas and experiences. As the political philosopher R. B. Friedman writes, following Weber's logic, the effectiveness of authority is derived from "some mutually recognized normative relationship" (1990:71). Its legitimacy is based on historically and culturally conditioned expectations about what constitutes appropriate conduct. A practical distinction between societal orders based on formal design and organization (e.g., the state) and more spontaneous orders that emerge from the mutual accommodations of many diverse and autonomous actors has long been a staple feature of Western social philosophy, going back to Bernard Mandeville's *Fable of the Bees*, first published in 1714. The unplanned, spontaneous model may be regarded as no less legitimate—no less *authoritative*—than the deliberately devised variety.

Governance, therefore, does not necessarily demand the tangible institutions of government. It may not even call for the presence of explicit actors, whether state-sponsored or private, to take responsibility for rulemaking and enforcement. To suffice, all that governance really needs is a valid social consensus on relevant rights and values. As summarized by James Rosenau:

> Governance refers to activities backed by shared goals that may or may not derive from legal and formally prescribed responsibilities and that do not necessarily rely on police powers to overcome defiance and attain compliance. Governance, in other words, is a more encompassing phenomenon than government. It embraces governmental institutions, but it also subsumes informal, non-governmental mechanisms. . . . Governance is thus a system of rule that is as dependent on intersubjective meanings as on formally sanctioned constitutions and charters. (1992:4)

Authority may be formally articulated in explicit rules outlining specific prescriptions or proscriptions for action. But it may also express itself more informally as implicit norms defining standards of behavior in terms of understood rights and obligations. Rules are normally enforced by "rightful" rulers, and since the Peace of Westphalia such rulers have been most closely identified with the territorial state. Norms, by contrast, tend to exercise their influence more through the power of social institutions, including such familiar arrangements as family, religion, and, of course, market. Both explicit rules and implicit norms are part of what we mean by governance. We do not face a vacuum whenever influence is redistributed from the former to the latter.

Admittedly, governance may not be as tidy when it is effectuated through social institutions. The greater ambiguity of norms, as compared with rules, leaves actors more room for strategic maneuver; absence of overt compliance mechanisms (police, judiciary, etc.) heightens the temptation to renege on commitments when it is convenient to do so. Outcomes, therefore, may be neither as stable nor as equitable as we might prefer. As I have indicated, Susan Strange is undoubtedly right when she suggests that many functions of governance are no longer being discharged as adequately as they could be. The certitude of formal government is replaced by the less predictable force of social convention. But that is not the same as "ungovernance." We must not confuse the *form* of authority with its *consequences*.

Hence it is not at all accurate to conclude, as Strange suggests, that no one now governs money's newly deterritorialized landscape. The monopoly power of states has been replaced not by anarchy but by the invisible hand of competition. The authority that once derived solely from legal-tender laws and other political interventions has come to be embodied more in the norms and expectations that rule the Darwinian struggle among currencies. The power of governance, in short, now resides in that social institution we call the market.

Supply or demand?

But that still leaves us with an underlying question: *Who* in the market governs? The market is not a unitary actor, after all; we must avoid the sin of reification. At least two sets of actors are involved here—the producers of money on the supply side, the users of money on the demand side. Who really is in charge?

In fact, *both* sides govern—producers of money as well as users. As in any market setting, it is supply and demand together, interacting synergistically, that determine the organization of currency space. The basic point was made many years ago by the renowned English economist Alfred Marshall, commenting on whether it is demand ("utility") or supply ("cost of production") that governs market outcomes ("value"): "We might as reasonably dispute whether it is the upper or the under blade of a pair of scissors that cuts a piece of paper, as whether value is governed by utility or cost of production" (1920:348). Likewise in our own time, we might just as reasonably dispute whether it is state or society that shapes the new geography of money. In reality, as with Marshall's scissors, it is both, each playing a critical and reciprocal role in an ongoing dialectical process. What links the two sides in their synergy are the transactional networks that define the functional domains of individual currencies. And what lies at the heart of these social spaces is the issue of trust: the reciprocal faith of a group of like-minded transactors in a money's general usefulness and future acceptability. Governance is provided by whatever may influence market confidence in individual currencies.

In this sense our exploration of money's imaginary landscape leads us back full circle to the meanings of geography and money first discussed in Chapter 1. If monetary spaces are understood in functional rather than physical terms—seen through the lens of a flow-based model of currency relations rather than a more traditional territorial model—it becomes clear that the power of national governments, while still substantial, is no longer automatically privileged over that of all other actors. If money is accurately comprehended as a social institution derived from self-reinforcing patterns of historical practice, it also becomes evident that neither formal organization nor explicit rules are required for the effective exercise of monetary authority. The system of governance is the collectivity of actors, public as well as private, that comprise both sides of the market. Through their ongoing interaction, it is these agents *together* who jointly, if uneasily, make the rules and shape the contours of today's monetary geography.

A crisis of legitimacy

In the end, the traditional Westphalian model has become as much a fiction in currency relations, a trap for the unwary, as it has in the broader arena of global politics. Chapter 1 noted how the organization of political space in the contemporary era has been transformed from the homonomous world of the territorial state to something much more like the heteronomous Middle Ages—a new medievalism, to borrow Hedley Bull's (1977) term. So, it appears, has the imaginary landscape of money, which today is governed by a patchwork of authority every bit as diffuse and contingent as that of medieval Europe. In currency matters too, we are witnessing the emergence of a new medievalism. Where the sovereign state once ruled, market forces now prevail.

Once more, therefore, we confront the question first posed in the Introduction to this book: Does it matter? By this time, the answer should be clear: it does indeed matter. Much more than a mere shrug of the shoulders is called for. Money affects us all, every day of our lives; its impacts are manifold and direct. At issue is the *legitimacy* of decisionmaking in this new, deterritorialized system of governance—a decidedly normative question. Should we be content with this dramatically new geography of power?

Many, particularly partisans of a more libertarian persuasion, might well respond Yes, since liberty appears to be promoted. Ever distrustful of excessive government authority, libertarians celebrate all limitations on political behavior imposed by the decentralized decisionmaking of the marketplace. For them, the market serves two valuable functions, dispersing power in society and also providing a potent counterweight to the awesome power of the state. Hence many would undoubtedly applaud such a passing of privilege from the public to the private sector—from despised politicans to competitive market forces. The monopoly appropriated by governments during the era of territorial money was frequently mismanaged or abused, as we well know, resulting in corrosive inflation or macroeconomic instability. Are we not all better off if states must now act as oligopolists, competing keenly with one another for the allegiance of market actors? In lieu of compulsory Loyalty, we now have the option of voluntary Exit. Instead of the arbitrary actions of public officials, we may now enjoy the fruits of market rationality.

Moreover, libertarians continue, markets are inherently democratic because they reflect the attitudes and decisions of millions of individual transactors, functioning in effect as a sort of perpetual opinion poll—Meigs's "automatic, nonpolitical system for grading [policy] performance" (1993:717). Why should we not be content with a governance structure that yields more power to the people?

The libertarian response, however, is seriously deficient in two respects. It neglects issues of both equity and accountability. It is true that cross-border competition gives many societal actors more Voice in relation to governmental authority: the right to vote with their feet if they disapprove of official policy. But such votes are distributed not by person—the traditional One person, One Vote—but by wealth. The notion of equality before the law is thus violated if not fatally compromised. In the words of economist Arthur Okun, writing of the "big trade-off" between the principles of democracy and capitalism, "money transgresses equal political rights" (1975:29). Those with the most money have the most votes. Such a skewed franchise is greatly inconsistent with contemporary views of political legitimacy.

Worse, there is less accountability in a system of governance that gives as much Voice to a select set of market agents as it does to elected officials. As an approach to political rule, such a change may be regarded as regressive or even pernicious, insofar as it subverts the will of the general electorate. Politicans may be ineffectual or unsavory, but in many countries—and certainly in representative democracies—they are supposed to govern with the consent of the governed. In other words they can, at least to some degree, be held accountable for their actions. Market actors, by contrast, are neither elected nor politically accountable, and they may not even be citizens. If the will of the majority, however poorly refracted through the lens of representative government, can be thwarted by the economic power of an anonymous minority, democracy itself is threatened. This too is at odds with contemporary views of legitimacy.

That economic globalization may threaten a crisis of legitimacy in political rule—what one source calls a "legitimacy deficit" (Underhill 1996:6)—has only recently begun to attract the attention of students of world politics.[22] The growing concern is well captured by the title of a book by Louis Pauly: *Who Elected the Bankers?* As Saskia Sassen puts the point:

> Central banks and governments appear now to be increasingly concerned about pleasing the financial markets rather than setting goals for social and economic well-being. . . . Do we want the global capital market to exercise this discipline over our governments? And to do so at all costs—jobs, wages, safety, health—and without a public debate? While it is true that these markets are the result of multiple decisions by multiple investors and thus have a certain democratic aura, all the "voters" have to own capital . . . This leaves the vast majority of a country's citizens without any say. (1996a:50–51)

No one who believes in either equity or accountability in politics should be content with such a structure of authority. Currency deterritorialization *does* matter.

᠃

The issue is not that states have lost all role in the management of currency relations. They are still part of money's implicit system of governance. But in the new medievalism that has supplanted the old Westphalian model, governments must consciously adapt to a dramatic transformation of their status, from monopolists to oligopolists, if they are adequately to represent the interests of all their citizens in monetary affairs. As in the centuries before the era of territorial money, so now sovereignty has become increasingly contested; notions of authority and legitimacy have grown as subtly intricate and ambiguous as they ever were during the Middle Ages. Can public policy cope?

EIGHT

Can Public Policy Cope?

"**M**oney, now shorn of its reference to specific subjectivities, has been largely deprived of its sovereign vestiges."

Michael J. Shapiro, *Reading "Adam Smith,"* 1993

The current transformation of money's landscape is real. Monetary geography is increasingly determined by impersonal transactional networks and authority relationships that, in true medieval fashion, are largely indifferent to the territorial frontiers of states. Michael Shapiro's remark is right on target. Governments can no longer rely on an automatic subjective linkage between currency and country—the keystone of the traditional Westphalian model—in seeking to realize their goals. As a result, ordinary citizens can no longer rely on their elected representatives to respond, however imperfectly, to the express will of the majority. The consequence of this legitimacy deficit is a myriad of new tensions and insecurities around the globe, posing threats to stability as well as promising opportunities for cooperation.

Yet national sovereignty remains the central organizing principle of world politics. Tempted though we may be to contemplate new, nonstate forms of governing institutions, we must be realistic. Society still looks first to the state for some kind of solution to its problems. Hence we too must look to established governments for constructive responses to the growing deterritorialization of money. Today public policy is challenged in nearly every sovereign nation, wherever it ranks in the Currency Pyramid: in the small number of countries whose moneys are most widely used, including the United States, members of the European Union, and Japan; as well as in the much larger number of countries with less competitive currencies. What can governments do to cope?

No Easy Solutions

Broad policy options are easy to identify but difficult to implement. Recall again the two limiting cases defined by a flow-based model of monetary geography. At one extreme, governments can simply surrender their monetary sovereignty to market forces, formally abdicating all responsibility for currency affairs: the Hayekian solution of denationalized currencies. At the other extreme, they can actively seek to recreate the traditional Westphalian model, reasserting their control in money's imaginary landscape either on their own or collectively: a "*re*territorialization" of currencies. Though opposed in intent—one negating state authority, the other celebrating it—both approaches share the appeal of clarity and intellectual elegance, offering neat, clean remedies for some of the world's messiest ailments. For precisely that reason, however, neither is likely to occur in reality, where complexity and politics prevail. Only the Candides of this world put their faith in such easy solutions.

Friedrich Hayek's laissez-faire vision, for example, assumes on the part of contemporary governments a passivity that is impossible to imagine. True, national control of money has long since been eroded by cross-border competition. Many of the benefits of a strictly territorial currency have already been lost to market forces. Moreover, governments may have no option if and when electronic cash, as yet embryonic, emerges to challencge conventional legal tender. That day, however, is still a long way off; and in the meantime most states remain wedded to monetary sovereignty in principle, even if they are able to exploit its promise less in practice. So long as they can squeeze any power out of the privilege that money represents, few governments will opt voluntarily for formal denationalization.[1]

Conversely, any attempt to recreate the full Westphalian model—maximum autarky for individual states or groups of states—assumes a degree of government activism that seems equally farfetched. Superficially, insofar as we are talking about representative government, total reterritorialization might seem attractive: a logical way to remedy money's emerging legitimacy deficit. Through the democratic franchise, the general electorate would once again gain a dominant Voice in the policy process. When Dorothy, that lost little girl, wanted to leave the Land of Oz, all she had to do was repeat "There's no place like home." In no time at all, she found herself back in comfortable, familiar Kansas. For governments, however, the task is not so simple. Practical politics makes either unilateral or collective action on this scale difficult and perhaps impossible.

Unilateral action would require each state to restore all of its traditional monopoly by whatever means necessary. Such an approach is not infeasible. Indeed, as long as absolute sovereignty prevails as a juridical norm, autarky will remain a viable option. All it needs is the will to replicate the enormous and sustained governmental effort that accomplished the earlier territorialization of money. As Pauly (1995:373) has suggested, "states can still defy markets" if they wish. In today's world, however, where opportunities for substitution between currencies are far greater than they ever were in the nineteenth century, the costs of coming "home," economic as well as administrative, would be astronomical—almost certainly higher than most states are prepared to tolerate. As a practical matter, unilateral initiatives to reterritorialize money are likely only in the most dire of circumstances, such as a deep depression or a national-security crisis.

Alternatively, states could act collectively, aiming not to restore but to merge their individual monetary monopolies—in effect, to cartelize their present oligopoly by creating a single world currency, as Richard Cooper (1984) has suggested. But we have already seen, in Chapter 4, how difficult it is to create or sustain a monetary alliance among even a limited number of countries. How much more challenging would an agreement be that encompasses all, or even a majority, of the two hundred sovereign states around the globe? To ask the question is to answer it. A single universal money is not politically feasible either.

As much as we may want to repeat "There's no place like home," we are reminded of the title of a Thomas Wolfe novel: *You Can't Go Home Again.* The legitimacy deficit cannot be corrected by turning back the clock. Some degree of cross-border currency competition is here to stay. If governments, therefore, are determined to retain the formality of monetary sovereignty and yet respond constructively to the equity and accountability issues raised by deterritorialization, they will have to do so *within* the power structure of the market, not in opposition to it. To put the point differently, they will now have to accept the practical reality of the new system of governance, the dialectical interaction of state and society, that shapes the geography of money today.

The bottom line is clear. Governments must learn how to *manage* their oligopolistic rivalry, not make futile attempts to evade or suppress it. That lesson is true for states at the top of the Currency Pyramid as well as for others near the bottom. All governments are challenged by today's new galactic structure of money. Not all of the problems are unfamiliar. Indeed, some have festered for years, if not decades, because of misperceptions engendered by the outmoded Westphalian model. But all are serious and call for fresh insight and understanding. A brief look at some of these challenges through the lens of a flow-based model of currency space can shed illuminating new light for policymakers.

The Future of the Dollar

We begin with the dollar—the world's Top Currency for well over half a century. Though not unaware of potential risks, U.S. policymakers have long preferred to stress the manifold benefits of the greenback's popularity. As one Treasury official said not long ago: "The U.S. dollar is the most favored currency. Why would we want to lose that franchise?"[2] More recently, however, as competition has heated up, tarnishing some of the dollar's earlier luster, new worries have arisen about adverse consequences for the people of the United States. Washington is learning, as never before in the twentieth century, that it must concern itself explicitly with the market share of its currency. In the words of Lawrence Lindsey, a member of the Federal Reserve Board of Governors:

> We in the United States cannot . . . assume that the international role of the dollar is unassailable. Unlike during the years immediately following the Second World War, our institutions do not have a near-monopoly on global confidence. The position of the dollar in the world must no longer be taken for granted. It must be earned, it is not automatic. (1996:306–307)

The advantages of the dollar's still leading position are plain. Extensive international use promotes America's status and prestige around the world. It also generates considerable opportunities for seigniorage as well as policy leverage on foreign governments. Such gains are real, even if difficult to measure. But the gradually growing appeal of key rivals, such as the DM and yen, makes costs more evident, in the form of tightened constraints on the exercise of national power. Both flexibility at home and influence abroad have been compromised, to some degree, by the increased availability of viable currency substitutes. The issue for public policy is: How should Washington respond?

In good part, the answer depends on what we assume about market sentiment—how relevant societal actors see the future attractiveness of the dollar as compared with its chief foreign competitors. Here we see the real significance of the transformation of government's role from monopolist to oligopolist. Not even the issuer of the world's Top Currency can disregard market preferences for long if it wishes adequately to represent the interests of its citizens.

What are the market's preferences? Trends are not clear. Though global dollar circulation, in absolute magnitude, has never been greater, the greenback's relative popularity, as we saw in Chapter 5, does seem to have diminished somewhat. For some observers that erosion, though so far modest, is a sign of irreversible decline: the dollar's day is over—or soon will be. More than a decade ago Charles Kindleberger was already predicting that "the dollar will end up on history's ashheap, along with sterling, the guilder, florin, ducat, and if you choose to go way back, the Levantine bezant."[3] More recently, the historian Diane Kunz has written in a similar vein of "the death of the dollar order" (1995:26), and economist Paul Craig Roberts has described the dollar as "a dying reserve currency" (1995:22). Obituaries for the greenback appear with increasing frequency.

Like reports of Mark Twain's demise, however, such alarmist accounts are at best premature, at worst wildly misleading—"a bit too much ado about relatively little," as former Federal Reserve governor Alan Blinder puts it (1996:136). In fact, there is a lot of life yet in America's two-century-old currency. Much of what looks like erosion of the dollar's preeminence is little more than a natural diversification of investment portfolios, partly induced by regulatory and tax changes, as the authoritative Bank for International Settlements has recently emphasized (1995:26). Movement into other currencies has been slow and certainly shows no signs of acceleration. Indeed, as the evidence in Chapter 5 makes clear, the greenback's share of international currency use has in some respects actually increased rather than decreased during the 1990s. Recall that the value of U.S. banknotes in circulation abroad, at last count, was at least $250 billion and growing at an increasing pace. Likewise, the dollar remains the preferred vehicle for nearly one-half of world trade and for well over one-third of all international assets.

What accounts for the greenback's enduring popularity? Much of the credit undoubtedly goes to America's political stability and impressive record of inflation control, as well as to the continued efficiency and openness of U.S. financial markets—all familiar attributes stressed in the conventional economics literature. But even more critical, it seems evident, is the dollar's well-established transactional network, literally spanning the globe, which tends to discourage switching to other, less widely circulated currencies. As the flow-based approach to monetary geography makes clear, network externalities, reinforced by mimesis, give incumbency a significant advantage.

Also important is the absence of any obvious alternative. There is no fully qualified understudy in the wings, waiting impatiently for an opportunity to leap to center stage, as there was when sterling started into its decline after World War I. Neither the DM, its future clouded by uncertainties about EMU, nor the yen, still a distant third among international moneys, seems ready to climb soon to the apex of the Currency Pyramid. As Jeffrey Frankel, a vocal champion of the dollar, has optimistically predicted: "It is a fairly safe call that in the year 2020 the dollar will still be the world's favorite reserve currency. None of the alternative candidates is plausible" (1995b:14).

Less sanguine predictions are possible, of course. Precisely because of the possibility of multiple equilibria in such matters, reflecting the strategic interdependencies of decisionmaking on both sides of the market, we cannot entirely exclude a sudden flight from the dollar, as Paul Krugman has noted:

> The troublesome possibilities are either that the dollar's fundamental advantages will drop to some critical point, leading to an abrupt unraveling of its international role, or that a temporary disruption of world financial markets will permanently impair the dollar's usefulness. These are not purely academic speculations, since they have precedent in the history of sterling's decline. The disruption of World War I led to a permanent reduction in sterling's role, while the gradual relative decline of Britain's

importance in the world was reflected not in a smooth decline in sterling's role but in surprising persistence followed by abrupt collapse. (1992:179)

Short of such low-probability events, however, the more credible prospect is that the dollar will remain the world's favorite for some time to come—perhaps even for the next quarter-century that Frankel suggests. The dollar's day is by no means over, its many obituaries notwithstanding, though it is clear that high noon is past and the shadows are beginning to lengthen. Cross-border use will surely go on growing, but so too, most probably, will shifts at the margin into rival moneys elsewhere. The Top Currency's superiority will continue to show modest signs of erosion. Even Frankel acknowledges that "a return to the gentle downward trend of the 1970s and 1980s would not be surprising" (1995b:16). Other possible developments, as we shall see, including birth of the Euro and a potential yen bloc in the Asian Pacific, might also cut into the dollar's authoritative domain.

In this light, what is the best policy response from Washington? In principle, at one extreme, one might envision a stance of benign neglect[4]—essentially a strategy of inaction, relying on the dollar's past glories to sustain its future popularity. As attractive alternatives become available, however, such an approach could be a prescription for disaster, triggering exactly the kind of "abrupt unraveling" feared by Krugman, if unanticipated shocks threaten U.S. political or economic stability or the openness of its financial markets. In the words of *The Economist*: "If policy-makers continue to neglect the greenback . . . this could turn into a stampede, sending the dollar into a spin and pushing interest rates sharply higher. Such instability would harm the whole world economy—not just America" (1994d). History is littered with the carcasses of formerly dominant currencies left to wither by their issuing governments.

At the opposite extreme one might imagine an aggressive policy of market promotion—an activist, targeted strategy designed to discourage any decline in the dollar's role. As I indicated in the previous chapter, governments can deploy a variety of tactics to strengthen demand for a currency, including higher interest rates, convertibility guarantees, and special tax advantages, as well as financial-market initiatives to enhance exchange convenience and capital certainty. The greenback has an established brand name, and it would not take much effort to sustain confidence in its continued usefulness and reliability.

Such measures could prove counterproductive, however, if they merely serve to raise doubts about the dollar's future competitiveness. Why, market actors might well ask, would a strong currency need special measures of support? The dollar's reputation might actually suffer as a result (as sterling's reputation suffered from London's futile efforts to hold together the sterling area after World War II). Worse, a predatory approach could provoke retaliation from the EU and Japan, concerned about market shares for their own moneys. Global stability might be threatened if U.S. policies generated open confrontation among suppliers of the world's elite currencies.

In practice, therefore, neither inaction nor overreaction is warranted. In a world of accelerating competition, the United States will certainly not enjoy the benefits of Top-Currency status forever. But it does Americans no good at all to invite either sudden flight or a policy fight. Washington will best serve its citizenry if it consciously aims to accommodate the revealed preference of the marketplace: namely, sustained dollar leadership together with continued diversification at the margin. Most attractive, accordingly, would be a middle course of prudent caution, emphasizing programs that effectively sustain the political and economic foundations of the greenback's popularity—credible strategies to minimize inflation and inflation variability, promote savings, and maximize the breadth, depth, and resiliency of U.S. financial markets. As *The Economist* has written: "In the long run, it may be inevitable that investors diversify out of dollars. The speed at which they do this—and the havoc it causes—depends on America's leaders" (1994d). One can only hope that our leaders are up to this challenge.

Europe and the Euro

For the leaders of the European Union, the challenge is rather different—not how to protect an old currency but how to promote a new one. If implemented successfully, EMU will build on the already extensive authoritative domains of the DM and other participating moneys. But the Euro will not be created in a vacuum. It enters a world of intense competition, a world in which the dollar, still broadly popular for many uses, has long pervaded Europe's nominal monetary space. The greenback's established foothold in Europe may severely limit the benefits as well as complicate the process of currency merger for participating members. Alternatively, an ascendant EMU could seriously threaten the present market share of the dollar, compounding tensions in U.S.-European relations.

Much has been written about the implications of EMU for the future of the dollar.[5] The general consensus holds that monetary union in Europe will indeed threaten the greenback's hitherto predominant role. Predicts one source: "The most visible effect of EMU at the global level will be the emergence of a second global currency" (Gros and Thygesen 1992:295). Concludes another: "In the long term, the emergence of a European pole may lead to the creation of a new international monetary architecture" (Bénassy et al. 1994:9). The conventional wisdom is clear. If EMU is successful, the dollar will face a potent rival.

Indeed, the only questions seem to be: How great a rival, and how soon? For Fred Bergsten, a former U.S. Treasury official, the answers are: Very great, and very soon. Because of the inherent strengths of the European economy, Bergsten declares, the Euro will achieve full parity with the dollar in as little as five to ten years. A massive portfolio shift will occur in private financial markets that could exceed a half-trillion dollars.[6] In a similar vein, the economists George Alogoskoufis and Richard Portes argue that "the fundamentals point toward a potentially large shift in favor of the Euro. . . . The dollar would immediately lose its importance as a vehicle currency" (1997:4). Particularly influential in their estimation are the large domestic markets and extensive foreign-trade ties of prospective EMU participants, which should generate instant network externalities for Europeans and non-Europeans alike.

Most other observers are more cautious, stressing factors that might slow movement from the dollar to the Euro. Large-scale portfolio shifts, for example, are likely to be inhibited, at least initially, for two reasons. First is the fragmentation of Europe's financial markets, few of which (apart from the City of London) can match those of the United States for sheer size, openness, and operational efficiency. Undoubtedly, in time, a single currency will increase the homogeneity and liquidity of European markets, enhancing scale economies and lowering costs. But existing differences in national institutions and practices across the EU are unlikely to be eliminated quickly; it could be a very long time before all traces of segmentation disappear. In the words of one authority: "The European capital market will not become seamless as a result of monetary union; further harmonization and deregulation will be necessary before it rivals the American capital market in breadth and depth" (Henning 1997:13). Moreover, as two IMF economists have recently emphasized, the process is unlikely to be quick. Any movement by dollar investors toward the Euro is apt to be gradual (Prati and Schinasi 1997).

Second is the negative effect of monetary union on the composition of existing portfolios, many of which historically have been designed to balance risks by including a variety of EU currencies. When these moneys merge, reducing diversification, many risk-averse investors may delay acquiring yet more Euro-denominated assets. Indeed, some may actually prefer to sell off a portion of their Euro holdings in order to preserve customary portfolio targets, although according to Prati and Schinasi (1997:32) such reverse shifts are unlikely to be substantial.

Likewise, any sizable amount of switching to the Euro for transactions purposes will probably be limited at first mainly to the EU's immediate neighbors in East-Central Europe and the Mediterranean, whose foreign trade is dominated by the European Union. In other regions, where commercial ties are less heavily concentrated on Europe, the dollar will continue to enjoy significant incumbency advantages. Concludes one careful study: "The information collected . . . does not hint at dramatic changes in the currency composition of international trade after full monetary union. Rather, what one might expect is a gradual increase of Euro invoicing after a start from a relatively low level compared to the importance of the U.S. dollar" (Hartmann 1996:16).

Even with these caveats, however, few doubt the considerable potential of the Euro over the long term. The mainstream view is best summarized by Randall Henning:

> When it is introduced, there will probably be no large, precipitous displacement of the dollar. Nonetheless, much of the increased role of the new European currency can be expected to come at the dollar's expense, and this would reinforce the gradual historical decline in the role of the dollar exhibited over the last several decades. (1996:93).

But is even this more cautious expectation justified? Overlooked are the formidable competitive advantages that the dollar already enjoys *within* Europe's nominal monetary space, let alone elsewhere. To be sure, no evidence suggests any significant use of dollars for conventional *domestic* purposes inside EU countries. Dollarization is a phenomenon characteristic of the high-inflation economies of the developing world or former Soviet bloc, not of Western Europe. But for *international* purposes the greenback is still employed widely by many Europeans in preference to their own national moneys or even the DM, the local hegemon. To this extent the dollar's authoritative domain significantly overlaps the physical territory of its principal European rivals.

That overlap is certainly apparent in the foreign-trade area, where the dollar continues to be a favored vehicle despite the well-known preference in most industrial countries for home-currency invoicing of exports. Across Europe today, as we saw in Chapter 5, the dollar still accounts for a significant proportion of export contracts, outdoing the DM even in France and the Netherlands. On the import side, only Germany uses its own currency more than the dollar. Statistics are less clear in the investment area, since no disaggregation of published data is available to identify the currency distribution of financial assets in Europe alone. But we know that globally the greenback still accounts for over half of all international banking assets, as compared with a DM share of little more than 15 percent; and as much as two-fifths of the global bond market, as compared with a DM share of 10 percent. It is difficult to imagine that the dollar is less competitive in Europe for these purposes than it is elsewhere in the world.

The dollar's competitive advantage inside Europe is important because it poses a critical extra obstacle to successful implementation of EMU. In effect, Europeans will be under pressure to alter established patterns of behavior that have presumably yielded considerable savings on transactions costs in the past. If the dollar is already being used within Europe in preference to local moneys (including the DM), it must be because of its superior network externalities for at least some cross-border purposes. Put differently, the reach of the greenback's authoritative domain must already have made it a more efficient medium for some range of local-market uses. The economist Polly Allen calls this a money's "in-place network externality," which in an uncertain world makes a familiar currency like the dollar obviously more attractive to market agents than some newly created and untested alternative like the Euro. In her words:

> In a world of great uncertainty, the relative externalities of an in-place network become greater. . . . The expected network externalities from a new competing currency are likely to be small and uncertain. . . . [Hence] its lack of *in-place* network externalities and uncertain *current* externalities will dominate its still uncertain expected *future* network externalities. (1993:172–173)

The advantages of the dollar for Europeans will of course be minimal for purely domestic transactions or for trade within the group—especially if, as we may expect, the Euro is supported by restrictive legal-tender legislation. But as a vehicle for exports to the United States and elsewhere, as well as for imports, or as a store of value in banking and securities markets, the greenback will undoubtedly enjoy an initial edge, particularly if the new common money seems less credible than existing EU currencies. Reputations take time to develop, after all. Can widespread confidence in the Euro's prospective network externalities be generated instantly? Can political stability or a high degree of liquidity and predictability of asset value be immediately assured? In practice, market agents, at least at the outset, might be rational to prefer the tried-and-true to the experimental. Inertias similar to those that prolonged the life of other international currencies in the past are highly likely to manifest themselves again.

The persistent competitiveness of the dollar, in turn, will reduce other potential benefits of EMU. Continuing use of the greenback would inhibit growth of a stock of generalized Euro claims that might help ease payments adjustments vis-à-vis countries elsewhere; it would also restrict the base for levying an inflation tax in case of need. Neither macroeconomic flexibility nor the capacity for seigniorage will be enhanced as much as they would be if the Euro were being created in a vacuum.

In time, of course, things could change. Experience may bring increased credibility and confidence in the usefulness of the new money. Eventually, its network value to Europeans may indeed come to rival or perhaps even exceed that of the dollar, whose dominant global position, as we know, is by no means invulnerable. A favorable outcome for the Euro is particularly likely if growing use within the EU is reinforced by parallel adoptions elsewhere. No single configuration of monetary space is optimal for all circumstances, as I indicated previously, and multiple equilibria are possible.

Getting from one equilibrium to another, however, can be costly and, given the conservative bias introduced by mimesis, will almost certainly be delayed unless

EU governments promote the switch with vigor. The problem is one of collective action—a coordination dilemma. Individually, European market actors have little incentive to switch quickly from one currency to another (except where compelled to do so by legal-tender requirements) unless they have reason to expect many others to do the same. In a setting of decentralized decisionmaking, network externalities will not be generated instantaneously. In the short term, widespread displacement of the dollar will occur only if an aggressive EU marketing strategy is designed to expand networks for cross-border use of the Euro. Market share may be promoted, for example, by sponsoring the development of debt markets denominated in the new currency or by subsidizing the Euro's use as a vehicle for third-country trade. This is one circumstance where, in the ongoing dialectic between political authority and markets, public policy can make a real difference.

If it chose to do so, however, the EU would pose a direct threat to the authoritative domain of the dollar—and thus put itself on track for open confrontation with the United States. Predatory policy initiatives could provoke retaliatory countermeasures with each side endeavoring to defend or promote the competitiveness of its own money. In the long term, Americans as well as Europeans may well benefit from a successful EMU. The game need not be zero-sum. But at the outset a contest for market share could trigger serious policy frictions. As Robert Mundell has suggested: "A successful movement toward European Monetary Union would mean that the [Euro] area will be a rival to the dollar. . . . Each of the two major blocs would strive to build up its own currency area" (1995:31–32). The risks are real.

But so too are the risks of doing too little—an EU version of benign neglect—if the game is to be worth the candle for Europeans. In principle, participating governments could adopt a passive strategy, leaving it entirely to the marketplace to decide the Euro's future global role. However unlikely, such an approach might conceivably appeal to policymakers as a way to avert overt conflict with Washington. But it might also mean foregoing many of the benefits of a formal monetary merger. The longer inertia in market practice is tolerated, the more will anticipated gains be limited, despite the massive effort involved in creating a common currency. The Euro's entry onto the world stage must be explicitly managed.

As on the U.S. side, therefore, the most attractive option is a middle course, a prudent caution that emphasizes general measures to promote the fundamental soundness of the new money rather than either overreaction or inaction. In effect, the EU too must accommodate market sentiment—which for the moment appears to combine a preference for continued dollar preeminence with some diversification at the margin—if it is truly to serve the interests of its citizens. Even better would be joint measures with the United States to ensure smooth introduction of the Euro. Conflict is not the only possible outcome of the EU's momentous monetary project. EMU could also open up a dramatic new opportunity for international cooperation—if leaders on both sides of the Atlantic are prepared to seize it.

Toward a Yen Bloc?

Japan too is challenged by the new geography of money. For Tokyo, however, the issue is not *how* to manage the internationalization of its currency but *whether* to do so. Observers have long predicted the emergence of a yen bloc in the Asian Pacific that might rival existing monetary zones grouped around the dollar and DM/Euro.[7] Progress to date, however, has been limited, as evidence in chapters 3 and 5 amply testifies. Cross-border use of Japan's money, whether as a nominal anchor for exchange rates or as a medium for trade and investment, remains far below what we might expect of such an economic powerhouse, thus depriving the Japanese of benefits of high rank in the Currency Pyramid. Tokyo may feel it has no choice but to promote a greater market share for the yen. If it does, however, Japan too risks open confrontation with the United States, its main oligopolistic competitor.

The yen is ripe for internationalization, and the notion is hardly controversial. Japan is already the world's second-largest national economy, third-biggest exporter, and top international creditor. It can also claim an enviable record of success in controlling inflation and has made significant strides in opening and modernizing its domestic financial markets. Yet for all these advantages, the yen still runs far behind the dollar and even the DM for most cross-border purposes. In international asset markets, the yen's share in total financial wealth is barely one-third that of America's greenback (and no more than three-quarters that of the mark). In trade invoicing, the Japanese currency plays a modest role at best. Nowhere, not even in Japan itself, is the yen used as much as the dollar for denominating export and import contracts. By almost any measure, the yen is underutilized relative to the size and stature of the Japanese economy.

Might this situation change? For some observers, there is no doubt. Birth of a flourishing yen bloc is only a matter of time and indeed may already have begun. In the words of the economist David Hale: "The role of the yen in the global financial system has increased significantly during the past decade and will probably continue to expand in the future" (1995:156). Particularly important, in Hale's view, is the dynamic growth expected in the economies of East Asia, customarily regarded as Japan's economic hinterland. Expanding commercial and financial ties with Japan will naturally promote more widespread use of the yen for trade and investment purposes. Although "the dollar will continue to be the world's primary medium of exchange," Hale confidently concludes, "there will be more competition from the yen because of [these] changing economic circumstances" (1995:170).

Such confidence may, however, be misplaced. In fact, there are real grounds for doubt. It is true that cross-border circulation of the yen expanded significantly in the 1980s. But it is not true that the trend has continued into the 1990s. Japan's "bubble economy" burst in 1989, and subsequent years saw stagnation in Japanese domestic growth. In fact, in recent years the yen's share of international currency use has, in many respects, actually decreased rather than increased, mirroring the dollar's relative gains. Moreover, formal analysis of the risk and return characteristics of the two currencies gives little reason for either traders or investors to prefer the yen. "The fundamentals," concludes one study, "do not provide much support for the idea of a yen currency area."[8]

Skepticism regarding the yen's prospects is justified for much the same reason as it is for the Euro—namely, the dollar's still considerable in-place network externalities, which in Asia as in Europe continue to give it a formidable competitive advantage. Asians have long exhibited a preference for the dollar. Hence they too are unlikely to quickly alter established patterns of behavior that have yielded valuable savings in the past. For them the United States remains a dominant trading partner. The dollar's unparalleled authoritative domain will undoubtedly inhibit any large-scale switching to Japan's less widely circulated yen. Network externalities, therefore, are no more likely to be generated instantaneously in the Asian Pacific than they are in Europe. Here too uncertainty reinforced by mimesis will make for a significant incumbency advantage. As the Japanese economist Takatoshi Ito has written: "Inertia associated with scale economies may preserve the key currency status of the dollar for a long time. . . . The continued expansion of Japan's economy and its international trade may yet lead to an expanded role for the yen as a key currency, though not for some time" (1994:330).

Will Tokyo be prepared to wait? Most sharply at issue is reform of Japanese financial markets, which despite recent improvements have long lagged behind the U.S. and even many European markets in terms of openness and efficiency. Indeed, only two decades ago, Japan's financial system was the most tightly regulated and protected in any industrial nation, inhibiting wider use of the yen. Strict exchange controls were maintained on both inward and outward movements of capital, securities markets were relatively underdeveloped, and financial institutions were rigidly segmented. In the mid-1970s a process of liberalization began, prompted in part by a slowing of domestic economic growth and in part by pressure from the United States. Exchange controls were largely eliminated, new instruments and markets developed, and institutional segmentation greatly relaxed.[9] As a result, the yen's exchange convenience and capital certainty have been enhanced. But the process is by no means complete, as numerous sources have emphasized (Hale 1995; Garber 1996; Tavlas 1996a).

Further reforms are expected. Under a government plan announced in the fall of 1996, dubbed the Big Bang (in imitation of the swift deregulation of Britain's financial markets a decade earlier), additional steps are to be pursued over the next several years to reduce costs and interventionist regulations and to improve market depth and resiliency. A formal timetable for the Big Bang was laid down in mid-1997. Measures include termination of all remaining exchange restrictions and further liberalization of trading in equities and securities, all to be completed before the end of the decade. The yen, as a result, will become steadily more competitive in the Darwinian struggle among currencies.

Tokyo could simply stop there, ignoring any more direct measures to advance internationalization—its own variant of benign neglect. To do so, though, would mean foregoing many of the benefits that the Japanese people might rightfully expect to derive from the already elevated rank of their currency. These benefits include not only the status and prestige associated with widespread acceptance but also new opportunities for international seigniorage and political influence. Forbearance may be difficult to sustain.

Historically, Japanese policymakers have been ambivalent about yen internationalization, fearing especially the increased constraints on domestic policy that an ever-growing overhang of foreign liabilities might impose. The earlier examples of sterling and the dollar have weighed heavily. More recently, however, thinking appears to have swung, stressing advantages rather than disadvantages (Hale 1995:160–163). To a degree, this change merely acquiesces to the inevitable: it is a belated acknowledgment that an economy of such standing in the world cannot permanently suppress wider use of its currency. Certainly that view helps explain the government's new-found willingness to open its financial markets to foreign participation. But even more important is a far-reaching and fundamental transformation of official attitudes regarding Japan's overall place in the world—a coming of age. For a new generation of politicians and bureaucrats, the time has arrived to normalize the country's international status by assuming more of the role of a great commercial and financial power. As a Bank of Japan official puts it:

> Generally speaking, it is natural to expect that the larger economic presence of a country tends to lead to a stronger influence of that country on the world economy in terms of goods, capital and labor, which in turn will expand a basis for the currency of that country to be used internationally. Therefore, Japan's growing status in the world economy has certainly contributed to a wider use of the yen. (Maehara 1993:160)

The possibility exists, therefore, that Tokyo might be tempted to adopt a decidedly more aggressive strategy, to promote rather than merely await a growing market share for its currency. One straw in the wind was a series of agreements signed in 1996 with nine neighboring countries, to lend their central banks yen when needed to help stabilize exchange rates. Informed sources had no doubt that these pacts were deliberately designed to increase Japanese influence among potential members of a yen bloc. "It's a manifest attempt to take leadership," said one bank economist in Tokyo.[10] Equally suggestive was the critical role that Japan played when a severe currency crisis struck Thailand in mid-1997. In cooperation with the IMF, Tokyo moved quickly to mobilize financial assistance from around the region, providing some $4 billion of its own money to help support the Thai baht. In subsequent months Japan even tried, unsuccessfully, to float a plan for a special regional fund, limited to Asian nations only, to cope with similar threats in the future. Such an arrangement would of course have been dominated by Tokyo.

Greater cross-border use of the yen may also be encouraged by further development of yen-denominated debt markets or by subsidized use of the currency as a vehicle for trade in the region. Already as much as half of all Japanese exports to the Asian Pacific are denominated in yen, in contrast to little more than 15 percent of sales to the United States (Ostrom 1995). Japanese trade and investment are already so important to neighboring countries that it might not take much further effort to achieve the economies of scale needed to trigger a wholesale switch away from the dollar. Full-scale internationalization of Japan's currency could be hastened considerably.

But here too, as in Europe, such a proactive strategy would put the Japanese on track for a dangerous confrontation with the United States. Even a yen-bloc enthusiast like David Hale acknowledges that "there is also a risk that [such measures] will be interpreted as a threat by some Americans [and] could intensify the economic conflicts that are already straining U.S.-Japan relations" (1995:162). Far preferable, clearly, would be the prudent caution already suggested for Washington and the EU, emphasizing general measures to promote fundamental currency soundness rather than more specific initiatives designed to contest existing market shares. And here too it is desirable to substitute cooperation for conflict, consulting on joint measures to ensure a smoother transition. Collaborative management of the oligopolistic rivalry among the Big Three currencies is the best way to serve the interests of all the countries involved.

Coping with Currency Invasion

What about the many countries lower down the Currency Pyramid, particularly those with relatively uncompetitive Plebeian, Permeated, or Quasi-Currencies? Prospects for the Big Three currencies matter because of the extensiveness of their authoritative domains. Any conflict involving the United States, the EU, and Japan is bound to have serious ramifications far beyond their own borders. But difficult as the problems of the Big Three may be, they can be only a source of envy to governments whose moneys lose rather than win from deterritorialization—the currencies whose authoritative domains have been shrunken and constricted, sometimes quite dramatically, by more popular foreign rivals. For these governments, the challenge is far more central to their effectiveness and legitimacy: not how to preserve or promote the appeal of their currencies abroad but, rather, how to defend or retain any vestiges of monetary sovereignty at home. In short what, if anything, can they do or should they do to cope with the invasion of their nominal monetary space?

Such governments have two broad alternatives. One, an appealing choice to some, is to do nothing—a passive policy of market followership, simply acceding to high levels of currency substitution or influence from abroad. After all, extensive encroachment by another country's money is not without its advantages, as we have already noted. A strategy of forebearance can be readily implemented, either implicitly or explicitly.

The implicit version involves no more than a calculated tolerance of market-driven CS in the local economy. Particularly for citizens of states that have a long history of inflationary excesses, the availability of an alternative to local money is attractive for the discipline it provides over governmental abuse of the seigniorage privilege. As one source suggests, "dollarization is the ultimate repudiation of inflationary policy" (Melvin and Peiers 1996:39). The public gains from greater monetary stability and, insofar as financial repression is eased, quite probably from a more efficient allocation of capital resources as well. Economists in particular favor this strategy where more orthodox approaches to macroeconomic stabilization have already failed.[11] As indicated, the logic of such a "market-enforced monetary reform" (Melvin 1988a) is precisely what James Meigs had in mind when he advocated hiring a foreign currency in circumstances of financial infirmity.

Explicit implementation involves formal subordination to the authority of a strong foreign central bank via a currency board or firm exchange-rate rule. It aims to borrow credibility and respectability from abroad by overtly tying the government's hands at home. Such an approach is especially inviting to citizens of states with a new or untested currency, as I suggested in Chapter 3. The public gains not only sounder money but, at the symbolic level, a new source of national pride and accomplishment as well. Not surprisingly many economists subscribe to some variant of this strategy too, differing mainly over how much trade-off there ought to be between credibility and flexibility. Currency-board enthusiasts such as Steve Hanke and his associates argue that nothing less than the tightest possible linkage will fully persuade market actors of the government's sincerity.[12] Others fear that too tight a linkage will increase financial vulnerability by depriving the local banking system of a discretionary lender of last resort at time of crisis (Brand 1993; Calvo and Vegh 1992, 1996).

Whatever advantages market followership may offer, however, there are also disadvantages, as by now we well know. Not only is the government shorn of its capacity for effective macroeconomic management on its own. Deprived of seigniorage, it also loses the single most flexible instrument of taxation available for mobilizing resources in an emergency, leaving the country more vulnerable to political coercion from abroad. Most seriously, such an approach substitutes the judgment of anonymous market actors or foreign central banks for the considered deliberations of the citizenry's own government representatives, in effect ratifying the subversive impact of money's new galactic structure on the general will of the electorate. What the public gains in terms of financial stability, it loses in terms of democratic accountability. Acquiescence does nothing to correct for the legitimacy deficit generated by cross-border currency competition.

The alternative is a proactive policy designed to challenge directly the local market share of a dominant foreign money; in effect, a strategy to reconfigure currency space in favor of one's own money—*partial* reterritorialization. The more the local currency's authoritative domain can be enhanced, diminishing the influence and use of foreign money, the greater will be the opportunity to make official actions responsive, through the institutions of representative government, to the public's own revealed preferences. Results may not always be as conducive to efficiency or stability as we might like, but insofar as more democratic societies are concerned, at least they can lay claim to some degree of political legitimacy. At a minimum, private citizens would now have a better idea of whom to blame for outcomes not to their liking.

There are of course limits to how much currency space can be reconfigured in this way. As I noted at the outset of this chapter, a complete reterritorialization of money—absolute autarky—is not, in principle, infeasible. In practical terms, however, the high costs involved clearly make such an approach unlikely except in the direst of circumstances. Much more realistic are policies that aspire to something less than a full restoration of monopoly powers, balancing costs with prospective benefits—measures to compete more effectively rather than efforts to recreate the Westphalian model in one country. Here too initatives may be either unilateral or collective, and may combine elements of persuasion and coercion.

Unilateral action—a strategy of market neutrality—might, as suggested in Chapter 7, include a selection of more or less narrowly targeted measures to promote a currency's use as well as a broader commitment to orthodox monetary and fiscal policies. It might also include more coercive measures of financial repression designed to neutralize rather than cultivate market sentiment. Collective action—a strategy of market alliance—would aim to strengthen the role of local money by joining forces in some kind of monetary union in emulation of the East Caribbean Currency Area or the CFA Franc Zone. Where a handful of separate currencies might lack market appeal, one single money may prove more popular. In fact, the range of possible initiatives is remarkably wide.

Not all such policy actions will prove equally effective, of course, as our earlier discussion has made clear. Efforts to promote the reputation of a currency, whether unilateral or collective, may not always persuade the market; measures of financial repression may, as we well know, backfire, eroding rather than reinforcing confidence in a money's continued usefulness. One important determinant of outcomes is the degree and duration of CS in the local economy, which affects the likelihood of hysteresis. Dollarization is a costly process. The more extensive and long-lived an invasion by foreign money, the more difficult it will be to induce the public to switch back again. Another important determinant is the government's own previous record in monetary affairs, which will certainly condition the way market agents react to any new promises or threats by policymakers. Other determinants include the degree of market orientation in the economy as a whole, the level of development in financial markets, and the stability of political institutions. No one recipe is apt to work for all currencies. For dollarized economies, as one source has commented, "it is . . . not possible to give clear-cut or generally valid recommendations to policy-makers. . . . The best policy option can only be chosen against the the background of a particular country case."[13]

Whatever strategy is chosen, however, it is essential that any effort to reterritorialize currencies does not provoke outright policy conflict between nations—yet another way of stressing the importance of the need for governments to manage their oligopolistic rivalry in currency relations. A flow-based model of monetary geography cannot tell us precisely how that objective can be accomplished. But it does vividly highlight the central issues that policymakers must confront if they are to adequately serve the interests of their constituents in today's world.

⌒

The growing deterritorialization of money has by no means eliminated a role for public policy in the management of currency relations. It has, however, greatly complicated the task facing governments long accustomed to the privilege of national monetary sovereignty. Where once states claimed the rights of monopoly, they must now act like oligopolists, vying endlessly for the favor of market agents. Where once monetary politics was largely a matter of state intercourse, today the invisible hand of competition penetrates to the very core of official decisionmaking. The transformation of money's imaginary landscape demands that governments now, more than ever, incorporate private-market processes—the driving force behind cross-border competition—as a central element in the public policy process.

The traditional Westphalian model of monetary geography discounts the role of markets. Currencies are presumed to be effectively national, managed in monopolistic fashion by each separate government; and markets are expected to operate within a framework defined in strictly territorial terms. The policy process is conceived first and foremost in terms of relations among sovereign nations, and only secondarily in terms of an uneasy dialectic between political authority and markets. States exercise power, and governments govern.

Once we acknowledge the growth of cross-border competition, however, that state-centric model looks increasingly inadequate, if not wholly misleading. The more widely currencies come to be used across, and not just within, political frontiers, the more pivotal becomes the independent role of market forces in global monetary governance. Market agents too exercise power, and they increasingly rival governments as direct determinants of currency outcomes. The strategic interaction between the public and private sectors, not between states alone, becomes the primary locus of authority in monetary affairs.

If public policy is to remain at all effective, therefore, we must update our mental maps of money to close the widening gap between image and fact—between the conventional myth of One Nation/One Money and the reality of a deterritorialized galactic structure of currency. Westphalia's territorial trap must be avoided. We all need to learn to think anew about the spatial organization of monetary relations.

Notes

1. The Meaning of Monetary Geography

1. Allen and Massey 1995:2.

2. For a particularly useful discussion of poststructural theory, see Cmiel 1993.

3. See also Elkins 1995; Biersteker and Weber 1996. Ruggie acknowledges adapting the term from Foucault's *The Order of Things* (Ruggie 1993:157, n. 89). "Social episteme" shares origins with the term epistemology, conventionally defined as the theory or science of the method and grounds of knowledge, and is derived from the Greek word for knowledge. Ruggie (1975) had previously used the same root to develop the concept of an "epistemic community," which enjoyed a brief vogue in the literature of international political economy (e.g., Haas 1992).

4. In this book the terms "money" and "currency" are used interchangeably. "Cash" denotes coins and notes in circulation.

5. While agreeing that all three functions are integral to the definition of money, monetary theorists have long disagreed over which is essential, some arguing that the medium-of-exchange role is paramount (e.g., Meltzer 1995), others stressing the primacy of money's use as a unit of account (e.g., Aschheim and Tavlas 1996). Fortunately, there is no need to resolve this age-old debate here.

6. Marcel Mauss, "Les Origines de la notion de monnaie," *Institut Français d'Anthropologie,* Compte rendu des séances, vol. 2 (1914), as quoted in Zelizer 1994:25. Notable recent discussions by sociologists include Baker 1987; Zelizer 1989, 1994; Dodd 1994, 1995.

7. For a recent example, see Eichengreen and Flandreau 1996.

8. See also Johnston 1986.

9. Agnew 1994b:89. For some examples, see Agnew 1994a; Agnew and Corbridge 1995; Taylor 1993, 1994, 1995; Camilleri, Jarvis, and Paolini 1995; Elkins 1995; Shapiro and Alker 1996; Murphy 1996. Agnew, Corbridge, Taylor, and Murphy are geographers; the others are political scientists.

10. The ascendance of absolute territoriality was not instantaneous, of course. Even after 1648 a few anomalous practices remained, including some vestigial extraterritorial rights accorded the Holy Roman Empire and the Papacy. But as Daniel Philpott (1995:364) has written, "the anomalies were just that—traces of the past." Most exceptions gradually disappeared over the next two centuries.

11. Scholars differ on when the modern epoch actually began. Most political scientists simply distinguish broadly between the medieval and modern periods; modernism began with Westphalia. Others, particularly historians or humanists—many taking their cue from Foucault (1970)—insist on a further distinction between the classical age that was the immediate successor of medievalism and the truly modern epoch, which we are told did not really begin until early in the nineteenth century.

12. The terms "homonomous" and "heteronomous" in this context have been popularized by Ruggie, who explains:

> The term "heteronomous" refers to systems wherein the parts are subject to different biological laws or modes of growth and "homonomous" to systems wherein they are subject to the same laws or modes of growth. . . . In the original, biological sense of the terms, the fingers on a hand would exhibit homonomous growth—for a current international relations meaning, read "all states are functionally alike"—and the heart and hands of the same body heteronomous growth—read "all states are functionally different." (1993:151, n. 63)

13. See especially the outstanding work of Stephen Krasner (1988, 1993, 1995/96) and John Ruggie (1983, 1989, 1993). Other notable contributions include A. James 1986; Kratochwil 1986; Caporaso 1989; Jackson 1990; Walker and Mendlovitz 1990; Rosenau and Czempiel 1992; Camilleri and Falk 1992; Walker 1993; Rosenberg 1994a; Spruyt 1994; Guehenno 1995; C. Weber 1995; Biersteker and Weber 1996. Ironically, this analytical challenge is occurring at the very same time that the territorial boundaries of existing states have, in practice, become more fixed than ever before. Today, territory is no longer traded between states or treated as a legitimate prize of military force; and the only internationally recognized changes of national frontiers are those, such as in the former Soviet Union and Czechoslovakia, that follow the lines of existing internal borders (Jackson and Zacher 1996).

14. For that reason, some sources (e.g., Andrews 1994) insist on a firm linguistic distinction between the legal principle of control, for which the term *sovereignty* seems most appropriate, and the empirical issue of practical authority, perhaps better described by words like *autonomy* or *independence.* My own preference is for a more relaxed use of language, so long as the distinction between principle and practice is made clear in each context.

15. Much of this literature owes its inspiration to the early writings of the economist Raymond Vernon (1971) and the political scientists Robert Gilpin (1975) and Robert Keohane and Joseph Nye (1977). For some recent examples, reflecting a variety of viewpoints, see Gilpin 1987; Hirst and Thompson 1992, 1995, 1996; Strange 1994, 1995, 1996; Axford 1995; Bryan 1995; Jones 1995; Ohmae 1995; Boyer and Drache 1996; Sassen 1996a; Rodrik 1997. Michael Shapiro describes the issue as "a contention between the impulses of sovereignty and exchange. . . . The *sovereignty impulse* tends toward drawing firm boundaries around the self in order unambiguously to specify individual and collective identities. . . . In contrast, the *exchange impulse* encourages flows and thus (often) the relaxation of specifications of eligible subjectivities and territorial boundaries" (1993: 2–3).

16. For examples, see Bull 1977; Ruggie 1989, 1993; Cerny 1993b; Jarvis and Paolini 1995; Helleiner 1996a, 1997a; Kobrin 1996. Some scholars prefer the term "unbundled." See Kratochwil 1986; Ruggie 1993; Elkins 1995; Sassen 1996a.

17. The term "territorial currency," defined as a currency that is "homogenous and exclusive within the territorial boundaries of a state," was first coined by Helleiner (1996a). Elsewhere, I have used the more awkward term "insular national money" for the same purpose (B. Cohen 1997a, 1997b). Andrew Leyshon, a geographer, describes this as "homogenization of financial space within the borders of a nation-state" (1995a:38). For more on territorial currencies, see below, Chapter 2.

18. Eric Helleiner, in a pioneering commentary, refers to the "unravelling of territoriality" in the monetary sphere (1997a: 18–22). Helleiner also emphasizes the relatively recent origin of the historical notion of territorial currencies, which I take up in more detail in Chapter 2.

19. Dicken and Lloyd 1990:7.

20. Structural approaches to economic geography are mostly derived from theories of dependency and "unequal" exchange, and in particular from the world-systems model of Immanuel Wallerstein (1984). Major recent examples include Taylor 1993; Knox and Agnew 1994. For discussion, see Dicken and Lloyd 1990.

21. Though largely neglected in contemporary analysis, hints of both ideas have emerged in some historical discussions. See e.g., Boyer-Xambeu et al. (1994:10), who in discussing the "monetary geography" of Renaissance Europe speak of "a hierarchy of areas, each of which possesses an organic unit of its own." Regrettably, such thinking has not yet made much of an impact on conventional representations of currency space in our own era.

22. Notable examples include Daly and Logan 1988; Corbridge, Martin and Thrift 1994; Leyshon 1995a; Thrift 1995; Germain 1997; Leyshon and Thrift 1997. For a recent two-part survey of work along these lines, mostly by geographers and sociologists, see Leyshon 1995b, 1997.

23. Leyshon (1995b) labels these topics, respectively, the "geopolitical economy of finance" and the "geoeconomics of finance."

24. Scholars lately have busied themselves declaring the "end" of just about everything—from nature and science to architecture and economics—as Mihir Desai (1996) recently noted. See contributions by Camilleri and Falk (1992), Ohmae (1995), and Guehenno (1995). A good part of the inspiration for this latest generation of "endism" probably comes from Francis Fukuyama's notorious 1989 article, written in the first flush of celebration at the end of the Cold War, declaring nothing less than end of history. Or perhaps the trend has something to do with the coming of the millennium.

25. See e.g., R. Martin 1994; Cable 1995; Leyshon 1995a.

26. Martin 1994:264. See also Sassen 1996b.

27. Examples include Gill and Law 1989; Underhill 1991; Cerny 1993a, 1994a, 1994b; Goodman and Pauly 1993; Andrews 1994; Strange 1994.

28. The earliest use of the terms "space-of-flows" and "space-of-places" that I have found is Castells 1989. Four years later John Ruggie (1993) proposed the same distinction; his references show a clear awareness of Castells's earlier work. For more recent use, see e.g., Thrift 1995.

29. The term "virtual geography" I borrow from Australian commentator McKenzie Wark (1994), who distinguishes the "perceptions at a distance" produced by global communications media (television, telecommunications and the like) from our more familiar—and mundane—"geography of experience."

30. Perhaps the most notable exception was an early essay by economists Joseph Aschheim and Y. S. Park (1976), who wrote of the role that nonstate units of account—so-called artifical currency units (ACUs)—might play in creating "functional currency areas." Little attention has been paid to their suggestion, however.

31. Aglietta and Deusy-Fournier 1994; Thygesen et al. 1995. In fact, these two sources might be considered one, since the relevant texts are virtually identical and evidently owe their composition to Pierre Deusy-Fournier, who was a coauthor on both publications.

32. This definition refines, and slightly revises, versions of the concept of authoritative domain that I proposed in earlier attempts to explore the geography of money (B. Cohen 1994, 1997a, 1997b).

33. See e.g., Black 1990, 1993; Tavlas 1991, 1993a, 1996b; Tavlas and Ozeki 1992; Hakkio

1993; Thygesen et al. 1995; Frankel 1995a; Eichengreen and Frankel 1996. For more discussion, see below, Chapter 5.

34. Indeed, I too have been guilty of posing the issue this way, as Philip Cerny (1994c) critically noted in a review of B. Cohen 1993b. The present book is a further refinement of my thinking.

35. For some examples, see B. Klein 1974; Vaubel 1977, 1984; Greenfield and Yeager 1983; Yeager 1983; White 1983, 1984, 1988, 1989; Rahn 1986, 1989; Glasner 1989; Dowd 1992; Selgin and White 1994.

2. Territorial Money

1. According to Barry Eichengreen, "Mussa is fond of describing how, each time he walks to the IMF cafeteria, down the corridor where the currency notes of the member states are arrayed, he rediscovers one of the most robust regularities of monetary economics: the one-to-one correspondence between countries and currencies" (1996b:12). In Mussa's own words: "A stroll along the first floor corridor at the International Monetary Fund's Washington headquarters reveals the fundamental and indisputable fact [that] the empirical regularity is one country, one money" (1997:217). Eichengreen, an accomplished economic historian, is rightly more skeptical.

2. For some useful discussions of early monetary history, see Ederer 1964; Groseclose 1976; Wisely 1977; Braudel 1982; Chown 1994; Davies 1994.

3. The maxim is attributed to Sir Thomas Gresham (1519–1579), an English businessman and founder of London's Royal Exchange. He was also for a time financial adviser to Queen Elizabeth I. For some technical qualifications of Gresham's Law, see Rolnick and Weber 1986.

4. One source refers to these as "prestige-coins" (Ederer 1964:85). This long-term process of natural selection was very similar to present-day currency internationalization and currency substitution, which have been described as a Gresham's Law in reverse (Streissler 1992; Guidotti and Rodriguez 1992; Sturzenegger 1994). For more discussion, see Chapter 5.

5. As Wisely notes, the denarius did become "the dominant monetary standard of Western Europe," where the influence of Greek civilization was least marked (1977:10). But despite Roman conquests its effect was clearly eclipsed in the eastern Mediterranean and beyond by the historical prestige of the drachma.

6. The Islamic dinar, in turn, was imitated by the short-lived Crusader kingdoms, whose gold coins became known back in Italy as "saracen bezants" (*bisanti saracenati*) or simply "saracenati" (Lane and Mueller 1985:271).

7. Vilar 1976: chap. 3. Until the end of the seventh century, Cipolla suggests, "we can safely say that the Mediterranean was a 'nomisma area'. . . . After the late seventh century the Mediterranean world had two strong coins that enjoyed a predominant international prestige" (1967:16, 20), the bezant and the Islamic dinar.

8. According to one source (Larson, 1939:58), this may also account for the origin of the familiar dollar sign. The "S" with a stroke through it may have begun as an "8" for the eight bits in a silver peso.

9. As cited in Rolnick and Weber 1986:187.

10. Day 1954:15–16. For more on the history of sterling, see Polk 1956; B. Cohen 1971a; Walters 1992.

11. Ghost moneys prevailed throughout Europe for nearly a thousand years, from the time of Charlemagne until the French Revolution, with a few lingering even longer, such as the guinea in Britain (worth 21 shillings when the pound was still divided into 20 shillings worth 12 pence

each). Ghost moneys had their origin in the eighth-century Carolingian reforms that established the libra (one pound of silver) as the basic unit of monetary measure. Though meant to reduce currency confusion, ghost moneys sometimes had the reverse effect when several such units existed and competed within the same general area. For more discussion, see Einaudi 1936, 1937; Cipolla 1967; Bordo and Schwartz 1989; Boyer-Xambeu et al. 1994.

12. The emergence of territorial currencies has been discussed most recently by Eric Helleiner in an important series of papers (1996a, 1996b, 1997a, 1997b). Helleiner prefers the term "territorial currency order," rather than Westphalian model, in order to underscore the lateness of this historical transformation of monetary relations. As he writes:

Although the practice of "territoriality" is often said to have originated in the Westphalian age in seventeenth century Europe, I emphasize that monetary systems were not organized along territorial lines until the nineteenth century . . . [and were] linked to the broader historical processes that encouraged the emergence of "nation-states" in the nineteenth century. For this reason, it seems more accurate to link the rise of territorial currencies with the creation of the nation-state than with the transformations of the Westphalian age. (1996a:2, 6)

Helleiner is right, of course, about the practical timing of these developments. Strong nation-states did not in fact emerge as a general phenomenon until the nineteenth century. In principle, however, the inspiration and claims of legitimacy for the nation-state can certainly be traced back further, to the Peace of 1648. Moreover, as Helleiner himself emphasizes, early theorists of state sovereignty, such as the Frenchman Jean Bodin, were inspired by Westphalia well before the nineteenth century to advocate uniform and exclusive national currencies. Hence Westphalian model seems no less fitting a term for the monetary geography of the period than for its political geography.

13. As quoted by Berliner 1995.

14. As quoted by Goodhart 1995:455.

15. As quoted in Nash 1995:C5.

16. As quoted in Shlaes 1997:190.

17. Eckhard Fuhr, a columnist for the *Frankfurter Allgemeine Zeitung,* as quoted in the *New York Times,* June 12, 1997:A12.

18. A provisional Croatian dinar had been introduced as early as December 1991 but had not succeeded in supplanting the Yugoslav dinar.

19. In fact, the common practice of equating seigniorage and the inflation tax overlooks a slight technical difference between the two. In formal theory, seigniorage includes the resource transfer from increased private holdings of money as well as the inflation tax. See Blanchard and Fischer 1989:179.

20. Also known as the theory of optimal taxation or optimal (or rational) public finance, the idea of optimal seigniorage was initially developed by Bailey (1956) and Phelps (1973), following Milton Friedman (1953, 1969, 1971). Other key contributions include Auernheimer 1974; Gordon 1975; Calvo 1978; Chappell 1981; Fischer 1982; Kimbrough 1986; Vegh 1989; Canzoneri and Rogers 1990; Canzoneri and Diba 1992; Aizenman 1992; Goff and Toma 1993.

21. Fischer 1982; Dornbusch 1988; Drazen 1989; Grilli 1989a, 1989b; Giavazzi 1989; Giavazzi and Giovannini 1989; European Commission 1990; Bacchetta and Caminal 1992. For the same four countries, seigniorage as a percentage of tax revenues has ranged from 6 to 14 percent. For empirical purposes, seigniorage is most often calculated using the change in central bank claims on the government (known as high-powered money, reserve money, or the monetary base), though alternative measures are available and have been used. For some discussion, see

Fischer 1982; Klein and Neumann 1990; Cukierman et al. 1992; Gros 1993b; Gros and Vandille 1995.

22. Gros 1993b; Gros and Vandille 1995. The only exception, according to these sources, is Greece, where seigniorage remained steady from the early 1980s to the mid-1990s. This general trend has led some economists to question the practical relevance of the optimal-seigniorage idea in industrialized nations. Suggests Barry Eichengreen: "It is hard to imagine that such countries attach much value to the inflation tax" (1996b:14).

23. Financial repression, a term with obvious pejorative connotations, is part of the standard language of the technical economics literature. First suggested by Ronald McKinnon (1973), the term is meant to describe the combination of capital controls, interest-rate restrictions, high reserve requirements, and other regulations that many developing nations have used to control the activities of domestic financial intermediaries. One consequence of financial repression is a lower cost of funding for governments—in effect, a device to increase inflationary fiscal revenues. See e.g., Aizenman 1986; Dornbusch 1988; Drazen 1989; Bacchetta and Caminal 1992; Giovannini and De Melo 1993; Aizenman and Guidotti 1994; Dooley 1996.

24. Strictly speaking, the exchange rate is expenditure-changing as well as expenditure-switching. In the short term, the effect of altering the exchange rate is indeed mostly to shift expenditures between home and foreign goods. But over the longer term, as the domestic price level rises (in the case of devaluation) or falls (in the case of revaluation), altering the purchasing power of money balances, the aggregate level of spending will be affected as well, in what is technically known as the real-balance effect. For some discussion, see Caves et al. 1996: chaps. 19–20. The distinction between expenditure-changing and expenditure-switching policies was first introduced by Harry Johnson (1961: chap. 6).

25. Say's Law asserts that in market-based economies there can never be a general and permanent deficiency of aggregate demand; that is, there will always be a tendency toward full-employment equilibrium in the long run. Attributed to Jean-Baptiste Say, an early nineteenth-century French businessman turned economist, the Law was a fundamental tenet of the neo-classical economic tradition that Keynes attacked so vigorously in the *General Theory*.

26. Technically, an economist would say that we must be able to assume a negative slope to what is known as the Phillips curve—a graphic device used to illustrate the inflation-unemployment trade-off geometrically, with inflation measured on the vertical axis and unemployment on the horizontal axis.

27. Panama's dependence on the dollar goes back to an agreement between the two countries in 1904, implemented under terms of Panamanian Law No. 84, passed in the same year. Panama agreed to accept the dollar as legal tender and to issue no paper currency of its own. Balboa notes have been issued just once, during the brief presidency of nationalist Arnulfo Arias Madrid in 1941, and were quickly withdrawn from circulation following his overthrow (engineered, it is generally believed, with aid from Washington). For more detail, see H. Johnson 1973:223–28; Collyns 1983: chap. 6; Zimbalist and Weeks 1991.

28. In a similar vein, see Collyns 1983: chap. 6; Fieleke 1992.

29. Ambler H. Moss, Jr. in testimony before the U.S. Congress in 1989, as quoted in Kirshner 1995:162. For further discussion and detail, see Kirshner 1995:159–66; Hufbauer et al. 1990:249–67.

3. Subordinating Monetary Sovereignty

1. I avoid associating the term "integration" with such unions because, in currency relations among sovereign states, integration is a characteristic of vertical hierarchies as well as of horizontal alliances.

2. Kiribati (previously the Gilbert Islands) was a dependency of Great Britain and currently uses the Australian dollar. The Marshall Islands and Micronesia, once United Nations trust territories administered by the United States, still make use of the U.S. dollar. See Table 3.1.

3. Alan James (1986) uses a similar term, "permeated state."

4. Foreign-currency deposits, or Euro-deposits, are simply deposits in banks outside the borders or beyond the formal regulatory control of the country where the currency originates. Despite the label, the Euro-market is in fact global in scope and operates 24 hours a day. For some background, see Park and Zwick 1985; Aliber 1987.

5. B. Cohen 1963:613. A similar argument involving the pound sterling was made a few years later by British economist Peter Coffey (1968). Sterling, he asserted, had become a form of European currency as a result of agreements among Common Market central banks to hold pounds and accept them in settlement of mutual debts.

6. Meigs 1993:714, 716. See also Rahn 1989; Chown and Wood 1992–93; Dornbusch 1994. An alternative strategy, inspired by the idea of denationalized money advocated by Friedrich Hayek, might be not to hire one single currency but rather to allow a free competition of currencies in order to achieve monetary stability. See e.g., P. Schwartz 1993; A. Anderson 1993, 1995; Hefeker 1995b.

7. Precisely because of the risk of such confusion, the *Economist* (1996b) has proposed, not entirely tongue-in-cheek, that the label Euro-currency be changed to xeno-currency (from the Greek for foreign).

8. "Base money" is high-powered because in a fractional-reserve banking system, variations in circulating cash or commercial-bank reserves will have a multiple effect on the level of bank deposits—the major component of the nominal money supply in most countries today—depending on such factors as the portfolio choices of individuals and applicable reserve requirements. Full foreign-currency backing for base money, therefore, does not mean full backing for the aggregate stock of money in circulation, though of course there is a direct link between them.

9. For more discussion of the mechanics and operating principles of currency boards, see Fieleke 1992; Walters and Hanke 1992; Osband and Villanueva 1993; Liviatan 1993; Bennett 1994, 1995; Humpage and McIntire 1995; Williamson 1995; *IMF Survey* 1997.

10. For discussion, see Ow 1985; Jao and King 1990; Fieleke 1992; A. Schwartz 1992, 1993; Williamson 1995. Hanke et al. (1993: appendix C) provide a useful list of currency board experiences over the last century.

11. Singapore, exceptionally, has combined its currency board with a managed float rather than a fixed exchange rate. Brunei pegs its currency to the Singapore dollar. Both countries had previously participated in Britain's Malayan Currency Board, which also included the Malay States, Sarawak, and North Borneo (Sabah). The latter three entities are now combined in the sovereign state of Malaysia. For more detail, see Ow 1985.

12. For evaluations of Argentina's Convertibility Plan, see Liviatan 1993; Schweickert 1994; Zarazaga 1995a; Hanke 1996.

13. In 1985 the old peso had been replaced by the "austral," which in turn was succeeded by the "new" austral before the new peso was introduced.

14. The Estonian kroon was pegged directly to the DM; the Lithuanian litas, to the dollar. For more detail, see Bennett 1993; Hansson 1993a; Camard 1996.

15. During the years of military conflict leading up to the Dayton agreement, several currencies circulated in various parts of Bosnia & Herzegovina, among them the Yugoslav dinar in Serb-controlled areas, the Croatian kuna in Croat-populated regions, and a Bosnia & Herzegovina dinar that was introduced in October 1994. According to the Dayton agreement, the Yugoslav and Croatian moneys were to be withdrawn from circulation and a new central bank set

up to act as a de facto currency board for a minimum of six years. The Bosnia & Herzegovina dinar was pegged firmly to the Deutschemark.

16. The most tireless advocate of currency boards is the economist Steve Hanke, who with a varying cast of colleagues—labeled "monetary evangelicals" by John Williamson (1995:1)—has urged consideration of the currency-board option by countries as diverse as Mexico (Hanke 1996), Russia (Hanke et al. 1993), Russia's former allies in East-Central Europe (Hanke and Schuler 1991), and even China (Hanke and Walters 1993), as well as for the whole of Latin America (Hanke and Schuler 1993) and for developing nations in general (Hanke and Schuler 1994, 1996).

17. Giavazzi and Pagano 1988. The use of a firm exchange-rate link—up to and including a formal currency board—to lend credibility to domestic anti-inflationary policies once was known among monetary specialists as the "strong-currency option" (Cohen 1992a). More recently a currency-board strategy has been likened to a "poison pill," the well-known device used by corporations to ward off hostile takeovers, since such a commitment is difficult to reverse without a substantial risk of financial turmoil (Aslund et al. 1996:280–283).

18. The key issues, apart from the initial choice of anchor currency and exchange rate, are: (1) what liabilities to back with foreign currency; (2) how much backing to provide; and (3) who should have access to the resources of the board. For more discussion, see Bennett 1994, 1995; Camard 1996.

19. B. Cohen 1993c. Andrew Rose (1996) prefers the term Holy Trinity. Adding free trade to the equation produces what Tommaso Padoa-Schioppa (1988) calls the Inconsistent Quartet.

20. The theme of rules versus discretion, along with related issues of reputation and credibility, has long pervaded the theoretical literature on international macroeconomics, going back to early contributions of Kydland and Prescott (1977) and Barro and Gordon (1983). More recent contributions formalize the trade-off between credibility and flexibility in terms of conditional or contingent policy rules, otherwise known as rules with escape clauses—rules that can be overridden in exceptional circumstances. For useful discussion, see Cukierman, Kiguel, and Liviatan 1992; Corden 1994: chap. 5; De Grauwe 1994: chap. 2; Isard 1995: chap. 9.

21. Prior to the 1970s there were only two exceptions to this general practice, Canada and Lebanon, both of which maintained a floating exchange rate for periods of time.

22. The story of the breakdown of the old Bretton Woods system is well told by historian Harold James (1996: chaps. 8–9).

23. In the words of one researcher (Savvides 1993:112), "the IMF system is the only comprehensive and continuous system available."

24. The reasons for this are explored more fully in Chapter 5.

25. See e.g., Giavazzi and Giovannini 1989; Herz and Roger 1992; Welfens 1996. For some contrary opinions, see De Grauwe 1991; Fratianni and von Hagen 1992. On balance, the evidence seems to confirm a high degree of asymmetry in the ERM, though not total German dominance. Concludes one careful study: "The overall picture that emerges is . . . that Germany has a strong influence on the other EMS countries, but there is also some weak influence the other way round" (Gros and Thygesen 1992:150).

26. Additional results derived from these studies, both part of broader research programs, are reported in Frankel 1993; Frankel and Wei 1995b; Bénassy-Quéré and Deusy-Fournier 1995; Bénassy-Quéré 1996a, 1996b.

27. Examples include Fischer 1983; Dornbusch 1988; Giavazzi 1989; Grilli 1989a, 1989b; Cukierman, Kiguel, and Liviatan 1992; Willett and Banaian 1996.

28. Key early contributions include Boyer 1978b; Frenkel and Aizenman 1982; Aizenman and Frenkel 1985. For more recent discussion, see Collier and Joshi 1989; Argy and De Grauwe 1990; Aghevli et al. 1991: chap. 3; Flood and Marion 1992; Alogoskoufis 1994.

29. A useful survey of some early econometric work is provided by Edison and Melvin (1990). Other contributions include G. Weil 1983; Bosco 1987; Savvides 1990, 1993; Honkapohja and Pikkarainen 1992. For two rare exceptions that incorporate political variables as well as economic characteristics into the analysis, see Al-Marhubi and Willett 1996; Edwards 1996.

30. Modern analysis of the domestic politics of exchange rates has been pioneered by Frieden in a series of influential papers (1991, 1993a, 1994, 1996). Other important recent contributions include Ruland and Viaene 1993; Stephan 1994; Hefeker 1996, 1997.

31. This excludes members of the European Monetary System, which is a very special case.

32. For more detail on these trends, see the annual reports of the International Monetary Fund. For some discussion, see Collier and Joshi 1989; Flickenschild et al. 1992; Quirk et al. 1995.

33. Zarazaga 1995b:6, 9. See also Eichengreen 1994: chap. 5; Zarazaga 1995a; Williamson 1995.

4. Sharing Monetary Sovereignty

1. General discussions of monetary alliances and mergers in the nineteenth century can be found in Kramer 1970; Bartel 1974; Graboyes 1990; De Cecco 1992; Perlman 1993; Gallarotti 1994, 1995; Hefeker 1995a, 1997.

2. The only tangible result of the conference was a ceremonial coin minted by the French government carrying the inscription "5 dollars, 25 francs, 1867" on its reverse side. For more detail on the universal-currency idea, as well as the 1867 proceedings and succeeding conferences, see Reti 1994; Gallarotti 1995.

3. Useful recent discussions of the LMU include Griffiths 1992; Flandreau 1993, 1995; Gallarotti 1994, 1995; Redish 1994. In addition to Greece several other states—including Austria, Romania, and Spain—also associated themselves with the Latin Monetary Union in one manner or another, though never becoming formal members. By 1880 some eighteen states used the franc, the core monetary unit of the LMU, as the basis for their own currency systems (Bartel 1974:697).

4. The SMU experience has been evaluated most recently by Jonung 1987; Bergman et al. 1993.

5. The thaler and florin in turn were linked by a ghost money called the Cologne mark—an abstract currency unit expressed as equivalent to a certain quantity of silver ("mark fine by Cologne definition"). The mark (Reichsmark) of course became the common currency of the new German Empire, replacing thalers and florins alike, after political unification was completed in 1871.

6. For more discussion of the German nineteenth-century experience, see Kramer 1970; Bartel 1974; Holtfrerich 1989, 1993; De Cecco 1992; Hefeker 1995a, 1997.

7. Relatively little has been written on the Belgium-Luxembourg Economic Union. The most useful sources include Meade 1956; van Meerhaeghe 1987.

8. Belgium's population is some 25 times that of Luxembourg; its GDP is roughly twenty times larger.

9. Benin, Burkina Faso, Côte d'Ivoire, Mali, Niger, Senegal, and Togo. The West African Monetary Union was formally established in 1962.

10. The six members of the Central African group are Cameroon, Central African Republic, Chad, Congo, Equatorial Guinea (a former Spanish colony), and Gabon. Although the Bank of Central African States was not formally established until 1964, the West African central bank had been created earlier, in 1959. In the Central African group, the bank issues an identifiable currency for each member, although each country's currency is similar in appearance, carries the

same name ("franc de la Coopération Financière en Afrique Centrale"), and is legal tender throughout the region. This is in contrast to the West African group, where the central bank issues a single currency that circulates freely in all seven states.

11. Anguilla, Antigua and Barbuda, Dominica, Grenada (from 1967), St. Kitts-Nevis, St. Lucia, St. Vincent and the Grenadines.

12. Prior to 1960, the Republic's currency was the South African pound.

13. These were: France, Germany, Italy, and the three Benelux nations.

14. The Treaty of Rome contained a chapter on the balance of payments in which the partners pledged to coordinate their policies in monetary matters "to the full extent necessary for the functioning of the Common Market." Members vowed to maintain overall payments equilibrium and to treat exchange-rate policy as a matter of mutual interest. But no further commitments were included other than a promise to set up a procedure for granting mutual financial assistance in the event of serious external imbalances. For more detail, see B. Cohen 1963; Tsoukalis 1977: chap. 4.

15. Numerous histories have been written of European monetary integration in the period since World War II. Among the most informative are Tsoukalis 1977, 1991; Ludlow 1982; Gros and Thygesen 1992; Kenen 1992, 1995; Ungerer 1997.

16. Schmidt's initiative was enthusiastically backed by Roy Jenkins, president of the European Commission, who first revived interest in the topic with a call for renewed monetary integration in October 1977, and by French president Valéry Giscard d'Estaing, Schmidt's close ally and confidant. Tsoukalis (1991:49) describes the EMS proposal, which emerged directly from private talks between the two heads of government, as "the crowning act of the close cooperation between Valéry Giscard d'Estaing and Helmut Schmidt." Which of the two actually came up with the idea remains uncertain. When asked who might be regarded as the father of the plan, Giscard d'Estaing is said to have replied with a quotation from Napoleon: "En matières de paternité, Monsieur, il n'y a que des hypothèses."

17. Greece, Portugal, and Spain were all admitted to the EC during the 1980s, followed by Austria, Finland, and Sweden in 1995. Some of the EC's financially weaker members, beginning with Italy and subsequently including Spain (1989), Britain (1990), and Portugal (1992), were allowed into the ERM within a broader band of movements of up to 6 percent in either direction—derisively labelled by some the "boa." (In 1990 Italy narrowed its band to the $+/-$ 2.25 percent sustained by the ERM's other original members.) Austria, Finland, and Sweden, meanwhile, even before formally joining the EC, were all closely associated with the snake on a de facto basis, shadowing the DM exchange rate and closely coordinating their interest rates with ERM countries.

18. The term "new EMS" was first coined by Giavazzi and Spaventa 1990.

19. The following quotations and interpretations are from European Union 1992, article 109j and a related protocol. All members meeting the four convergence criteria must participate in Stage Three except Britain and Denmark, each of which negotiated a right to opt out if it so desires.

20. The one exception was the Netherlands, which retained a narrow peg for its guilder vis-à-vis the DM. Austria joined the ERM in January 1995, Finland in October 1996. Italy was readmitted in November 1996. For more on the 1992 and 1993 crises, see Kenen 1995: chap. 7; Ungerer 1997: chap. 22; Salvatore 1997.

21. Less than two months after their amicable divorce on January 1, 1993, the Czech and Slovak republics each introduced a new currency, both named the koruna (crown), to replace the Czechoslovak koruna (plural: koruny). For some discussion, see Janackova 1994. In Yugoslavia, where separation was less peaceful, replacements for the Yogoslav dinar have been created not

only by Croatia (the kuna) and Slovenia (the tolar), as described in Chapter 2, but also by both Bosnia & Herzegovina (the dinar, described in Chapter 3) and Macedonia (the Macedonian denar). The Yugoslav dinar remains legal tender only in Serbia and Montenegro, the two remaining constituents of the rump Yugoslav federation.

22. The recent ruble experience has already produced a wealth of analytical discussions. See especially Centre for Economic Policy Research 1993; Gros 1993a; Hansson 1993b; Goldberg et al. 1994; Wolf 1994; Aslund 1995; Conway 1995; Granville 1995; Gros and Steinherr 1995; Willett et al. 1995; Hefeker 1997.

23. These were: Armenia, Azerbaijan, Belarus, Estonia, Georgia, Kazakhstan, Kirghizia, Latvia, Lithuania, Moldova, Russia, Tajikistan, Turkmenistan, Ukraine, and Uzbekistan.

24. All three, which had been independent states during the interwar period, were forcibly absorbed by the Soviet Union in 1940 under the terms of Joseph Stalin's nonaggression pact with Nazi Germany. Estonia's new currency, the kroon, was introduced in mid-1992 and those of Latvia (the lats) and Lithuania (the litas) in two-step programs concluded a year later. For more detail, see Girnius 1993.

25. In fact, an accord on a joint central-bank council was signed in May 1992 but never implemented owing to disagreement over the voting power to be attributed to each government in collective decisionmaking (Gros and Steinherr 1995:386–387).

26. A competition for seigniorage had been predicted as early as 1992 by two economists, Jeffrey Sachs and David Lipton, who wrote "there is *no realistic possibility* of controlling credit in a system in which several independent central banks each have the independent authority to issue credit" (1992:237).

27. Eichengreen (1994:125) speculates that Russia's attitude may have been shaped primarily by domestic political considerations. In his words: "Given that it is still seeking to establish its authority over breakaway regions within the Russian republic, Moscow will surely hesitate to give other republics a voice in the formulation of policy by the Central Bank of Russia for fear that regions within the Russian Federation will demand the same voice."

28. European Commission 1990; Alogoskoufis and Portes 1991, 1992; Alogoskoufis 1993; Benassy et al. 1994. Not everyone agrees with this last line of argument, however, as we shall see in Chapter 8.

29. See e.g., Dornbusch 1988; Giavazzi 1989; Giavazzi and Giovannini 1989; Grilli 1989a, 1989b; Canzoneri and Rogers 1990; Vegh and Guidotti 1990; Aizenman 1992; Bacchetta and Caminal 1992; Canzoneri and Diba 1992; Sibert 1992, 1994; Daniels and Van Hoose 1996; Willett and Banaian 1996.

30. Other important early contributions were made by Ronald McKinnon (1963) and Peter Kenen (1969). For useful recent surveys, see Gandolfo 1992; Masson and Taylor 1993; Tavlas 1993b, 1993c, 1994; De Grauwe 1994.

31. In addition to the motive of political integration, domestic distributional considerations are stressed by Frieden (1993b, 1996) and Hefeker (1996, 1997) as a factor shaping European policy preferences toward EMU. This conclusion is disputed by Giovannini (1993).

32. The remainder of this chapter draws heavily from B. Cohen 1993a. Sustainability, in this context, refers solely to the longevity of a monetary alliance. Other possible criteria by which to judge the success or failure of such commitments (e.g., impacts on price stability, employment, or economic growth) are not directly considered.

33. The same point is also suggested by a companion theoretical literature on the economics of investment under uncertainty, which stresses the importance of "sunk costs" as a barrier to exit: the greater the cost of starting up again in the future, the lower is the incentive to abandon an unprofitable investment in the present. See e.g., Dixit 1992.

34. Graboyes (1990:9) concurs, arguing that the fatal flaw of LMU was that it "decreed a common monetary policy but left each central bank to police its own compliance."

35. For a dissenting note, stressing the joint influence of economic and organizational variables rather than either of the two political characteristics I highlight, see Andrews and Willett 1997.

36. Only once has the Luxembourg government publicly asserted its own will on a major issue. That was in 1935, following a 28 percent devaluation of the Belgian franc. Luxembourg also devalued, but by only 10 percent, unilaterally changing the partners' bilateral exchange rate from par to a ratio of 1.25 Belgian francs per Luxembourg franc (Meade 1956:14–16). Over the long haul, however, that solitary episode has proved to be the exception rather than the rule. Since restoration of parity during World War II, Luxembourg has formally followed Belgium's lead on most matters (though reportedly it does not hesitate to make its views forcefully known in private).

37. While for some sources (e.g., Boughton 1993a, 1993b; Clement et al. 1996) the impact of France's role is on balance positive, promoting monetary discipline and stability, for others the effect is clearly for the worse insofar as it may perpetuate dependency, retard development, reinforce income inequality, or depress exports. See e.g., Hayter 1966; Yansane 1978/79; Martin 1986; van de Walle 1991; Usman and Savvides 1994; Monga 1997.

5. Currency Competition and Hierarchy

1. Useful sources on currency internationalization include Krugman 1992; Black 1990, 1993. General introductions to currency substitution include Calvo and Vegh 1992, 1993, 1996; Marquez 1992; Brand 1993; Giovannini and Turtelboom 1994; Mizen and Pentecost 1996.

2. Modestly, I may claim credit for first introducing this analytical typology into the literature (B. Cohen 1971a), as, among others, Kenen 1983 and Krugman 1992 acknowledge.

3. Among the best of these studies are Kindleberger 1973; Eichengreen 1990: chap. 11; Walter 1991; Gallarotti 1995.

4. Among the most notable are Strange 1971a, 1971b; Brown 1978, 1979; and Aliber 1987. For a brief formal treatment, see Fratianni 1992.

5. Strictly speaking this formulation, encompassing money substitutes as well as the core components of the money supply (coins, notes, and demand deposits), defines "broad" or "indirect" CS, which in formal models is usually distinguished from "narrow" or "direct" CS, referring to the interchangeability of core money alone (Copeland 1994: chap. 9; Giovannini and Turtelboom 1994). The distinction is due to McKinnon (1985) and has recently been revisited (McKinnon 1996). For our purposes, the broad definition seems more appropriate.

6. Although most sources treat CS and dollarization as synonymous terms, a few analysts have insisted on a distinction between the two. Calvo and Vegh (1992, 1996), for instance, define dollarization as the broader term, encompassing all three functions of money, and they limit CS to the role of medium of exchange alone. For them, "currency substitution is normally the last stage of the dollarization process" (1992:4). But this approach is disputed by others, as surveys have noted (Brand 1993:2; Giovannini and Turtelboom 1994:390–392). Our discussion follows the more common practice of treating the two terms as essentially equivalent.

7. See e.g., Guidotti and Rodriguez 1992; Sturzenegger 1992; Guidotti 1993; Peiers and Wrase 1995; Uribe 1995; Savastano 1996. But see also Sahay and Vegh (1995, 1996) and Mutch (1995) for evidence that the process is not always irreversible, particularly where CS has not gone on for very long. I return to this point below. Seizing on the point, Mueller (1994) has proposed

to use reversibility rather than, as do Calvo and Vegh (1992, 1996), monetary functions to distinguish between CS and dollarization. CS exists, he suggests, when the substitution process is reversible, dollarization when it is not (or reversible only to a limited degree). But this distinction has not caught on in the literature either, mainly because there is really no way of knowing whether or not the process is reversible until after the fact.

8. Reasons for the hysteresis frequently observed in the process of currency substitution are explored more fully in Chapter 7.

9. For recent surveys, see Marquez 1992; Copeland 1994: chap. 9; Giovannini and Turtelboom 1994; Mizen and Pentecost 1996. Classic sources include Calvo and Rodriguez 1977; Boyer 1978a; Miles 1978a, 1978b; Girton and Roper 1981; Kareken and Wallace 1981; Cuddington 1983; Calvo 1985.

10. See e.g., Girton and Roper 1980; Melvin 1985.

11. Prominent examples include Fratianni and Peters 1978; Vaubel 1978, 1990; Salin 1984; British Treasury 1989; Streissler 1992.

12. See e.g., Woodford 1991; P. Weil 1991; Canzoneri and Diba 1992; Canzoneri et al. 1993; De Grauwe 1994: chap. 6; Daniels and Van Hoose 1996.

13. Put differently, the process may be described not as Darwinian but as Gresham's Law in reverse, where more attractive ("good") money drives out less attractive ("bad") money. See e.g., Streissler 1992; Guidotti and Rodriguez 1992; Sturzenegger 1994. The reversal of Gresham's Law in conditions of high inflation has been labeled Thiers' Law by Bernholz (1989), after the nineteenth-century French historian Louis Thiers who noted the pattern at the time of the French Revolution.

14. From this point on, CI is defined to include the symmetrical variant of CS. The term CS refers to the asymmetrical variant alone unless otherwise specified.

15. Hartmann 1994:1. The key insight about the cost savings underlying CI is usually attributed to Swoboda (1968, 1969) and has formed the basis of numerous formal models, including Chrystal 1977, 1984; Krugman 1980, 1992; Black 1991.

16. Extrapolating from this point, Eichengreen uses the same concern for economies of scale, as they influence government decisionmaking, to explain the broader evolution of the international monetary system since the nineteenth century. "The international monetary arrangement that a country prefers," he argues, "will be influenced by arrangements in other countries. . . . [by] the network-externality characteristic of international monetary arrangements" (1996a:6).

17. Key sources include B. Cohen 1971a; Bergsten 1975; Tavlas 1991, 1996b; Krugman 1992; Frankel 1995a, 1995b; Eichengreen and Frankel 1996. For additional references, see Frenkel and Goldstein 1997:2–3.

18. For precisely that reason, the economist Roohi Prem (1997) has recently argued that the standard qualities cited in the literature, all of which are based on past performance, cannot wholly suffice to predict a currency's future attractiveness. Additionally, he contends, it is necessary to consider factors that will encourage the issuing government to preserve its money's overall competitiveness—"characteristics [that] embody information about the extent to which the issuer is committed against imprudence" (1997:7), such as an independent central bank. Such factors are described as "enforcement determinants" of the international role of a currency.

19. For some discussion, see Dominguez and Frankel 1993: chap. 5.

20. The number of reporting countries included in Table 5.10 is actually quite small—21 in 1989 and 26 in succeeding years. These countries account, however, for the vast majority of foreign-exchange transactions in the global market today.

21. A general preference for home-currency invoicing of exports has been subsequently confirmed as an empirical regularity by numerous other studies, including Page 1977, 1981;

Carse et al. 1980; Magee and Rao 1980; San Paolo Bank of Turin 1990; S. Black 1990, 1993; Thygesen et al. 1995; Tavlas 1996b. Analytical models to explain the choice between home- and foreign-currency invoicing have been developed by, among others, Magee and Rao 1980; Rao and Magee 1980; Bilson 1983; Donnenfeld and Zilcha 1991; Ahtiala and Orgler 1995. The main advantage of home-currency invoicing is avoidance of overt exchange-rate risk. The main advantage of invoicing in the foreign buyer's currency is the ability to minimize fluctuations of demand that might otherwise be caused by exchange-rate movements.

22. Reasons for Japan's distinct dollar preference, which has long made it unique among industrial countries, are discussed by Ito 1993, 1994; Taguchi 1994; Ostrom 1995. Most sources agree that the principal explanation is to be found in the "pricing-to-market" strategy typically followed by Japanese exporters, many of whom are still willing to bear a certain amount of exchange risk in order to maintain more stable production levels and preserve foreign market shares.

23. The calculation (47.6 percent) is for 1992, down from an estimated 56.1 percent in 1980. Just about all of the decline after 1980, however, was due to the decreasing relative importance of oil. In nonoil trade, the dollar's share has remained virtually unchanged. See also Blinder 1996.

24. Examples include the Hong Kong dollar in the coastal provinces of China (Yamazawa et al. 1992, n. 8; Gardner 1993; Lo 1996), the Singapore dollar in southeastern Asia, the Indian rupee in Bhutan and Nepal, and even for a time the Greek drachma in southern Albania (*Economist* 1993b). But these are obviously special cases, stemming from unique local circumstances, as compared with the far more popular Big Three. Currencies that for historical reasons circulate outside their country of origin, as described in Chapter 3, because of a grant of legal-tender status (the rand in southern Africa, the rupee in Nepal, the ruble in Belarus and Tajikistan), must also be considered special cases.

25. For a useful primer on the technical difficulties of measuring "cocirculation" of currencies, see Krueger and Ha 1996.

26. See e.g., Stekler 1991; Porter 1993; Sprenkle 1993; Feige 1994, 1996; Porter and Judson 1996.

27. Growing foreign circulation has also meant a growing problem of counterfeiting, owing to the greater difficulty of enforcing U.S. law outside the United States. Of particular concern in recent years has been the so-called Supernote or Superbill—$100 Federal Reserve Notes, originating somewhere in the Middle East, that were so perfectly forged that not even experts could tell them from the real thing. The threat from the Supernote was directly responsible for a sweeping redesign of all U.S. currency, starting with the $100 bill, begun in 1966 (Drew and Engelberg 1996).

28. *Business Week* 1993. Local nicknames are also popular among journalistic sources, such as the Castrodollar in Cuba (*Economist* 1993a) or the Ding Dong Dollar in Vietnam (*Far Eastern Economic Review* 1995).

29. A similar approach was used earlier by the Bundesbank, which argued that "cash returning from abroad . . . probably provides a relatively complete picture of the volume of Deutsche Mark notes circulating internationally" (Deutsche Bundesbank 1991:47).

30. A combined estimate of $300 billion is remarkably consistent with Wilson's early calculation (1992), which suggested a total "unexpected currency growth" in eight major countries— those most likely to have substantial cash outflows to other countries—of $279 billion between 1970 and 1990. Taking a different tack, however, and adding in the moneys of other industrial states as well, another source comes up with a much higher figure, guessing that in the developing world as a whole as much as $820 billion of foreign banknotes may presently be in use for transactions purposes (Sprenkle 1993). These calculations have not gone unchallenged (see e.g.,

Pieper 1994; Sumner 1994; Haughton 1995) and should probably be taken with the proverbial grain of salt.

31. Numerous other studies also exist but unfortunately fail to provide comparably detailed data. The empirical literature is reviewed by Brand 1993; Giovannini and Turtelboom 1994. Important recent contributions include Sahay and Vegh 1996 and Savastano 1996.

32. B. Cohen 1997a, 1997b. The notion of a currency region is useful to distinguish a functional image of monetary space from either the currency "areas" of OCA theory or the currency "unions" that are created by formal, interstate monetary alliances.

33. The term "key currency" was originated after World War II by economist John Williams. See e.g., Williams 1947.

34. The allusion to the movie *Back to the Future* was suggested by Stephen Kobrin, in a broader context, as a colorful way to characterize the perceived transition of the global political system from Westphalia to some form of post-Westphalian neomedievalism, as discussed in Chapter 1 (Kobrin 1996).

35. The term Top Currency is borrowed from Strange 1971a, 1971b.

36. A. James 1986. For an earlier suggestion along the same line, see Herz 1957. For Herz, speaking of the challenge of defending the territorial state at time of war, "territoriality" was defined as synonymous with "impermeability" or "impenetrability" (1957:474).

6. A New Structure of Power

1. See e.g., Melvin and Fenske 1992; Savastano 1992, 1996; Brand 1993; Claassen and De La Cruz Martinez 1994.

2. The foreign adviser was Ardo Hansson, a Swedish economist, as quoted in the *Economist* 1994d:59. See also Hansson 1993a.

3. These were the cruzeiro, first introduced in 1967, succeeded by the cruzado (1986), new cruzado (1989), another cruzeiro (1990), and the "cruzeiro real" (1993).

4. As quoted in B. Cohen 1971a:xi.

5. Technically, the magnitude of international seigniorage is a direct function of the size of current-account deficits financed in the country's currency and only indirectly related to the size of fiscal deficits monetized by the government (domestic seigniorage). The link between the two depends on the extent to which such budgetary shortfalls, by reducing net national savings, may be considered a contributing factor to external imbalance.

6. Cohen 1971a: chap. 2. In his classic 1982 article, Stanley Fischer labels these components respectively the "stock cost" and "flow rate" of seigniorage. The latter assumes that the extra expenditures go into profitable investment: the net saving represents the difference between interest paid on liabilities and the rate of return on capital, which is presumably higher.

7. For an example, see B. Cohen 1971b.

8. The broader applicability of the logic was recognized by James Ingram in an early proposal for financial integration—in effect, a currency union based on firmly fixed exchange rates—among the industrial nations of Europe and North America (Ingram 1962); and more recently was revived as the basis for a possible alternative route to monetary integration in Europe (Kregel 1990). But the logic holds, plainly, only so long as all exchange risk is indeed removed. Between currencies whose exchange rates are not irrevocably pegged, capital flows may be anything but equilibrating.

9. Strange 1971a:222. In the same vein, see also Block 1977; Brett 1983; Kirshner 1995: chap. 4.

10. For more detail on these two episodes of French systemic disruption, see Kindleberger 1972; Kirshner 1995: chap. 5. The term "exorbitant privilege" was coined by Charles De Gaulle, president of France during the 1960s, who expressed particular resentment of America's capacity, owing to the dollar's universal acceptability, to run payments deficits "without tears." De Gaulle's views on the subject were greatly influenced by the advice he received from the eminent French economist Jacques Rueff, an ardent advocate of a politically more neutral gold standard. See e.g., Rueff 1972.

11. Following this logic, economist George Tavlas (1996b) has recently demonstrated the direct relevance of OCA criteria to the determination of market-driven currency configurations which, as noted in Chapter 5, I have elsewhere labeled currency regions (B. Cohen 1997a, 1997b).

7. Governance Transformed

1. For recent surveys, see B. Cohen 1996; Andrews and Willett 1997.

2. In fact, much of Andrews's analysis is appropriately directed to qualifications and limits of the proposition. In his words: "Caution is warranted when generalizing about the effects of heightened capital mobility on individual states' monetary autonomy" (1994:193). Andrews does not concur unreservedly with the Capital Mobility Hypothesis, as I incorrectly implied in my 1996 survey (B. Cohen 1996:281).

3. Early examples of this line of argument include Bates and Lien 1985; Gill and Law 1989; Frieden 1991. For some recent discussion of empirical evidence, see Milner and Keohane 1996:249–251.

4. Alain Madelin, a political conservative, quoted in the *International Herald Tribune,* October 16, 1995, two months after he resigned from the government of Prime Minister Alain Juppé.

5. For some discussion, see Morehouse 1989; Solomon 1996.

6. Other examples include the IMF's SDR and an early predecessor of the ECU labeled the European Unit of Account (EUA). For more discussion, see Aschheim and Park 1976.

7. For some discussion, see Allen 1986, 1990, 1992, 1993; Masera 1987; De Grauwe and Peeters 1989; Fujita 1995.

8. For some discussion, see Levy 1994; *Business Week* 1995; Gleick 1996; Teitelman and Davis 1996; Kobrin 1997b.

9. See e.g., Vaubel 1977, 1978, 1984.

10. Dowd and Greenaway 1993a:1180. See also Dowd and Greenaway 1993b. For an empirical application, see Peiers and Wrase 1995.

11. Strange 1987:564. Strange contrasts this with the older, more traditional rivalry between states for such things as territory and the wealth-creating resources that might be located within territory. See also Strange 1995. A similar argument, posing a distinction between the older-style territorial state and a more modern "trading state," was proposed even earlier by Richard Rosecrance (1986).

12. Cerny 1994b:225. First introduced a few years earlier (Cerny 1990: chap. 8), Cerny's idea of the competition state has been explored in some detail in business studies and industrial economics but is only beginning to penetrate the literature of international political economy. For further discussion, see Palan and Abbott 1996.

13. See e.g., De Boissieu 1988. De Boissieu, a French economist, writes of an "oligopolistic monetary equilibrium" consisting of dollar, DM (or EU common currency), and yen. See also Aliber 1987; Erdman 1996.

14. For an early application of the analogy between oligopoly and international relations, see B. Cohen 1991: chap. 1. That chapter was originally published in 1968. For a more specific application to monetary relations among sovereign states, see B. Cohen 1977.

15. See also Klein and Melvin 1982; Melvin 1988b.

16. Most prominent is Neil Wallace (1983, 1988). For some discussion of this "legal restrictions theory," which is closely associated with the development of the so-called new monetary economics in the 1980s, see Cowen and Kroszner 1987; Harper and Coleman 1992; Laidler 1992; Selgin 1994; Selgin and White 1994. Numerous authors have highlighted the resemblance of legal restrictions theory to George Knapp's early "state theory of money" mentioned in Chapter 1.

17. Hirst and Thompson (1995, 1996) label such observers "extreme globalization theorists." See these sources for further references. Louis Pauly (1995) describes them as "global market enthusiasts."

18. See also Strange 1994, 1995.

19. Alternatively: "The proposition, in short, is that state authority has leaked away, upwards, sideways, and downwards. In some matters, it seems even to have gone nowhere, just evaporated" (Strange 1995:56).

20. See note 17, above.

21. The literature on authority is voluminous, involving specialists from several disciplines. Intense debate is attracted by the relationship of the concept of authority to notions of duty or obligation, on the one hand, and to issues of liberty, rights, and the autonomy of the individual on the other. For a useful survey, see Miller 1987. Notable recent contributions include Watt 1982; Pennock and Chapman 1987; Raz 1990; Lincoln 1994; Molnar 1995. For an application to issues of international political economy, see Cutler 1996.

22. See e.g., Held 1991; Held and McGrew 1993; Hirst and Thompson 1995; Pauly 1995; Underhill 1995; Sassen 1996a.

8. Can Public Policy Cope?

1. Government attitudes could eventually change, of course, as Professor Hayek himself once pointed out to me at a conference in the late 1970s, where I had the temerity to challenge his absolutist vision. States, I argued, could not be expected easily to surrender what has long been regarded as an essential attribute of sovereignty. Who would have thought, Hayek quietly replied, that four hundred years ago governments might have contemplated giving up control of religion? Clearly he had a point, though over a time horizon a good deal longer than is relevant to the discussion in this book.

2. As quoted in the *New York Times* 1994:A8.

3. Kindleberger 1985:308. Kindleberger's views have not changed. A decade later he was still writing that "the outlook . . . is dark, as the dollar follows sterling, the guilder, the ducat and the bezant" (1995:9).

4. In international monetary discussions the term "benign neglect" first originated in the late 1960s as a critical way to describe the policies of the U.S. government, which at the time was more concerned with waging war in Vietnam than with defending America's deteriorating balance of payments.

5. Key contributions include European Commission 1990; Alogoskoufis and Portes 1991, 1992, 1997; Gros and Thygesen 1992; Alogoskoufis 1993; Goodhart 1993; Bénassy et al. 1994; K. Johnson 1994; Kenen 1995; Ranki 1995; Thygesen et al. 1995; Bénassy-Quéré 1996b; Hartmann 1996; Henning 1996, 1997; Ilzkovitz 1996; Bergsten 1997.

6. Bergsten 1997. Portfolio shifts of a comparable order of magnitude have also been suggested by the European Commission 1990; Gros and Thygesen 1992; Henning 1997.

7. See e.g., Das 1993; Kwan 1994; Taguchi 1994; Hale 1995; Bowles and MacLean 1996. But for more skeptical views, see Tavlas and Ozeki 1992; Frankel 1993; Frankel and Wei 1993, 1994, 1995a; Ito 1993, 1994; Tavlas 1996a.

8. Melvin et al. 1994:344. See also Melvin and Peiers 1993.

9. A summary of the key elements of the liberalization process is provided by Tavlas 1996a.

10. As quoted in the *New York Times*, April 27, 1996:20.

11. See e.g., Melvin 1988a; Calvo and Vegh 1992, 1993, 1996; Cukierman, Kiguel, and Liviatan 1992; Hefeker 1995b.

12. For references, see Chapter 3.

13. Brand 1993:203. See also Calvo and Vegh 1992, 1996.

References

Agenor, Pierre-Richard, and Mohsin S. Kahn (1992). "Foreign Currency Deposits and the Demand for Money in Developing Countries." Working Paper WP/92/1. Washington: International Monetary Fund.

Aghevli, Bijan B., Mohsin S. Khan, and Peter J. Montiel (1991). "Exchange Rate Policy in Developing Countries: Some Analytical Issues." Occasional Paper no. 78. Washington: International Monetary Fund.

Aglietta, Michel, and Pierre Deusy-Fournier (1994). "Internationalisation des monnaies et organisation du système monétaire." *Économie Internationale* 59, no. 3: 71–106.

Agnew, John A. (1994a). "The Territorial Trap: The Geographical Assumptions of International Relations Theory." *Review of International Political Economy* 1, no. 1 (Spring): 53–80.

Agnew, John A. (1994b). "Timeless Space and State-Centrism: The Geographical Assumptions of International Relations Theory." In Stephen J. Rosow, Naeem Inayatullah, and Mark Rupert, eds., *The Global Economy as Political Space.* Boulder, Colo.: Lynne Rienner, chap. 4.

Agnew, John A., and Stuart Corbridge (1995). *Mastering Space: Hegemony, Territory and the International Political Economy.* London: Routledge.

Ahtiala, P., and Y. E. Orgler (1995). "The Optimal Pricing of Exports Invoiced in Different Currencies." *Journal of Banking and Finance* 19, no. 1 (April): 61–77.

Aizenman, Joshua (1986). "On the Complementarity of Commercial Policy, Capital Controls and the Inflation Tax." *Canadian Journal of Economics* 19, no. 1 (Feb.): 114–33.

—— (1992). "Competitive Externalities and the Optimal Seigniorage." *Journal of Money, Credit, and Banking* 24, no. 1 (Feb.): 61–71.

Aizenman, Joshua, and Jacob A. Frenkel (1985). "Optimal Wage Indexation, Foreign Exchange Intervention, and Monetary Policy." *American Economic Review* 75, no. 3 (June): 402–23.

Aizenman, Joshua, and Pablo E. Guidotti (1994). "Capital Controls, Collection Costs and Domestic Public Debt." *Journal of International Money and Finance* 13, no. 1 (Feb.): 41–54.

Al-Marhubi, Fahim, and Thomas D. Willett (1996). "Determinants of Exchange Rate Regime Choice" (manuscript).

Aliber, Robert Z. (1987). *The International Money Game,* 5th edition. New York: Basic Books.

Allen, John, and Doreen Massey (1995). "Introduction," in Allen and Massey, eds., *Geographical Worlds.* New York: Oxford University Press: 1–3.

Allen, Polly Reynolds (1986). "The ECU: Birth of a New Currency." Occasional Paper no. 20 Washington: Group of Thirty.

—— (1990). "The Private ECU Markets: What They Are, Why They Exist, and Where They May Go." *Journal of Banking and Finance* 14: 845–76.

—— (1992). "The ECU and the Transition to European Monetary Union." *International Economic Journal* 6, no. 1 (Spring): 83–99.

—— (1993). "Transactions Use of the ECU in the Transition to EMU: A Model of Network Externalities," *Recherches Économiques de Louvain* 59, nos. 1–2: 155–76.

Alogoskoufis, George (1993). "The ECU, the International Monetary System and the Management of Exchange Rates." In Leonce Bekemans and Loukas Tsoukalis, eds., *Europe and Global Economic Interdependence.* Brussels: European Interuniversity Press: 231–251.

—— (1994). "On Inflation, Unemployment, and the Optimal Exchange Rate Regime" In Frederick Van Der Ploeg, ed., *The Handbook of International Macroeconomics.* Oxford: Blackwell, chap. 7.

Alogoskoufis, George, and Richard Portes (1991). "International Costs and Benefits from EMU." *European Economy,* Special Issue, no. 1: 231–45.

—— (1992). "European Monetary Union and International Currencies in a Tripolar World." In Matthew B. Canzoneri, Vittorio Grilli, and Paul R. Masson, eds., *Establishing a Central Bank: Issues in Europe and Lessons from the U.S.* Cambridge: Cambridge University Press, chap. 9.

—— (1997). "The Euro, the Dollar and the International Monetary System." Paper prepared for an IMF conference on EMU and the International Monetary System, Washington, D.C., March (manuscript).

Anderson, Annelise (1993). "The Ruble Problem: A Competitive Solution," *Cato Journal* 12, (Winter): 633–49.

—— (1995). "Alternative Approaches to Monetary Reform in the Formerly Communist Countries: A Parallel Strategy." In Thomas D. Willett, Richard C. K. Burdekin, Richard J. Sweeney, and Clas Wihlborg, eds., *Establishing Monetary Stability in Emerging Market Economies.* Boulder, Colo: Westview, chap. 8.

Anderson, Benedict (1991). *Imagined Communities: Reflections on the Origins and Spread of Nationalism,* rev. ed. London: Verso.

Anderson, Perry (1974). *Lineages of the Absolutist State.* London: New Left Books.

Andrew, A. Piatt (1904). "The End of the Mexican Dollar." *Quarterly Journal of Economics* 18, no. 2 (May): 321–56.

Andrews, David M. (1994). "Capital Mobility and State Autonomy: Toward a Structural Theory of International Monetary Relations." *International Studies Quarterly* Vol. 38, (June): 193–218.

Andrews, David M., and Thomas D. Willett (1997). "Financial Interdependence and the State: International Monetary Relations at Century's End," *International Organization,* 51, no. 3 (Summer): 479–511.

Appadurai, Arjun (1990). "Disjuncture and Difference in the Global Cultural Economy." *Public Culture* 2, no. 2 (Spring): 1–24.

Arendt, Hannah (1968). "What is Authority?" In Arendt, *Between Past and Future: Eight Exercises in Political Thought.* New York: Viking Press: 91–141.

Argy, Victor, and Paul De Grauwe, eds. (1990). *Choosing an Exchange Rate Regime: The Challenge for Smaller Industrial Countries.* Washington: International Monetary Fund.

Aschheim, Joseph, and Y. S. Park (1976). "Artificial Currency Units: The Formation of Functional Currency Areas." *Essays in International Finance* no. 114. Princeton: International Finance Section.

Aschheim, Joseph, and George S. Tavlas (1996). "Monetary Economics in Doctrinal Perspective." *Journal of Money, Credit and Banking* 28, no. 3, part 1 (Aug.): 406–17.

Aslund, Anders (1995). *How Russia Became a Market Economy.* Washington: Brookings Institution.

Aslund, Anders, Peter Boone, and Simon Johnson (1996). "How to Stabilize: Lessons from Postcommunist Countries." *Brookings Papers on Economic Activity* no. 1: 217–91.

Auernheimer, Leonardo (1974). "The Honest Government's Guide to the Revenue from the Creation of Money." *Journal of Political Economy* 82 (May/June): 598–606.

Axford, Barrie (1995). *The Global System: Economics, Politics and Culture.* New York: St. Martin's.

Bacchetta, Philippe, and Ramon Caminal (1992). "Optimal Seigniorage and Financial Liberalization." *Journal of International Money and Finance* 11 (Dec.): 518–38.

Bagehot, Walter (1873). *Lombard Street: A Description of the Money Market,* 4th ed. London: Henry S. King & Co.

Bailey, Martin J. (1956). "The Welfare Cost of Inflationary Finance." *Journal of Political Economy* 64 (April): 93–110.

Baker, Wayne E. (1987). "What Is Money? A Social Structural Interpretation." In Mark S. Mizruchi and Michael Schwartz, eds., *Intercorporate Relations: The Structural Analysis of Business.* New York: Cambridge University Press, chap. 4.

Bank of Japan (1994). "The Circulation of Bank of Japan Notes." *Quarterly Bulletin* (Nov.): 89–118.

Bank for International Settlements (1995). "The Role of the Dollar in International Market Financing from a Longer-Term Perspective." *International Banking and Financial Market Developments* (Nov.): 23–26.

—— (1996). *Central Bank Survey of Foreign Exchange and Derivatives Market Activity.* Basel, Switzerland.

Barkin, J. Samuel, and Bruce Cronin (1994). "The State and the Nation: Changing Norms and the Rules of Sovereignty in International Relations," *International Organization* 48, no. 1 (Winter): 107–30.

Barro, Robert J., and David B. Gordon (1983). "Rules, Discretion, and Reputation in a Model of Monetary Policy." *Journal of Monetary Economics* 12: 101–21.

Bartel, Robert J. (1974). "International Monetary Unions: The XIXth-Century Experience." *Journal of European Economic History* 3, no. 3 (Winter): 689–704.

Bates, Robert H., and Da-Hsiang Donald Lien (1985). "A Note on Taxation, Development, and Representative Government." *Politics and Society* 14, no. 1 (March): 53–70.

Bayoumi, Tamim, and Barry Eichengreen (1993). "One Money or Many? On Analyzing Prospects for Monetary Unification in Various Parts of the World." Working Paper C93–030 Nov. Berkeley: Center for International and Development Economics Research, University of California.

Bénassy-Quéré, Agnès (1996a). *Exchange Rate Regimes and Policies in Asia,* Document de Travail no. 96–07. Paris: Centre d'Études Prospectives et d'Informations Internationales.

—— (1996b). *Potentialities and Opportunities of the Euro as an International Currency.* Document de Travail no. 96–09. Paris: Centre d'Études Prospectives et d'Information Internationales.

Bénassy-Quéré, Agnès, and Pierre Deusy-Fournier (1994). "La Concurrence pour le statut de monnaie internationale depuis 1973." *Économie Internationale* 59, no. 3: 107–44.

—— (1995). "Le Rôle international des grandes devises: 1974–1994." *Bulletin Économique et Financier* (Banque Internationale à Luxembourg) no. 42: 13–32.

Bénassy, Agnès, Alexander Italianer, and Jean Pisani-Ferry (1994). "The External Implications of the Single Currency." *Économie et Statistique,* Special Issue: 9–22.

Bennett, Adam G. G. (1993). "The Operation of the Estonian Currency Board." *International Monetary Fund Staff Papers* 40 (June): 451–70.

—— (1994). "Currency Boards: Issues and Experiences." International Monetary Fund. Paper on Policy Analysis and Assessment PPAA/94/18.

—— (1995). "Currency Boards: Issues and Experiences." *Finance and Development* 32: 39–42.

Bergman, Michael, Stefan Gerlach, and Lars Jonung (1993). "The Rise and Fall of the Scandanavian Currency Union, 1873–1920," *European Economic Review* 37 (April): 507–17.

Bergsten, C. Fred (1975). *The Dilemmas of the Dollar.* New York: New York University Press.

—— (1997). "The Impact of the Euro on Exchange Rates and International Policy Cooperation (Or: A 'Big Bang' for the Euro?)." Paper prepared for an IMF conference on EMU and the International Monetary System, Washington, D.C., March (manuscript).

Berliner, Nancy (1995). "The Faces on Money Change with the Face of the Map." *The New York Times,* March 5, p. 8F.

Bernholz, Peter (1989). "Currency Competition, Inflation, Gresham's Law and Exchange Rate." *Journal of Institutional and Theoretical Economics* Vol. 145, no. 3 (Sept.): 465–88.

Biersteker, Thomas J. and Cynthia Weber, eds. (1996). *State Sovereignty as Social Construct.* New York: Cambridge University Press.

Bilson, John F. O. (1983). "The Choice of an Invoice Currency in International Transactions." In Jagdeep S. Bhandari and Bluford H. Putnam, eds., *Economic Interdependence and Flexible Exchange Rates.* Cambridge: MIT Press. chap. 14.

Bixler, Raymond W. (1957). *The Foreign Policy of the United States in Liberia.* New York: Pageant Press.

Black, Stanley W. (1990). "The International Use of Currencies." In Yoshio Suzuki, Junichi Miyake, and Mitsuaki Okabe, eds., *The Evolution of the International Monetary System: How Can Efficiency and Stability Be Attained?* (Tokyo: University of Tokyo Press), ch. 7.

—— (1991). "Transactions Costs and Vehicle Currencies," *Journal of International Money and Finance* 10: 512–26.

—— (1993). "The International Use of Currencies." In Dilip K. Das, ed., *International Finance.* London: Routledge, chap. 29.

Blanchard, Olivier, and Stanley Fischer (1989). *Lectures on Macroeconomics.* Cambridge: MIT Press.

Blinder, Alan S. (1996). "The Role of the Dollar as an International Currency," *Eastern Economic Journal* 22, no. 2 (Spring): 127–36.

Block, Fred L. (1977). *The Origins of International Economic Disorder.* Berkeley: University of California Press.

Bookman, Milica Zarkovic (1992). *The Economics of Secession.* New York: St. Martin's Press.

Bordo, Michael D. and Anna J. Schwartz (1989). "The ECU—An Imaginary or Embryonic Form of Money: What Can We Learn from History?" In Paul De Grauwe and Theo Peeters, eds., *The ECU and European Monetary Integration.* London: Macmillan, chap. 1.

Bosco, Luigi (1987). "Determinants of the Exchange Rate Regimes in LDCs: Some Empirical Evidence" *Economic Notes* 16, no. 1: 119–43.

Boughton, James M. (1992). "The CFA Franc: Zone of Fragile Stability in Africa." *Finance and Development* (Dec.) 34–36.

—— (1993a). "The CFA Franc Zone: Currency Union and Monetary Standard" *Greek Economic Review* 15, no. 1 (Autumn): 267–312.

—— (1993b). "The Economics of the CFA Franc Zone." In Paul R. Masson and Mark P. Taylor, eds., *Policy Issues in the Operation of Currency Unions.* Cambridge: Cambridge University Press, chap. 4.

Bowles, Paul, and Brian MacLean (1996). "Regional Blocs: Can Japan Be the Leader?" In Robert Boyer and Daniel Drache, eds., *States against Markets: The Limits of Globalization.* New York: Routledge, chap. 6.

Boyer, Robert, and Daniel Drache, eds. (1996). *States against Markets: The Limits of Globalization.* New York: Routledge.

Boyer, Russell S. (1978a). "Currency Mobility and Balance of Payments Adjustment." In Bluford H. Putnam and D. Sykes Wilford, eds., *The Monetary Approach to International Adjustment.* New York: Praeger, chap. 13.

—— (1978b). "Optimal Foreign Exchange Market Intervention." *Journal of Political Economy* 86, no. 6 (Dec.): 1045–55.

Boyer-Xambeu, Marie-Thérèse, Ghislain Deleplace, and Lucien Gillard (1994). *Private Money and Public Currencies: The 16th Century Challenge.* Armonk, N.Y.: M. E. Sharpe.

Brand, Diana (1993). "Currency Substitution in Developing Countries: Theory and Empirical Analysis for Latin America and Eastern Europe." *Ifo-Studien zur Entwicklungsforschung* no. 24. Munich: Weltforum Verlag.

Braudel, Fernand (1982). *The Wheels of Commerce.* Vol. 2 of *Civilization and Capitalism: Fifteenth to Eighteenth Centuries.* New York: Harper and Row.

Brett, Edward A. (1983). *International Money and Capitalist Crisis: The Anatomy of Global Disintegration.* Boulder, Colo.: Westview.

British Treasury (1989). "An Evolutionary Approach to Economic and Monetary Union." Discussion paper. London: HM Stationary Office, 2 November.

Brooke, James (1994). "New Money No Novelty in Brazil." *New York Times*, July 9, pp. 17, 29.

Brown, Brendan (1978). *Money Hard and Soft: On the International Currency Markets.* New York: Wiley.

—— (1979). *The Dollar-Mark Axis: On Currency Power.* New York: St. Martin's Press.

Brozovic, Dalibor (1994). *The Kuna and the Lipa: The Currency of the Republic of Croatia.* Zagreb: National Bank of Croatia.

Bryan, Dick (1995). *The Chase across the Globe: International Accumulation and the Contradictions for Nation States.* Boulder, Colo.: Westview.

Bufman, Gil, and Leonardo Leiderman (1983). "Currency Substitution under Nonexpected Utility: Some Empirical Evidence." *Journal of Money, Credit, and Banking* 25, no. 3 (August, pt. 1): 320–35.

Bull, Hedley (1977). *The Anarchical Society: A Study in World Politics.* London: Macmillan.

Business Week (1993). "The Global Greenback." Aug. 9: 40, 44.

—— (1995). "The Future of Money." June 12: 66–78.

Cable, Vincent (1995). "The Diminished Nation-State: A Study in the Loss of Economic Power." *Daedalus* 124, no. 2 (Spring): 23–53.

Cagan, Phillip (1992). "Monetarism." In Peter Newman, Murray Milgate, and John Eatwell, eds., *The New Palgrave Dictionary of Money and Finance.* London: Macmillan. 2: 719–24.

Calvo, Guillermo A. (1978). "Optimal Seigniorage from Money Creation: An Analysis in Terms of the Optimum Balance of Payments Deficit Problem." *Journal of Monetary Economics* 4, no. 3 (Aug.): 503–17.

—— (1985). "Currency Substitution and the Real Exchange Rate: The Utility Maximization Approach." *Journal of International Money and Finance* 4, no. 2: 175–88.

Calvo, Guillermo A., and Carlos A. Vegh, eds. (1992). "Convertibility and Currency Substitution." *Revista de Análisis Económico,* Special Issue 7, (June).

Calvo, Guillermo A., and Carlos A. Vegh (1993). "Currency Substitution in High Inflation Countries." *Finance and Development* 30, (March): 34–37.

—— (1996). "From Currency Substitution to Dollarization and Beyond: Analytical and Policy Issues." In Guillermo A. Calvo, ed., *Money, Exchange Rates, and Output.* Cambridge: MIT Press, chap. 8.

Calvo, Guillermo A., and Carlos A. Rodriguez (1977). "A Model of Exchange Rate Determination under Currency Substitution and Rational Expectations," *Journal of Political Economy* 85 (June): 617–24.

Camard, Wayne (1996). "Discretion with Rules? Lessons from the Currency Board Arrangement in Lithuania." International Monetary Fund Paper on Policy Analysis and Assessment PPAA/96/1.

Camilleri, Joseph A., and Jim Falk (1992). *The End of Sovereignty? The Politics of a Shrinking and Fragmenting World.* Aldershot, U.K.: Edward Elgar.

Camilleri, Joseph A., Anthony P. Jarvis, and Albert J. Paolini, eds. (1995), *The State in Transition: Reimagining Political Space.* Boulder, Colo.: Lynne Rienner.

Canzoneri, Matthew B. and Carol Ann Rogers (1990). "Is the European Community an Optimal Currency Area? Optimal Taxation Versus the Cost of Multiple Currencies," *American Economic Review* 80, no. 3 (June): 419–433.

Canzoneri, Matthew B., and Behzad T. Diba (1992). "The Inflation Discipline of Currency Substitution." *European Economic Review* 36, no. 4 (May): 827–45.

Canzoneri, Matthew B., Behzad T. Diba, and Alberto Giovannini (1993). "Currency Substitution: From the Policy Questions to the Theory and Back." In Francisco Torres and Francesco Giavazzi, eds., *Adjustment and Growth in the European Monetary Union.* Cambridge: Cambridge University Press, chap. 10.

Caporaso, James A., ed. (1989). *The Elusive State: International and Comparative Perspectives.* Newbury Park, Calif.: Sage.

Carse, Stephen, John Williamson, and Geoffrey E. Wood (1980). *The Financing Procedures of British Foreign Trade.* London: Cambridge University Press.

Castells, Manuel (1989). *The Informational City: Information Technology, Economic Restructuring, and the Urban-Regional Process.* Oxford: Blackwell.

Caves, Richard E., Jeffrey A. Frankel, and Ronald W. Jones (1996). *World Trade and Payments: An Introduction.* New York: HarperCollins.

Centre for Economic Policy Research (1993). *The Economics of New Currencies.* London.

Cerny, Philip G. (1990). *The Changing Architecture of Politics: Structure, Agency, and the Future of the State.* London: Sage.

—— (1993a). *Finance and World Politics: Markets, Regimes and States in the Post-Hegemonic Era.* Aldershot: Edward Elgar.

—— (1993b). "Plurilateralism: Structural Differentiation and Functional Conflict in the Post-Cold War World Order." *Millennium: Journal of International Studies* 22: 27–51.

—— (1994a). "The Dynamics of Financial Globalization: Technology, Market Structure, and Policy Response." *Policy Sciences* 27: 319–42.

—— (1994b). "The Infrastructure of the Infrastructure? Toward 'Embedded Financial Orthodoxy' in the International Political Economy." In Ronan P. Palan and Barry Gills, eds.,

Transcending the State-Global Divide: A Neostructuralist Agenda in International Relations.
Boulder, Colo.: Lynne Reinner, chap. 12.
—— (1994c). "Money and Finance in the International Political Economy: Structural Change and Paradigmatic Muddle." *Review of International Political Economy* 1, no. 3 (Autumn): 587–92.
—— (1995). "Globalization and the Changing Logic of Collective Action." *International Organization* 49, no. 4 (Autumn): 595–625.
Chappell, David (1981). "On the Revenue Maximizing Rate of Inflation." *Journal of Money, Credit, and Banking* 13, no. 3 (Aug.): 391–92.
Chown, John (1994). *A History of Money.* London: Routledge.
Chown, John, and Geoffrey Wood (1992–93). "Russia's Currency—How the West Can Help." *Central Banking* 3, no. 1 (Winter): 39–46.
Chrystal, K. Alec (1977). "Demand for International Media of Exchange." *American Economic Review* 67, no. 5 (Dec.): 840–50.
—— (1984). "On The Theory of International Money." In J. Black and G. Dorrance, eds., *Problems of International Finance.* New York: St. Martin's Press: 77–92.
Cipolla, Carlo M. (1967). *Money, Prices, and Civilization in the Mediterranean World: Fifth to Seventeenth Century.* New York: Gordian Press.
—— (1989). *Money in Sixteenth-Century Florence.* Berkeley: University of California Press.
Claassen, Emil-Maria, and Justino De La Cruz Martinez (1994). "Dollarization and Its Impact on the Economy: Argentina, Bolivia, and Uruguay." Working Paper no. 168. Washington: Inter-American Development Bank.
Clement, Jean A. P. (1994). "Striving for Stability: CFA Franc Realignment," *Finance and Development* 31, no. 2 (June): 10–13.
—— (1995). "Aftermath of the CFA Franc Devaluation." *Finance and Development* 32, no. 2 (June): 24–27.
Clement, Jean A. P., et al. (1996). *Aftermath of the CFA Franc Devaluation,* Occasional Paper no. 138. Washington: International Monetary Fund.
Cmiel, Kenneth (1993). "Poststructural Theory." In Mary Kupiec Cayton, Elliot J. Gorn, and Peter W. Williams, eds., *Encyclopedia of American Social History.* New York: Charles Scribner's Sons. 1: 425–33.
Coffey, Peter (1968). "Sterling and a Common Market Currency." *Loughborough Journal of Social Studies* (June).
Cohen, Benjamin J. (1963). "The Euro-Dollar, the Common Market, and Currency Unification," *Journal of Finance* 18, no. 4 (Dec.): 605–21.
—— (1971a). *The Future of Sterling as an International Currency.* London: Macmillan.
—— (1971b). "The Seigniorage Gain of an International Currency: An Empirical Test." *Quarterly Journal of Economics,* 85, no. 3 (Aug.): 494–507.
—— (1977). *Organizing the World's Money: The Political Economy of International Monetary Relations.* New York: Basic Books.
—— (1981). "The European Monetary System: An Outsider's View." *Essays in International Finance* no. 142. Princeton: International Finance Section.
—— (1986). *In Whose Interest? International Banking and American Foreign Policy.* New Haven: Yale University Press.
—— (1991). *Crossing Frontiers: Explorations in International Political Economy.* Boulder, Colo.: Westview.
—— (1992a). "Currency Areas." In Peter Newman, Murray Milgate, and John Eatwell, eds., *The New Palgrave Dictionary of Money and Finance* London: Macmillan 1: 556–57.

—— (1992b). "Sterling Area." In Peter Newman, Murray Milgate, and John Eatwell, eds., *The New Palgrave Dictionary of Money and Finance*. London: Macmillan 3: 554–55.

—— (1993a). "Beyond EMU: The Problem of Sustainability." *Economics and Politics* 5, no. 2 (July): 187–202.

——, ed. (1993b). *The International Political Economy of Monetary Relations*. Aldershot: Edward Elgar.

—— (1993c). "The Triad and the Unholy Trinity: Lessons for the Pacific Region." In Richard Higgott, Richard Leaver, and John Ravenhill, eds., *Pacific Economic Relations in the 1990s: Cooperation or Conflict?* Boulder, Colo.: Lynne Rienner.

—— (1994). "The Geography of Money: Currency Relations among Sovereign States." OFCE Working Paper no. 94–07. Paris, France: Observatoire Français des Conjonctures Économiques.

—— (1996). "Phoenix Risen: The Resurrection of Global Finance" *World Politics* 48, no. 2 (Jan.): 268–96.

—— (1997a). "Optimum Currency Area Theory: Bringing the Market Back In." In Benjamin J. Cohen, ed., *International Trade and Finance: New Frontiers for Research*. New York: Cambridge University Press, chap. 8.

—— (1997b). "The Political Economy of Currency Regions." In Edward D. Mansfield and Helen V. Milner, eds., *The Political Economy of Regionalism*. New York: Columbia University Press.

Cohen, Roger (1994). "Croatia Currency's Name Protested." *New York Times,* May 28, p. 3.

Collier, Paul, and Vijay Joshi (1989). "Exchange Rate Policy in Developing Countries." *Oxford Review of Economic Policy* 5, no. 3 (Autumn): 94–113.

Collyns, Charles (1983). *Alternatives to the Central Bank in the Developing World*. Occasional Paper no. 20. Washington: International Monetary Fund.

Conway, Patrick (1995). "Currency Proliferation: The Monetary Legacy of the Soviet Union." *Essays in International Finance* no. 197. Princeton: International Finance Section.

Cooper, Richard N. (1984). "A Monetary System for the Future." *Foreign Affairs* 63, no. 1 (Fall): 166–184.

Copeland, Laurence S. (1994). *Exchange Rates and International Finance*. 2d ed. Reading, Mass.: Addison-Wesley.

Corbridge, Stuart, Ron Martin, and Nigel Thrift (1994). *Money, Power and Space*. Cambridge, Mass.: Blackwell.

Corden, W. Max (1972). "Monetary Integration." *Essays in International Finance* no. 93. Princeton: International Finance Section.

—— (1994). *Economic Policy, Exchange Rates, and the International System*. Chicago: University of Chicago Press.

Cowen, Tyler, and Randall Kroszner (1987). "The Development of the New Monetary Economics." *Journal of Political Economy* 95, (June): 567–90.

Cuddington, John T. (1983). "Currency Substitution, Capital Mobility and Money Demand." *Journal of International Money and Finance* 2, (Aug.): 111–33.

Cukierman, Alex, Sebastian Edwards, and Guido Tabellini (1992). "Seigniorage and Political Instability." *American Economic Review* 82, (June): 537–55.

Cukierman, Alex, Miguel A. Kiguel, and Nissan Liviatan (1992). "How Much to Commit to an Exchange Rate Rule? Balancing Credibility and Flexibility." *Revista de Análisis Económico* 7, (June): 73–89.

Cutler, A. Claire (1996). "Locating 'Authority' in the Global Political Economy." Paper prepared for the 1996 annual meeting of the American Political Science Association.

Daly, M. T. and M. I. Logan (1989). *The Brittle Rim: Finance, Business and the Pacific Region.* New York: Penguin.

Daniels, Joseph P. and David D. Van Hoose (1996). "Reserve Requirements, Currency Substitution, and Seigniorage in the Transition to European Monetary Union." *Open Economies Review* 7: 257–73.

Das, Dilip K. (1993). *The Yen Appreciation and the International Economy.* London: Macmillan.

Davies, Glyn (1994). *A History of Money: From Ancient Times to the Present Day.* Cardiff: University of Wales Press.

Day, A. C. L. (1954). *The Future of Sterling.* London: Oxford University Press.

De Boissieu, Christian (1988). "Concurrence entre monnaies et polycentrisme monétaire." In D. E. Fair and Christian De Boissieu, eds., *International Monetary and Financial Integration—The European Dimension.* Boston: Kluwer Academic, chap. 13.

De Cecco, Marcello (1992). "European Monetary and Financial Cooperation before the First World War." *Rivista di Storia Economica* 9: 55–76.

—— (1993). "Financial Relations: Between Internationalism and Transnationalism." In Roger Morgan, Jochen Lorentzen, Anna Leander, and Stefano Guzzini, eds., *New Diplomacy in the Post-Cold War World: Essays for Susan Strange.* New York: St. Martin's Press.

De Grauwe, Paul (1991). "Is the European Monetary System a DM-Zone?" In Alfred Steinherr and Daniel Weiserbs, eds., *Evolution of the International and Regional Monetary Systems.* London: Macmillan.

—— (1993). "The Political Economy of Monetary Union in Europe." *The World Economy* 16, no. 6 (Nov.): 653–61.

—— (1994). *The Economics of Monetary Integration,* 2d ed. New York: Oxford University Press.

De Grauwe, Paul, and Theo Peeters, eds. (1989). *The ECU and European Monetary Integration.* London: Macmillan.

De Palma, Anthony (1995). "In the Land of the Peso, the Dollar is Common Coin." *The New York Times,* Nov. 21: C1, C17.

Desai, Mihir (1996). "The End of Everything." *New York Times,* Aug. 24, p. 19.

Deutsche Bundesbank (1991). "Payments Media in Foreign Travel." *Monthly Report* 43, no. 7 (July): 43–48.

—— (1995). "The Circulation of Deutsche Mark Abroad." *Monthly Report* 47, no. 7 (July): 65–71.

Dicken, Peter (1992). *Global Shift: The Internationalization of Economic Activity.* 2d ed. London: Paul Chapman.

Dicken, Peter, and Peter E. Lloyd (1990). *Location in Space: Theoretical Perspectives in Economic Geography.* 3rd ed. New York: Harper and Row.

Dixit, Avinash (1992). "Investment and Hysteresis." *Journal of Economic Perspectives* 6, no. 1 (Winter): 107–132.

Dodd, Nigel (1994). *The Sociology of Money.* New York: Continuum.

—— (1995). "Money and the Nation-State: Contested Boundaries of Monetary Sovereignty in Geopolitics." *International Sociology* 10, no. 2: 139–54.

Dodsworth, J., M. A. El-Erian, and D. Hammann (1987). "Foreign Currency Deposits in Developing Countries—Origins and Economic Implications." Working Paper WP/87/12. Washington: International Monetary Fund.

Dodsworth, J., et al. (1996). *Vietnam: Transition to a Market Economy.* Occasional Paper no. 135. Washington: International Monetary Fund.

Dominguez, Kathryn M., and Jeffrey A. Frankel (1993). *Does Foreign Exchange Intervention Work?* Washington: Institute for International Economics.

Donnenfeld, Shabtai, and Itzhak Zilcha (1991). "Pricing of Exports and Exchange Rate Uncertainty," *International Economic Review* 32, no. 4 (Nov.): 1009–22.

Dooley, Michael P. (1996). "A Survey of Literature on Controls over International Capital Transactions." *International Monetary Fund Staff Papers* 43, no. 4 (Dec.): 639–87.

Dornbusch, Rudiger (1988). "The European Monetary System, the Dollar and the Yen." In Francesco Giavazzi, Stefano Micossi, and Marcus Miller, eds., *The European Monetary System*. New York: Cambridge University Press, chap. 2.

—— (1992). "Monetary Problems of Post-Communism: Lessons from the End of the Austro-Hungarian Empire." *Weltwirtschaftliches Archiv* 128, Heft 3: 391–424.

—— (1994). *Post-Communist Monetary Problems: Lessons from the End of the Austro-Hungarian Empire*. San Francisco: International Center for Economic Growth.

—— (1996). "Euro Fantasies." *Foreign Affairs* 75, no. 5 (Sept./Oct.): 110–24.

Dornbusch, Rudiger, Federico A. Sturzenegger, and Holger Wolf (1990). "Extreme Inflation: Dynamics and Stabilization." *Brookings Papers on Economic Activity* no. 2: 2–84.

Dowd, Kevin, ed. (1992). *The Experience of Free Banking*. London: Routledge.

Dowd, Kevin and David Greenaway (1993a). "Currency Competition, Network Externalities and Switching Costs: Towards an Alternative View of Optimum Currency Areas." *Economic Journal* 103 (Sept.): 1180–89.

—— (1993b). "A Single Currency for Europe?" *Greek Economic Review* 15, no. 1 (Autumn): 227–44.

Drainville, Andre C. (1995). "Of Social Spaces, Citizenship, and the Nature of Power in the World Economy," *Alternatives* 20, no. 1 (Jan.–March): 51–79.

Drazen, Allan (1989). "Monetary Policy, Capital Controls and Seigniorage in an Open Economy." In Marcello De Cecco and Alberto Giovannini, eds., *A European Central Bank? Perspectives on Monetary Unification after Ten Years of the EMS*. New York: Cambridge University Press, chap. 2.

Drew, Christopher, and Stephen Engelberg (1996). "Super-Counterfeit $100's Baffle U.S. Investigators." *New York Times*, Feb. 27, p. A4.

The Economist (1993a). "Hail to the Castrodollar." July 24, p. 46.

—— (1993b). "Last Chance, Sisyphus: A Survey of Greece." May 22.

—— (1993c). "Slip Me a Beak." April 24, p. 60.

—— (1994a). "Brazil's Poor Back Cardoso." Oct. 1, p. 51.

—— (1994b). "Electronic Money: So Much for the Cashless Society." Nov. 26, 21–23.

—— (1994c). "In a Bear's Paw." Nov. 19, 58–59.

—— (1994d). "Will the Buck Stop Here?" Nov. 12, p. 88.

—— (1996a). "All Lined Up." Sept. 7, p. 66.

—— (1996b). "Anyone for Xenobonds?" Nov. 9, p. 88.

—— (1996c). "Ecuador: Sane and Sober." Dec. 7, p. 40.

—— (1996d). "Slovenia: Much To Do." Nov. 2, 51–52.

Ederer, Rupert J. (1964). *The Evolution of Money*. Washington, D.C.: Public Affairs Press.

Edison, Hali J., and Michael Melvin (1990). "The Determinants and Implications of the Choice of an Exchange Rate System." In William S. Haraf and Thomas D. Willett, eds., *Monetary Policy for a Volatile Global Economy*. Washington, D.C.: AEI Press, pp. 1–44.

Edwards, Sebastian (1996). "Exchange Rates and the Political Economy of Macroeconomic Discipline." *American Economic Review* 86 (May): 159–163.

Edwards, Sebastian and Guido Tabellini (1991). "Explaining Fiscal Policies and Inflation in

Developing Countries." *Journal of International Money and Finance* 10, suppl. (March): S16–S48.

Eichengreen, Barry (1990). *Elusive Stability: Essays in the History of International Finance, 1919–1939.* Cambridge: Cambridge University Press.

—— (1994). *International Monetary Arrangements for the 21st Century.* Washington: Brookings Institution.

—— (1996a). *Globalizing Capital: A History of the International Monetary System.* Princeton: Princeton University Press.

—— (1996b). "A More Perfect Union? The Logic of Economic Integration." *Essays in International Finance* no. 198. Princeton: International Finance Section.

Eichengreen, Barry, and Marc Flandreau (1996). "The Geography of the Gold Standard." In Jorge Braga de Macedo, Barry Eichengreen, and Jaime Reis, eds., *Currency Convertibility: The Gold Standard and Beyond.* London: Routledge, chap. 5.

Eichengreen, Barry, and Jeffrey A. Frankel (1996). "The SDR, Reserve Currencies, and the Future of the International Monetary System." In Michael Mussa, James M. Boughton, and Peter Isard, eds., *The Future of the SDR in the Light of Changes in the International Financial System.* Washington: International Monetary Fund, chap. 9.

Eijffinger, Sylvester C. W., and Jakob De Haan (1996). "The Political Economy of Central–Bank Independence." *Special Papers in International Economics* no. 19. Princeton: International Finance Section.

Einaudi, Luigi (1936). "The Theory of Imaginary Money from Charlemagne to the French Revolution." *Rivista di Storia Economica* 1: 1–35.

—— (1937). "The Medieval Practice of Managed Currency." In A. D. Gayer, ed., *The Lessons of Monetary Experience.* New York: Farrar and Rinehart.

Eken, Sena, et al. (1995). *Economic Dislocation and Recovery in Lebanon.* Occasional Paper no. 120 (Washington: International Monetary Fund).

El-Erian, Mohamed (1988). "Currency Substitution in Egypt and the Yemen Arab Republic." *International Monetary Fund Staff Papers* 35. no. 1 (March): 85–103.

Elkins, David J. (1995). *Beyond Territoriality: Territory and Political Economy in the Twenty–First Century.* Toronto: University of Toronto Press.

Erdman, Paul (1996). *Tug of War: Today's Global Currency Crisis.* New York: St. Martin's Press.

European Commission (1990). "One Market, One Money." *European Economy* 44 (Oct.).

Far Eastern Economic Review (1995). "Ding Dong Dollar." March 30, p. 5.

Fasano-Filho, Ugo (1986). *Currency Substitution and Liberalization.* Brookfield, Vt.: Gower.

Feige, Edgar L. (1994). "The Underground Economy and the Currency Enigma." In Werner W. Pommerehne, ed., *Public Finance and Irregular Activities.* Supplement to *Public Finance/Finances Publiques* 49: 119–36.

—— (1996). "Overseas Holdings of U.S. Currency and the Underground Economy." In Susan Pozo, ed., *Exploring the Underground Economy: Studies of Illegal and Unreported Activity.* Kalamazoo, Mich.: W. E. Upjohn Institute for Employment Research, pp. 5–62.

Fieleke, Norman S. (1992). "The Quest for Sound Money: Currency Boards to the Rescue?" *New England Economic Review.* Nov./Dec. pp. 14–24.

Fischer, Stanley (1982). "Seigniorage and the Case for National Money," *Journal of Political Economy* 90, no. 2 (April): 295–313.

—— (1983). "Seigniorage and Fixed Exchange Rates: An Optimal Inflation Tax Analysis." In Pedro Aspe Armella, Rudiger Dornbusch, and Maurice Obstfeld, eds., *Financial Policies and the World Capital Market: The Problem of Latin American Countries.* Chicago: University of Chicago Press, chap. 3.

Flandreau, Marc (1993). "On the Inflationary Bias of Common Currencies: The Latin Union Puzzle." *European Economic Review* 37, nos. 2/3 (April): 501–6.

—— (1995). "Was the Latin Monetary Union a Franc Zone?" In Jaime Reis, ed., *International Monetary Systems in Historical Perspective.* London: Macmillan, chap. 3.

Flickenschild, Hans M., et al. (1992). *Developments in International Exchange and Payments Systems.* Washington: International Monetary Fund.

Flood, Robert P., and Nancy P. Marion (1992). "Exchange Rate Regime Choice." In Peter Newman, Murray Milgate, and John Eatwell, eds., *The New Palgrave Dictionary of Money and Finance.* London: Macmillan 2: 829–31.

Foucault, Michel (1970). *The Order of Things: An Archaeology of the Human Sciences.* New York: Pantheon Books.

Frankel, Jeffrey A. (1993). "Is Japan Creating a Yen Bloc in East Asia and the Pacific?" In Jeffrey A. Frankel and Miles Kahler, eds., *Regionalism and Rivalry: Japan and the United States in Pacific Asia.* Chicago: University of Chicago Press, chap. 2.

—— (1995a). "Is the Dollar Losing Its Role as a Reserve Currency and If So, What Does This Mean?" Unpublished (June).

—— (1995b). "Still the Lingua Franca." *Foreign Affairs* 74, no. 4 (July/Aug).: 9–16.

Frankel, Jeffrey A., and Shang–Jin Wei (1993). "Is There a Currency Bloc in the Pacific?" In Adrian Blundell–Wignall, ed., *The Exchange Rate, International Trade and the Balance of Payments.* Sydney, Australia: Reserve Bank of Australia, 275–307.

—— (1994). "Yen Bloc or Dollar Bloc? Exchange Rate Policies of the East Asian Economies." In Takatoshi Ito and Anne O. Krueger, eds., *Macroeconomic Linkage: Savings, Exchange Rates, and Capital Flows.* Chicago: University of Chicago Press.

—— (1995a). "Emerging Currency Blocks." In Hans Genberg (ed.). *The International Monetary System: Its Institutions and Future.* New York: Springer-Verlag, chap. 5.

—— (1995b). "European Integration and Regionalization of World Trade and Currencies: The Economics and the Politics." In Barry Eichengreen, Jeffry A. Frieden, and Jürgen von Hagen (eds.). *Monetary and Fiscal Policy in an Integrated Europe.* New York: Springer–Verlag.

Frankel, Jeffrey A., and Charles Wyplosz (1995/96). "A Proposal to Introduce the ECU First in the East." *European Parliamentary Yearbook.*

Fratianni, Michele (1992). "Dominant and Dependent Currencies." In Peter Newman, Murray Milgate, and John Eatwell, eds., *The New Palgrave Dictionary of Money and Finance.* London: Macmillan Press, 1: 702–4.

Fratianni, Michele, and Theo Peeters, eds. (1978). *One Money for Europe.* London: Macmillan.

Fratianni, Michele, and Jürgen von Hagen (1992). *The European Monetary System and European Monetary Union.* Boulder, Colo.: Westview.

Fratianni, Michele, Jürgen von Hagen, and Christopher Waller (1992). "The Maastricht Way to EMU." *Essays in International Finance* no. 187. Princeton: International Finance Section.

French, Howard W. (1996). "A Neglected Region Loosens Ties to Zaire." *New York Times,* Sept. 18, p. A1.

—— (1997). "Hard Times for Zaire: It Can't Give Cash Away." *New York Times,* Feb. 16, p. Y9.

Frenkel, Jacob A., and Joshua Aizenman (1982). "Aspects of the Optimal Management of Exchange Rates." *Journal of International Economics* 13, no. 3 (Sept.): 231–56.

Frenkel, Jacob A., and Morris Goldstein (1997). "The International Role of the Deutsche Mark." Paper prepared for *Fifty Years of the Deutsche Mark,* sponsored by Deutsche Bundesbank (manuscript).

Frick, Robert L. (1996). "Alternative Monetary Systems: The Ithaca HOUR." *Durell Journal of Money and Banking* 8, no. 2 (Spring): 29–35.

Frieden, Jeffry A. (1991). "Invested Interests: The Politics of National Economic Policies in a World of Global Finance." *International Organization* 45, no. 4 (Autumn): 425–52.

—— (1993a). "The Dynamics of International Monetary Systems: International and Domestic Factors in the Rise, Reign, and Demise of the Classical Gold Standard." In Jack Snyder and Robert Jervis, eds., *Coping with Complexity in the International System.* Boulder, Colo.: Westview, pp. 137–162.

—— (1993b). "Economic and Monetary Union: What Happened? Exploring the Political Dimension of Optimum Currency Areas—Discussion." In G. de la Dehesa et al., eds., *The Monetary Future of Europe.* London: Centre for Economic Policy Research.

—— (1994). "Exchange Rate Politics: Contemporary Lessons from American History." *Review of International Political Economy* 1, no. 1 (Spring): 81–103.

—— (1996). "The Impact of Goods and Capital Market Integration on European Monetary Politics." *Comparative Political Studies* 29, no. 2 (April): 193–222.

Friedman, Milton (1953). "Discussion of the Inflationary Gap." In Milton Friedman, *Essays in Positive Economics.* Chicago: University of Chicago Press.

—— (1969). "The Optimum Quantity of Money." In Milton Friedman, *The Optimum Quantity of Money and Other Essays.* Chicago: Aldine.

—— (1971). "Government Revenue from Inflation," *Journal of Political Economy* 79, no. 4 (July/Aug.): 846–56.

Friedman, R. B. (1990). "On the Concept of Authority in Political Philosophy." In Joseph Raz, ed., *Authority,* Oxford: Blackwell, chap. 3.

Friedman, Thomas L. (1994). "Never Mind Yen: Greenbacks are the New Gold Standard." *New York Times,* July 3, p. E5.

Fujita, Seiichi (1995). "The ECU as 'Artificial Currency.'" *Kobe University Economic Review* 41 (1995): 15–29.

Fukuyama, Francis (1989). "The End of History?" *National Interest* no. 16 (Summer): 3–18.

Gallarotti, Guilio M. (1994). "The Scramble for Gold: Monetary Regime Transformation in the 1870s." In Michael D. Bordo and Forrest Capie, eds., *Monetary Regimes in Transition.* New York: Cambridge University Press, chap. 2.

—— (1995). *The Anatomy of an International Monetary Regime: The Classical Gold Standard, 1880–1914.* New York: Oxford University Press.

Gandolfo, Giancarlo (1992). "Monetary Unions." In Peter Newman, Murray Milgate, and John Eatwell, eds., *The New Palgrave Dictionary of Money and Finance.* London: Macmillan. 2: 765–70.

Garber, Peter M. (1996). "The Use of the Yen as a Reserve Currency." *Bank of Japan Monetary and Economic Studies* 14 (Dec.): 1–21.

Garber, Peter M., and Michael G. Spencer (1994). "The Dissolution of the Austro–Hungarian Empire: Lessons for Currency Reform." *Essays in International Finance* no. 191. Princeton: International Finance Section.

Gardner, Charles S. (1993). "Whither Hong Kong?" *International Economic Insights* 4, no. 1 (Jan./Feb): 38.

Germain, Randall D. (1997). *The International Organization of Credit: States and Global Finance in the World-Economy.* New York: Cambridge University Press.

Giavazzi, Francesco (1989). "The Exchange Rate Question in Europe." In Ralph C. Bryant et al., eds., *Macroeconomic Policies in an Interdependent World.* Washington: Brookings Institution, chap. 7.

Giavazzi, Francesco, and Alberto Giovannini (1989). *Limiting Exchange Rate Flexibility: The European Monetary System.* Cambridge: MIT Press.

Giavazzi, Francesco, and Marco Pagano (1988). "The Advantage of Tying One's Hands: EMS Discipline and Central Bank Credibility." *European Economic Review* 32: 1055–82.

Giavazzi, Francesco, and Luigi Spaventa (1990). "The 'New' EMS." In Paul De Grauwe and Lucas Papademos, eds., *The European Monetary System in the 1990's.* London: Longman, chap. 4.

Gill, Stephen R., and David Law (1989). "Global Hegemony and the Structural Power of Capital." *International Studies Quarterly* 33, no. 4 (Dec.): 475–99.

Gilpin, Robert (1975). *U.S. Power and the Multinational Corporation: The Political Economy of Foreign Direct Investment.* New York: Basic Books.

—— (1987). *The Political Economy of International Relations.* Princeton: Princeton University Press.

Giovannini, Alberto (1993). "Economic and Monetary Union: What Happened? Exploring the Political Dimension of Optimum Currency Areas." In G. de la Dehesa et al., eds., *The Monetary Future of Europe.* London: Centre for Economic Policy Research.

Giovannini, Alberto, and Martha de Melo (1993). "Government Revenue from Financial Repression." *American Economic Review* 83, no. 4 (Sept.): 953–63.

Giovannini, Alberto, and Bart Turtleboom (1994). "Currency Substitution." In Frederick Van Der Ploeg, ed., *The Handbook of International Macroeconomics.* Oxford: Blackwell, chap. 12.

Girnius, Saulius (1993). "Establishing Currencies in the Baltic States." *RFE/RL Research Report* 2, no. 22 (May): 35–39.

Girton, Lance, and Don Roper (1980). "The Theory of Currency Substitution and Monetary Unification." *Économie Appliquée* 33, no. 1: 135–60.

—— (1981). "Theory and Implications of Currency Substitution." *Journal of Money, Credit, and Banking* 13, no. 1 (Feb.): 12–30.

Glasner, David (1989). *Free Banking and Monetary Reform.* Cambridge: Cambridge University Press.

Gleick, James (1996). "Dead as a Dollar." *New York Times Magazine,* June 16, pp. 26–30, 35–54.

Goff, Brian L., and Mark Toma (1993). "Optimal Seigniorage, the Gold Standard, and Central Bank Financing." *Journal of Money, Credit, and Banking* 25, no. 1 (Feb.): 79–95.

Goldberg, Linda S., Barry W. Ickes, and Randi Ryterman (1994). "Departures from the Ruble Zone: The Implications of Adopting Independent Currencies." *The World Economy* 17, no. 3 (May): 293–322.

Goodhart, Charles A. E. (1988). *The Evolution of Central Banks* Cambridge: MIT Press.

—— (1993). "The External Dimension of EMU." In Leonce Bekemans and Loukas Tsoukalis, eds., *Europe and Global Economic Interdependence.* Brussels: European Interuniversity Press.

—— (1995). "The Political Economy of Monetary Union." In Peter B. Kenen, ed., *Understanding Interdependence: The Macroeconomics of the Open Economy.* Princeton: Princeton University Press, chap. 12.

Goodhart, Charles A. E., Forrest Capie, and Norbert Schnadt (1994). "The Development of Central Banking." In Forrest Capie, Charles A. E. Goodhart, Stanley Fischer, and Norbert Schnadt, eds., *The Future of Central Banking: The Tercentenary Symposium of the Bank of England.* New York: Cambridge University Press, chap. 1.

Goodman, John B., and Louis W. Pauly (1993). "The Obsolescence of Capital Controls? Economic Management in an Age of Global Markets." *World Politics* 46, no. 1 (Oct.): 50–82.

Gordon, Robert J. (1975). "The Demand for and Supply of Inflation." *Journal of Law and Economics* 18, no. 3 (Dec.): 807–36.

Gottlieb, Gidon (1993). *Nation against State: A New Approach to Ethnic Conflicts and the Decline of Sovereignty.* New York: Council on Foreign Relations.

Graboyes, Robert F. (1990). "The EMU: Forerunners and Durability," *Federal Reserve Bank of Richmond Economic Review* July/Aug.: 8–17.

Granville, Brigitte (1995). "Farewell, Ruble Zone." In Anders Aslund, ed., *Russian Economic Reform at Risk.* London: Pinter, chap. 4.

Grassman, Sven (1973a). *Exchange Reserves and the Financial Structure of Foreign Trade.* Westmead: Saxon House.

—— (1973b). "A Fundamental Symmetry in International Payment Patterns." *Journal of International Economics* 3, no. 2 (May): 105–16.

—— (1976). "Currency Distribution and Forward Cover in Foreign Trade." *Journal of International Economics* 6, no. 2 (May): 215–21.

Greenfield, Robert L., and Leland B. Yeager (1983). "A Laissez–Faire Approach to Monetary Stability." *Journal of Money, Credit, and Banking* 15, no. 3 (Aug.): 302–15.

Griffiths, Mark (1992). "Monetary Union in Europe: Lessons from the Nineteenth Century— An Assessment of the Latin Monetary Union." Nuffield College, Oxford.

Grilli, Vittorio (1989a). "Exchange Rates and Seigniorage." *European Economic Review* 33, no. 1 (March): 580–87.

—— (1989b). "Seigniorage in Europe." In Marcello De Cecco and Alberto Giovannini, eds., *A European Central Bank? Perspectives on Monetary Unification after Ten Years of the EMS.* New York: Cambridge University Press, chap. 3.

Gros, Daniel (1993a). "Costs and Benefits of Economic and Monetary Union: An Application to the Former Soviet Union." In Paul R. Masson and Mark P. Taylor, eds., *Policy Issues in the Operation of Currency Unions.* Cambridge: Cambridge University Press, chap. 2.

—— (1993b). "Seigniorage and EMU: The Fiscal Implications of Price Stability and Financial Market Integration." *European Journal of Political Economy* 9: 581–601.

Gros, Daniel, and Alfred Steinherr (1995). *Winds of Change: Economic Transition in Central and Eastern Europe.* New York: Longman.

Gros, Daniel, and Niels Thygesen (1992). *European Monetary Integration: From the European Monetary System to European Monetary Union.* London: Longman.

Gros, Daniel, and Guy Vandille (1995). "Seigniorage and EMU: The Fiscal Implications of Price Stability and Financial Market Integration." *Journal of Common Market Studies* 33, no. 2 (June): 175–96.

Groseclose, Elgin (1976). *Money and Man: A Survey of Monetary Experience,* 4th ed. Norman: University of Oklahoma Press.

Guehenno, Jean–Marie (1995). *The End of the Nation–State.* Minneapolis: University of Minnesota Press.

Guidotti, Pablo E. (1993). "Currency Substitution and Financial Innovation." *Journal of Money, Credit, and Banking* 25, no. 1 (Feb.): 109–24.

Guidotti, Pablo E., and Carlos A. Rodriguez (1992). "Dollarization in Latin America: Gresham's Law in Reverse?" *International Monetary Fund Staff Papers* 39, no. 3 (Sept.): 518–44.

Haas, Peter, ed. (1992). "Knowledge, Power, and International Policy Coordination" *International Organization* 46, no. 1 (Winter). special issue.

Hakkio, Craig S. (1993). "The Dollar's International Role." *Contemporary Policy Issues* 11, no. 2 (April): 62–75.

Hale, David D. (1995). "Is It a Yen or a Dollar Crisis in the Currency Market?" *Washington Quarterly* 18, no. 4 (Autumn): 145–71.

Hanke, Steve H. (1996). "Don't Cry for Me: What Mexico Can Learn from the Recent Argentine Experience." *International Economy* (March/April): 46–51, 71.

Hanke, Steve H., Lars Jonung, and Kurt Schuler (1993). *Russian Currency and Finance: A Currency Board Approach to Reform.* London: Routledge.

Hanke, Steve H., and Kurt Schuler (1991). "Currency Boards for Eastern Europe." *Heritage Lectures* no. 355. Washington: Heritage Foundation.

—— (1993). "Currency Boards for Latin America." In Nissan Liviatan, ed., *Proceedings of a Conference on Currency Substitution and Currency Boards.* Washington: World Bank, 13–21.

—— (1994). *Currency Boards for Developing Countries: A Handbook.* San Francisco: International Center for Economic Growth.

—— (1996). "Monetary Systems and Inflation in Developing Countries." In James A. Dorn and Roberto Salinas–Leon, eds., *Money and Markets in the Americas: New Challenges for Hemispheric Integration.* Vancouver, Canada: Frasier Institute, chap. 14.

Hanke, Steve H., and Alan Walters (1993). "Ping Pong Peg: How to End China's Economic Roller Coaster Ride." *International Economy* (July/Aug.): 31–33, 62–63.

Hansson, Ardo H. (1993a). "The Estonian Kroon: Experiences of the First Year." In Centre for Economic Policy Research, *The Economics of New Currencies.* London, 85–107.

—— (1993b). "The Trouble with the Ruble: Monetary Reform in the Former Soviet Union." In Anders Aslund and Richard Layard, eds., *Changing the Economic System in Russia.* London: Pinter, chap. 10.

Harmelink, Herman (1972). letter to *The New York Times,* Jan. 12, p. 38.

Harper, Ian R., and Andrew Coleman (1992). "New Monetary Economics." In Peter Newman, Murray Milgate, and John Eatwell, eds., *The New Palgrave Dictionary of Money and Finance* London: Macmillan, 3: 28–31.

Hartmann, Philipp (1994). "Vehicle Currencies in the Foreign Exchange Market." Document de travail du seminaire Delta no. 94–13. Paris: École Normale Superieure.

—— (1996). "The Future of the Euro as an International Currency: A Transactions Perspective." Research Report no. 20. Brussels: Center for European Policy Studies.

Haughton, Jonathan (1995). "Adding Mystery to the Case of the Missing Currency." *Quarterly Review of Economics and Finance* 35 (special issue): 595–602.

Hawtrey, Sir Ralph (1928). *Currency and Credit,* 3rd ed. New York: Longmans, Green.

Hayek, Friedrich A. (1976). "Choice in Currency: A Way to Stop Inflation." Occasional Paper no. 48. London: Institute of Economic Affairs.

—— (1990). *Denationalisation of Money—The Argument Refined.* 3rd ed. London: Institute of Economic Affairs.

Hayter, Teresa (1966). *French Aid.* London: Overseas Development Institute.

Hefeker, Carsten (1995a). "Interest Groups, Coalitions and Monetary Integration in the XIXth Century." *Journal of European Economic History* 24, no. 3 (Winter): 489–536.

—— (1995b). "Monetary Union or Currency Competition? Currency Arrangements for Monetary Stability in East and West," *Constitutional Political Economy* 6: 57–69.

—— (1996). "The Political Choice and Collapse of Fixed Exchange Rates." *Journal of Institutional and Theoretical Economics* 152, no. 2: 360–79.

—— (1997). *Interest Groups and Monetary Integration: The Political Economy of Exchange Rate Choice.* Boulder, Colo.: Westview.

Held, David (1991). "Democracy, the Nation–State and the Global System." *Economy and Society* 20, no. 2 (May): 138–72.

Held, David and Anthony McGrew (1993). "Globalization and the Liberal Democratic State." *Government and Opposition* 28, no. 2 (Spring): 261–85.

Helleiner, Eric (1994). *States and the Reemergence of Global Finance: From Bretton Woods to the 1990s.* Ithaca, NY: Cornell University Press.

—— (1996a). "Historicizing Territorial Currencies: Monetary Structures, Sovereignty and the Nation–State." Paper prepared for the 1996 annual meeting of the International Studies Association.

—— (1996b). "Money and the Nation–State in North America." Paper prepared for the 1996 annual meeting of the Canadian Political Science Association.

—— (1997a). "A Challenge to the Sovereign State? Financial Globalization and the Westphalian World Order." Paper prepared for a workshop on State and Sovereignty in the World Economy, Laguna Beach, Calif., Feb.

—— (1997b). "National Currencies and National Identities." Paper prepared for the 1997 annual meeting of the American Political Science Association.

Henning, C. Randall (1996). "Europe's Monetary Union and the United States." *Foreign Policy* no. 102 (Spring): 83–100.

—— (1997). *Cooperating with Europe's Monetary Union.* Washington, D.C.: Institute for International Economics.

Hernandez–Cata, Ernesto (1995). "Russia and the IMF: The Political Economy of Macrostabilization." In Daniel A. Citrin and Ashok K. Lahiri, eds., *Policy Experiences and Issues in the Baltics, Russia, and Other Countries of the Former Soviet Union.* Washington: International Monetary Fund.

Herz, Bernhard, and Werner Roger (1992). "The EMS is a Greater Deutschemark Area." *European Economic Review* 36, no. 7 (Oct.): 1413–25.

Herz, John H. (1957). "Rise and Decline of the Territorial State." *World Politics* Vol. 9, no. 4 (July): 473–93.

Hicks, Sir John (1969). *A Theory of Economic History.* Oxford: Clarendon.

Hirsch, Fred (1969). *Money International,* rev. ed. London: Penguin.

Hirschman, Albert O. (1970). *Exit, Voice and Loyalty: Responses to Decline in Firms, Organizations, and States.* Cambridge: Harvard University Press.

Hirst, Paul, and Grahame Thompson (1992). "The Problem of 'Globalization': International Economic Relations, National Economic Management and the Formation of Trading Blocs." *Economy and Society* 21, no. 4 (Nov.): 357–96.

—— (1995). "Globalization and the Future of the Nation State." *Economy and Society* 24, no. 3 (Aug.): 408–42.

—— (1996). *Globalization in Question: The International Economy and the Possibilities of Governance.* Cambridge: Polity Press.

Hoffman, Ellen (1991). "One World, One Currency?" *Omni* (June): 50–56.

Holtfrerich, Carl–Ludwig (1989). "The Monetary Unification Process in 19th–Century Germany: Relevance and Lessons for Europe Today." In Marcello De Cecco and Alberto Giovannini, eds., *A European Central Bank? Perspectives on Monetary Unification after Ten Years of the EMS.* New York: Cambridge University Press. chap. 8.

—— (1993). "Did Monetary Unification Precede or Follow Political Unification of Germany in the 19th Century?" *European Economic Review* 37, nos. 2/3 (April): 518–24.

Honkapohja, Seppo, and Pentti Pikkarainen (1994). "Country Characteristics and the Choice of the Exchange Rate Regime: Are Mini–Skirts Followed by Maxis?" In Johnny Akerholm and Alberto Giovannini, eds., *Exchange Rate Policies in the Nordic Countries.* London: Centre for Economic Policy Research, chap. 3.

Honohan, Patrick (1992). "Price and Monetary Convergence in Currency Unions: The Franc and Rand Zones." *Journal of International Money and Finance* 11, no. 4 (Aug.): 397–410.

Hufbauer, Gary C., Jeffrey J. Schott, and Kimberly A. Elliott (1990). *Economic Sanctions Reconsidered: History and Current Policy.* 2d ed. Washington: Institute for International Economics.

Humpage, Owen F., and Jean M. McIntire (1995). "An Introduction to Currency Boards." *Federal Reserve Bank of Cleveland Economic Review* 31, no. 2 (Quarter 2): 2–11.

Ilzkovitz, Fabienne (1996). "Prospects for the Internationalization of the Euro." Doc. II/362/96-EN. Brussels: European Commission. June.

IMF (1997). "IMF Concludes Article IV Consultation with Bulgaria." Press Information Notice no. 97/15. Washington, July 29.

IMF Survey (1997). "Currency Board Arrangements More Widely Used," February 24: 54–57.

Ingram, James C. (1959). "State and Regional Payments Mechanisms." *Quarterly Journal of Economics* Vol. 73: 619–32.

—— (1962). "A Proposal for Integration in the Atlantic Community." In *Factors Affecting the United States Balance of Payments.* Compilation of studies prepared for the Subcommittee on International Exchange and Payments of the Joint Economic Committee of the Congress. Washington: U.S. Government Printing Office, 175–207.

Isard, Peter (1995). *Exchange Rate Economics.* New York: Cambridge University Press.

Ito, Takatoshi (1993). "The Yen and the International Monetary System." In C. Fred Bergsten and Marcus Noland, eds., *Pacific Dynamism and the International Economic System.* Washington: Institute for International Economics, chap. 9.

—— (1994). "On the Possibility of a Yen Bloc." In Reuven Glick and Michael M. Hutchison, eds., *Exchange Rate Policy and Interdependence: Perspectives from the Pacific Basin.* New York: Cambridge University Press, chap. 13.

Jackson, Robert H. (1990). *Quasi–States: Sovereignty, International Relations and the Third World.* Cambridge: Cambridge University Press.

Jackson, Robert H., and Mark W. Zacher (1996). "The Territorial Covenant: International Society and the Legitimization of Boundaries." Paper prepared for the 1996 annual meeting of the American Political Science Association.

James, Alan (1986). *Sovereign Statehood: The Basis of International Society.* London: Allen and Unwin.

James, Harold (1996). *International Monetary Cooperation since Bretton Woods.* Washington: International Monetary Fund.

Jameson, Kenneth P. (1990). "Dollar Bloc Dependency in Latin America: Beyond Bretton Woods." *International Studies Quarterly* 34, no. 4 (Dec.): 519–41.

Janackova, Stanislava (1994). "Parting with the Common State and Currency: First Steps of the Czech Republic." *Eastern European Economies* 32, no. 2 (March–April): 6–22.

Jao, Y. C. and Frank H. H. King (1990). *Money in Hong Kong: Historical Perspective and Contemporary Analysis.* Hong Kong: Centre of Asian Studies, University of Hong Kong.

Jarvis, Anthony P., and Albert J. Paolini (1995). "Locating the State." In Joseph A. Camilleri, Anthony P. Jarvis, and Albert J. Paolini, eds. (1995). *The State in Transition: Reimagining Political Space.* Boulder, Colo.: Lynne Rienner, chap. 1.

Johnson, Harry G. (1961). *International Trade and Economic Growth: Studies in Pure Theory.* Cambridge: Harvard University Press.

—— (1973). *Further Essays in Monetary Economics.* Cambridge: Harvard University Press.

Johnson, Karen H. (1994). "International Dimensions of European Monetary Union: Implications for the Dollar." International Finance Discussion Paper no. 469. (May). Washington: Federal Reserve Board of Governors.

Johnston, R. J. (1986). "Placing Politics." *Political Geography Quarterly* 5, no. 4: 563–78.

Jones, R. J. Barry (1995). *Globalisation and Interdependence in the International Political Economy: Rhetoric and Reality.* London: Pinter.

Jones-Hendrickson, S. B. (1989). "Financial Structures and Economic Development in the Organisation of Eastern Caribbean States." *Social and Economic Studies* 38, no. 4: 71–93.

Jonung, Lars (1987). "Swedish Experience under the Classical Gold Standard, 1873–1914." In Michael D. Bordo and Anna J. Schwartz, eds., *A Retrospective on the Classical Gold Standard, 1821–1931.* Chicago: University of Chicago Press, chap. 8.

Jovanovic, Miroslav N. (1992). *International Economic Integration.* London: Routledge.

Kamin, Steven B., and Neil R. Ericsson (1993). "Dollarization in Argentina." International Finance Discussion Paper no. 460. Washington: Federal Reserve Board of Governors.

Kann, E. (1937). "The Currencies of China: Old and New." In A. D. Gayer, ed., *The Lessons of Monetary Experience.* New York: Farrar and Rinehart.

Kareken, John, and Neil Wallace (1981). "On the Indeterminacy of Equilibrium Exchange Rates." *Quarterly Journal of Economics* 96, no. 2 (May): 207–22.

Kawai, Masahiro (1992). "Optimum Currency Areas." In Peter Newman, Murray Milgate, and John Eatwell, eds., *The New Palgrave Dictionary of Money and Finance* London: Macmillan, 3: 78–81.

Kenen, Peter B. (1969). "The Theory of Optimum Currency Areas: An Eclectic View." In Robert A. Mundell and Alexander K. Swoboda, eds., *Monetary Problems of the International Economy.* Chicago: University of Chicago Press, chap. 2.

—— (1983). "The Role of the Dollar as an International Currency." Occasional Paper no. 13. Washington: Group of Thirty.

—— (1992). *EMU after Maastricht.* Washington: Group of Thirty.

—— (1995). *Economic and Monetary Union in Europe: Moving Beyond Maastricht.* Cambridge: Cambridge University Press.

Keohane, Robert O., and Joseph S. Nye (1977). *Power and Interdependence: World Politics in Transition.* Boston: Little, Brown.

Keynes, John Maynard (1924). *Tract on Monetary Reform.* Reprinted in *The Collected Writings of John Maynard Keynes,* vol. 4. London: Macmillan, 1971.

Kimbrough, Kent P. (1986). "The Optimal Quantity of Money Rule in the Theory of Public Finance." *Journal of Monetary Economics* (Nov.), pp. 277–285.

Kindleberger, Charles P. (1969). *American Business Abroad.* New Haven: Yale University Press.

—— (1972). "The International Monetary Politics of a Near-Great Power: Two French Episodes, 1926–36 and 1960–70." *Economic Notes* 1, nos. 2–3: 30–44.

—— (1973). *The World in Depression, 1929–1939.* Berkeley: University of California Press.

—— (1985). "The Dollar Yesterday, Today and Tomorrow." *Banca Nazionale del Lavoro Quarterly Review* 38 (Dec.): 295–308.

—— (1995). "Dollar Darkness." *The International Economy* (May/June): 6–9.

Kirshner, Jonathan (1995). *Currency and Coercion: The Political Economy of International Monetary Power.* Princeton: Princeton University Press.

Klein, Benjamin (1974). "The Competitive Supply of Money." *Journal of Money, Credit, and Banking* 6, no. 4 (Nov.): 423–53.

Klein, Benjamin, and Michael Melvin (1982). "Competing International Monies and International Monetary Arrangements." In Michael B. Connolly, ed., *The International Monetary System: Choices for the Future.* New York: Praeger, chap. 9.

Klein, Lawrence R. (1993). "Some Second Thoughts on the European Monetary System." *Greek Economic Review* 15, no. 1 (Autumn): 105–14.

Klein, Martin, and Manfred J. M. Neumann (1990). "Seigniorage: What Is It and Who Gets It?" *Weltwirtschaftliches Archiv* 126, Heft 2: 205–21.

Knapp, George F. [1905] (1924). *The State Theory of Money.* London: Macmillan.

Knox, Paul, and John Agnew (1994). *The Geography of the World Economy: An Introduction to Economic Geography.* 2d ed. London: Edward Arnold.

Kobrin, Stephen J. (1996). "Back to the Future: Neomedievalism and the Post Modern World Economy." Paper prepared for the 1996 annual meeting of the International Studies Association.

—— (1997a). "The Architecture of Globalization: State Sovereignty in a Networked Global Economy." In John H. Dunning, ed., *Governments, Globalization, and International Business.* New York: Oxford University Press, 146–71.

—— (1997b). "Electronic Cash and the End of National Markets." *Foreign Policy* no. 107 (Summer): 65–77.

Kramer, Hans R. (1970). "Experience with Historical Monetary Unions." In Otmar Emminger et al., *Integration through Monetary Union?* Tubingen: J. C. B. Mohr, chap. 3.

Krasner, Stephen D. (1988). "Sovereignty: An Institutional Perspective." *Comparative Political Studies* 21, no. 1 (April): 66–94.

—— (1993). "Westphalia and All That." In Judith D. Goldstein and Robert O. Keohane, eds., *Ideas and Foreign Policy: Beliefs, Institutions, and Political Change.* Ithaca: Cornell University Press, chap. 9.

—— (1995/96). "Compromising Westphalia." *International Security* 20, no. 3 (Winter): 115–51.

Kratochwil, Friedrich (1986). "Of Systems, Boundaries, and Territoriality: An Inquiry into the Formation of the State System." *World Politics* 34, no. 1 (Oct.): 27–52.

Kregel, J.A. (1990). "The EMS, the Dollar and the World Economy," in Piero Ferri, ed., *Prospects for the European Monetary System* New York: St. Martin's Press, chap. 12.

Krueger, Russell, and Jiming Ha (1996). "Measurement of Cocirculation of Currencies." In Paul D. Mizen and Eric J. Pentecost, eds., *The Macroeconomics of International Currencies: Theory, Policy and Evidence.* Brookfield, Vt.: Elgar, chap. 4.

Krugman, Paul R. (1980). "Vehicle Currencies and the Structure of International Exchange." *Journal of Money, Credit, and Banking* 12, no. 3 (Aug.): 513–26.

—— (1992). "The International Role of the Dollar." In Paul R. Krugman, *Currencies and Crises.* Cambridge and London: MIT Press, chap. 10.

—— (1993). "What Do We Need to Know about the International Monetary System? *Essays in International Finance* no. 190. Princeton: International Finance Section.

Kunz, Diane B. (1995). "The Fall of the Dollar Order." *Foreign Affairs* 74, no. 4 (July/Aug.): 22–26.

Kwan, C.H. (1994). *Economic Interdependence in the Asia-Pacific Region: Towards a Yen Bloc.* London: Routledge.

Kydland, Finn E., and Edward C. Prescott (1977). "Rules Rather than Discretion: The Inconsistency of Optimal Plans." *Journal of Political Economy* 85, no. 3 (June): 473–92.

Laidler, David (1992). "Fiat Money." In Peter Newman, Murray Milgate, and John Eatwell, eds., *The New Palgrave Dictionary of Money and Finance.* London: Macmillan Press, 2: 20–21.

Lane, Frederic C., and Reinhold C. Mueller (1985). *Money and Banking in Medieval and Renaissance Venice.* Volume 1, *Coins and Moneys of Account.* Baltimore: John Hopkins University Press.

Larson, Henrietta M. (1939). "Note on Our Dollar Sign." *Bulletin of the Business Historical Society* 13, no. 4 (Oct.): 57–58.

Letiche, John M. (1974). "Dependent Monetary Systems and Economic Development: The Case of Sterling East Africa." In Willy Sellekaerts, ed., *Economic Development and Planning: Essays in Honor of Jan Tinbergen*. White Plains, NY: International Arts and Sciences Press, chap. 9.

Levy, Steven (1994). "E-Money (That's What I Want)." *Wired* 2, no. 12 (Dec.): 174–79, 213–19.

Leyshon, Andrew (1995a). "Annihilating Space? The Speed-Up of Communications." In John Allen and Chris Hamnett, eds., *A Shrinking World? Global Unevenness and Inequality*. New York: Oxford University Press, chap. 1.

—— (1995b). "Geographies of Money and Finance I," *Progress in Human Geography* 19, no. 4 (Dec.): 531–43.

—— (1997). "Geographies of Money and Finance II." *Progress in Human Geography* 21, no. 2 (June): 278–89.

Leyshon, Andrew, and Nigel Thrift (1997). *Money/Space: Geographies of Monetary Transformation*. London: Routledge.

Lincoln, Bruce (1994). *Authority: Construction and Corrosion*. Chicago: University of Chicago Press.

Lindsey, Lawrence B. (1996). "The Future of the Dollar as an International Currency." In James A. Dorn and Roberto Salinas-León, eds., *Money and Markets in the Americas: New Challenges for Hemispheric Integration*. Vancouver, Canada: Frasier Institute, chap. 16.

Lipton, David, and Jeffrey D. Sachs (1992). "Prospects for Russia's Economic Reforms," *Brookings Papers on Economic Activity* no. 2: 213–65.

Liviatan, Nissan, ed. (1993). *Proceedings of a Conference on Currency Substitution and Currency Boards*. Washington: World Bank.

Lo, Chi (1996). "China's Two Currencies." *International Economy*, (Sept./Oct): 54–55.

Lopez, Robert S. (1951). "The Dollar of the Middle Ages." *Journal of Economic History* 11, no. 3 (Summer): 209–34.

Ludlow, Peter (1982). *The Making of the European Monetary System*. London: Butterworths.

Maehara, Yasuhiro (1993). "The Internationalization of the Yen and Its Role as a Key Currency." *Journal of Asian Economics* 4, no. 1: 153–70.

Magee, Stephen P., and Ramesh K. S. Rao (1980). "Vehicle and Nonvehicle Currencies in International Trade." *American Economic Review* 70, no. 2 (May): 368–73.

Marquez, Jaime (1992). "Currency Substitution." In Peter Newman, Murray Milgate, and John Eatwell, eds., *The New Palgrave Dictionary of Money and Finance*. London: Macmillan, 2: 565–67.

Marshall, Alfred [1920] (1948). *Principles of Economics*. 8th ed. New York: Macmillan.

Martin, Guy (1986). "The Franc Zone, Underdevelopment and Dependency in Francophone Africa." *Third World Quarterly* 8, no. 1 (Jan.): 205–35.

Martin, Ron (1994). "Stateless Monies, Global Financial Integration and National Economic Autonomy: The End of Geography." In Stuart Corbridge, Nigel Thrift, and Ron Martin, eds., *Money, Power and Space*. Cambridge, Mass.: Blackwell, chap. 11.

Marx, Karl [1864] (1984). *Das Kapital*, vol. 1. Edited by Friedrich Engels. New York: International Press.

Masera, Rainer Stefano (1987). "An Increasing Role for the ECU: A Character in Search of a Script." *Essays in International Finance* no. 167. Princeton: International Finance Section.

Massey, Doreen (1995). "Imagining the World." In John Allen and Doreen Massey, eds., *Geographical Worlds.* New York: Oxford University Press, chap. 1.

Masson, Paul R., and Mark P. Taylor (1993). "Currency Unions: A Survey of the Issues." In Paul R. Masson and Mark P. Taylor, eds., *Policy Issues in the Operation of Currency Unions.* Cambridge and New York: Cambridge University Press, chap. 1.

Matsuyama, Kiminori, Nobuhiro Kiyotaki, and Akihiko Matsui (1993). "Toward a Theory of International Currency." *Review of Economic Studies* Vol. 60, no. 2 (April) pp. 283–307.

Mbogoro, D. A. K. (1985). "Regional Grouping and Economic Development: Some Lessons from the East African Integration Scheme." In W. A. Ndongko, ed., *Economic Cooperation and Integration in Africa.* Dakar, Senegal: CODESRIA, chap. 8.

McClean, A. Wendell A. (1975). *Money and Banking in the East Caribbean Currency Area.* Kingston, Jamaica: Institute of Social and Economic Research, University of the West Indies.

McKinnon, Ronald I. (1963). "Optimum Currency Areas" *American Economic Review* 53, no. 4 (Sept.): 717–25.

—— (1973). *Money and Capital in Economic Development.* Washington: Brookings Institution.

—— (1979). *Money in International Exchange: The Convertible Currency System.* New York: Oxford University Press.

—— (1985). "Two Concepts of International Currency Substitution." In Michael D. Connolly and J. McDermott, eds., *The Economics of the Caribbean Basin.* New York: Praeger, pp. 101–18.

—— (1996). "Direct and Indirect Concepts of International Currency Substitution." In Paul D. Mizen and Eric J. Pentecost, eds., *The Macroeconomics of International Currencies: Theory, Policy and Evidence.* Brookfield, Vt: Elgar, chap. 3.

Meade, James E. (1956). "The Belgium-Luxembourg Economic Union, 1921–1939: Lessons from an Early Experiment." *Essays in International Finance* no. 25. Princeton: International Finance Section.

Meigs, A. James (1993). "Eurodollars: A Transition Currency." *Cato Journal* Vol. 12, no. 3 (Winter): 711–27.

Meltzer, Allen H. (1995). "What is Money?" *Economic Affairs* 15, no. 4 (Autumn): 8–14.

Melvin, Michael (1985). "Currency Substitution and Western European Monetary Unification," *Economica* 52 (Feb.): 79–91.

—— (1988a). "The Dollarization of Latin America as a Market-Enforced Monetary Reform: Evidence and Implications." *Economic Development and Cultural Change* Vol. 36, no. 3 (April): 543–58.

—— (1988b). "Monetary Confidence, Privately Produced Monies, and Domestic and International Monetary Reform." In Thomas D. Willett, ed., *Political Business Cycles: The Political Economy of Money, Inflation, and Unemployment.* Durham, N.C.: Duke University Press, chap. 18.

Melvin, Michael, and Kurt Fenske (1992). "Dollarization and Monetary Reform: Evidence from the Cochabamba Region of Bolivia." *Revista de Análisis Económico* 7, no. 1 (June): 139–52.

Melvin, Michael, Michael Ormiston, and Bettina Peiers (1994). "Economic Fundamentals and a Yen Currency Area for Asian Pacific Rim Countries." In Reuven Glick and Michael M. Hutchison, eds., *Exchange Rate Policy and Interdependence: Perspectives from the Pacific Basin.* New York: Cambridge University Press, chap. 14.

Melvin, Michael, and Bettina Peiers (1993). "On the Possibility of a Yen Currency Bloc for Pacific-Basin Countries: A Stochastic Dominance Approach." *Pacific-Basin Finance Journal* 1: 309–33.

—— (1996). "Dollarization in Developing Countries: Rational Remedy or Domestic Dilemma?" *Contemporary Economic Policy* 14, no. 3 (July): 30–40.

Miles, Marc A. (1978a). "Currency Substitution, Flexible Exchange Rates, and Monetary Independence." *American Economic Review* 68, no. 3 (June): 428–36.

—— (1978b). "Currency Substitution: Perspectives, Implications, and Empirical Evidence." In Bluford H. Putnam and D. Sykes Wilford, eds., *The Monetary Approach to International Adjustment.* New York: Praeger, chap. 12.

Miller, David, ed. (1987). "Authority." *The Blackwell Encyclopedia of Political Thought.* Oxford: Basil Blackwell, pp. 28–31.

Milner, Helen V., and Robert O. Keohane (1996). "Internationalization and Domestic Politics: A Conclusion." In Robert O. Keohane and Helen V. Milner, eds., *Internationalization and Domestic Politics.* New York: Cambridge University Press, chap. 10.

Mintz, Norman N. (1970). *Monetary Union and Economic Integration.* New York: New York University Press.

Mizen, Paul D., and Eric J. Pentecost, eds. (1996). *The Macroeconomics of International Currencies: Theory, Policy and Evidence.* Brookfield, Vt.: Elgar.

Molnar, Thomas (1995). *Authority and Its Enemies.* New Brunswick, N.J.: Transaction.

Monga, Celestin (1997). "A Currency Reform Index for Western and Central Africa." *World Economy* 20, no. 1 (Jan.): 103–25.

Morehouse, Ward, ed. (1989). *Building Sustainable Communities: Tools and Concepts for Self-Reliant Economic Change.* New York: Bootstrap.

Morgan, E. Victor (1965). *A History of Money.* Baltimore: Penguin.

Mueller, Johannes (1994). "Dollarization in Lebanon" Working Paper WP/94/129. Washington: International Monetary Fund.

Mugomba, Agrippah T. (1978). "Regional Organisations and African Underdevelopment: The Collapse of the East African Community." *Journal of Modern African Studies* 16, no. 2: 261–72.

Mundell, Robert A. (1961). "A Theory of Optimum Currency Areas." *American Economic Review* Vol. 51, no. 3 (Sept.): 657–65.

—— (1973). "Uncommon Arguments for Common Currencies." In Harry G. Johnson and Alexander K. Swoboda, eds., *The Economics of Common Currencies.* London: George Allen and Unwin, chap. 7.

—— (1983). "International Monetary Options." *Cato Journal* 3, no. 1 (Spring): 189–210.

—— (1993). "EMU and the International Monetary System: A Transatlantic Perspective." Working Paper no. 13. Vienna: Austrian National Bank.

—— (1995). "Prospects for the International Monetary System and Its Institutions." In Hans Genberg, ed. *The International Monetary System: Its Institutions and Future.* New York: Springer-Verlag, chap. 2.

Murphy, Alexander B. (1996). "The Sovereign State System as Political-Territorial Ideal: Historical and Contemporary Considerations." In Thomas J. Biersteker and Cynthia Weber, eds., *State Sovereignty as Social Construct.* New York: Cambridge University Press.

Murphy, Craig N., and Cristina Rojas de Ferro (1995). "The Power of Representation in International Political Economy." *Review of International Political Economy* 2, no. 1 (Winter): 63–69.

Mussa, Michael (1991). "Macroeconomic Policy Implications of Currency Zones: Commentary." In *Policy Implications of Trade and Currency Zones.* Kansas City: Federal Reserve Bank of Kansas City, pp. 213–19.

—— (1995). "One Money for How Many?" In Peter B. Kenen, ed., *Understanding Interdependence: The Macroeconomics of the Open Economy.* Princeton: Princeton University Press, chap. 3.

—— (1997). "Political and Institutional Commitment to a Common Currency." *American Economic Review* 87, no. 2 (May): 217–20.

Mutch, David (1995). "World Makes the US Dollar Go 'Round." *The Christian Science Monitor,* Dec. 20: 1, 10.

Nascimento, Jean-Claude (1994). "Monetary Policy in Unified Currency Areas: The Cases of the CAMA and ECCA during 1976–90." Working Paper WP/94/11. Washington: International Monetary Fund.

Nash, Nathaniel C. (1995). "What Fits in Europe's Wallet?" *The New York Times,* July 11: C1, C10.

Nayman, Laurence, and Jean Pisani-Ferry (1996). "Élus et exclus de la monnaie unique." *La Lettre du CEPII* 43 (Feb.): 1–4.

Newlyn, W. T. (1962). *Theory of Money.* Oxford: Clarendon Press.

Newman, Peter, Murray Milgate, and John Eatwell, eds. (1992). *The New Palgrave Dictionary of Money and Finance.* London: Macmillan.

New York Times (1994). "Greenbacks to Get High-Tech Makeover," July 14, p. A8.

North, Douglass C. (1990). "Institutions and a Transaction-Cost Theory of Exchange." In James E. Alt and Kenneth A. Shepsle, eds., *Perspectives on Positive Political Economy.* New York: Cambridge University Press.

O'Brien, Richard (1992). *Global Financial Integration: The End of Geography.* New York: Council on Foreign Relations.

Ohmae, Kenichi (1993). "The Rise of the Region State." *Foreign Affairs* 72, no. 2 (Spring): 78–87.

—— (1995). *The End of the Nation State.* New York: Free Press.

Okun, Arthur M. (1975). *Equality and Efficiency: The Big Tradeoff.* Washington: Brookings Institution.

O'Mahony, David (1984). "Past Justifications for Public Interventions." In Pascal Salin, ed., *Currency Competition and Monetary Union.* The Hague: Martinus Nijhoff, pp. 127–30.

Oppenheimer, Peter M. (1966). "Monetary Movements and the International Position of Sterling." In D.J. Robertson and L. C. Hunter, eds., *The British Balance of Payments.* Edinburgh: Oliver and Boyd.

Orléan, Andre (1989). "Mimetic Contagion and Speculative Bubbles." *Theory and Decision* Vol. 27, Nos. 1–2: 63–92.

Osband, Kent, and Delano Villanueva (1993). "Independent Currency Authorities," *International Monetary Fund Staff Papers* 40, no. 1 (March): 202–16.

Ostrom, Douglas (1995). "Yen's Role in Trade Increasing." *JEI Report* no. 23B (June 23): 5–7.

Ow, Chwee-huay (1985). "The Currency Board Monetary System—The Case of Singapore and Hong Kong." Ph.D. dissertation, Johns Hopkins University.

Padoa-Schioppa, Tommaso (1988). "The European Monetary System: A Long-Term View." In Francesco Giavazzi, Stefano Micossi, and Marcus Miller, eds., *The European Monetary System.* Cambridge: Cambridge University Press, chap. 12.

—— (1993). "Tripolarism: Regional and Global Economic Cooperation" Occasional Paper no. 42. Washington: Group of Thirty.

Page, S. A. B. (1977). "Currency of Invoicing in Merchandise Trade." *National Institute Economic Review* no. 81 (Aug.): 77–81.

—— (1981). "The Choice of Invoicing Currency in Merchandise Trade." *National Institute Economic Review* no. 98 (Nov.): 60–72.

Palan, Ronan and Jason Abbott (1996). *State Strategies in the Global Political Economy*. London: Pinter.

Park, Yoon S., and Jack Zwick (1985). *International Banking in Theory and Practice*. Reading, Mass.: Addison–Wesley.

Pauly, Louis W. (1995). "Capital Mobility, State Autonomy and Political Legitimacy." *Journal of International Affairs* 48, no. 2 (Winter): 369–88.

—— (1997). *Who Elected the Bankers? Surveillance and Control in the World Economy*. Ithaca: Cornell University Press.

Peiers, Bettina, and Jeffrey Wrase (1995). "Dollarization Hysteresis and the Role of Network Externalities." CIBER Working Paper no. 95–4. Los Angeles: UCLA Center for International Business Education and Research.

Pennock, J. Roland, and John W. Chapman, eds. (1987). *Authority Revisited*. New York: New York University Press.

Perlman, M. (1993). "In Search of Monetary Union." *Journal of European Economic History* 22, no. 2 (Fall): 313–32.

Perroux, François (1950). "Economic Space: Theory and Applications." *Quarterly Journal of Economics* Vol. 64, no. 1 (Feb.): 89–104.

Phelps, Edmund (1973). "Inflation in the Theory of Public Finance." *Swedish Journal of Economics* 75, no. 1 (March): 67–82.

Philpott, Daniel (1995). "Sovereignty: An Introduction and Brief History." *Journal of International Affairs* 48, no. 2 (Winter): 353–368.

Pieper, Paul (1994). "The Case of the Missing Currency." *Journal of Economic Perspectives* 8, no. 4 (Fall): 203–6.

Polanyi, Karl (1944). *The Great Transformation*. Boston: Beacon.

Polk, Judd (1956). *Sterling: Its Meaning in World Finance*. New York: Harper and Brothers.

Pond, Shepard (1940). "The Ducat: Once an Important Coin in European Business." *Bulletin of the Business Historical Society* 14, no. 2 (April): 17–19.

—— (1941a). "The Maria Theresa Thaler: A Famous Trade Coin." *Bulletin of the Business Historical Society* 15, no. 2 (April): 26–31.

—— (1941b). "The Spanish Dollar: The World's Most Famous Silver Coin." *Bulletin of the Business Historical Society* 15, no. 1 (Feb.): 12–16.

Porter, Richard D. (1993). "Estimates of Foreign Holdings of U.S. Currency—An Approach Based on Relative Cross-Country Seasonal Variations." In *Nominal Income Targeting with the Monetary Base as Instrument: An Evaluation of McCallum's Rule*. Finance and Economics Discussion Series Working Study no. 1. Washington: Federal Reserve Board of Governors.

Porter, Richard D., and Ruth A. Judson (1996). "The Location of U.S. Currency: How Much Is Abroad?" *Federal Reserve Bulletin* 82, no. 10 (Oct.): 883–903.

Prati, Alessandro, and Garry J. Schinasi (1997). "European Monetary Union and International Capital Markets: Structural Implications and Risks." Working paper WP/97/62. Washington: International Monetary Fund.

Prem, Roohi (1997). "International Currencies and Endogenous Enforcement—An Empirical Analysis." Working Paper WP/97/29. Washington: International Monetary Fund.

Quirk, Peter J., et al. (1995). *Issues in International Exchange and Payments Systems*. Washington: International Monetary Fund.

Rahn, Richard W. (1986). "Time to Privatize Money." *Policy Review* no. 36: 55–57.

—— (1989). "Private Money: An Idea whose Time Has Come." *Cato Journal* 9, no. 2 (Fall): 353–62.

Ranki, Sinimaaria (1995). "On the Role of the Single Currency ECU." *Geld und Währung Working Papers* no. 40. Frankfurt: Goethe University, March.

Rao, Ramesh K. S., and Stephen P. Magee (1980). "The Currency of Denomination of International Trade Contracts." In Richard M. Levich and Clas G. Wihlborg, eds., *Exchange Risk and Exposure: Current Developments in International Financial Management*. Lexington, Mass.: D. C. Heath, chap. 3.

Ravenhill, John (1979). "Regional Integration and Development in Africa: Lessons from the East African Community." *Journal of Commonwealth and Comparative Politics* 17, no. 3 (Nov.): 227–46.

Raz, Joseph, ed. (1990). *Authority*. Oxford: Blackwell.

Redish, Angela (1994). "The Latin Monetary Union and the Emergence of the International Gold Standard." In Michael D. Bordo and Forrest Capie, eds., *Monetary Regimes in Transition*. New York: Cambridge University Press, chap. 3.

Reti, Steven (1994). "Doubtful Standards: The Political Economy of International Monetary Conferences." Ph.D. dissertation, University of California at Santa Barbara.

Ritter, Joseph A. (1995). "The Transition from Barter to Fiat Money." *American Economic Review* 85, no. 1 (March): 134–49.

Roberts, Paul Craig (1995). "The Inevitable Decline of a Reserve Currency." *The Wall Street Journal*, March 16, p. 22.

Rodriguez, Carlos A. (1993). "Money and Credit under Currency Substitution." *International Monetary Fund Staff Papers* 40, no. 2 (June): 414–26.

Rodrik, Dani (1997). *Has Globalization Gone Too Far?* Washington: Institute for International Economics.

Rolnick, Arthur J., and Warren E. Weber (1986). "Gresham's Law or Gresham's Fallacy?" *Journal of Political Economy* 94, no. 1 (Feb.): 185–99.

Rose, Andrew K. (1996). "Explaining Exchange Rate Volatility: An Empirical Analysis of 'The Holy Trinity' of Monetary Independence, Fixed Exchange Rates, and Capital Mobility." *Journal of International Money and Finance* 15, no. 6: 925–45.

Rosecrance, Richard (1986). *The Rise of the Trading State: Commerce and Conquest in the Modern World*. New York: Basic Books.

Rosenau, James N. (1992). "Governance, Order, and Change in World Politics." In James N. Rosenau and Ernst-Otto Czempiel, eds., *Governance without Government: Order and Change in World Politics*. New York: Cambridge University Press.

Rosenau, James N. and Ernst-Otto Czempiel, eds. (1992). *Governance without Government: Order and Change in World Politics*. New York: Cambridge University Press.

Rosenberg, Justin (1994a). *The Empire of Civil Society: A Critique of the Realist Theory of International Relations*. New York: Verso.

—— (1994b). "The International Imagination: IR Theory and 'Classic Social Analysis.'" *Millennium: Journal of International Studies* 23, no. 1: 85–108.

Rosow, Stephen J. (1994). "On the Political Theory of Political Economy: Conceptual Ambiguity and the Global Economy." *Review of International Political Economy* 1, no. 3 (Autumn): 465–88.

Rothchild, Donald (1974). "From Hegemony to Bargaining in East African Relations." *Journal of African Studies* 1, no. 4 (Winter): 390–416.

Rueff, Jacques (1972). *The Monetary Sin of the West*. New York: Macmillan.

Ruggie, John Gerard (1975). "International Responses to Technology: Concepts and Trends." *International Organization* 29, no. 3 (Summer): 557–83.

—— (1983). "Continuity and Transformation in the World Polity: Toward a Neorealist Synthesis." *World Politics* 35, no. 2 (Jan.): 261–85.

—— (1989). "International Structure and International Transformation." In Ernst-Otto Czempiel and James N. Rosenau, eds., *Global Changes and Theoretical Challenges: Approaches to World Politics for the 1990s.* Lexington, Mass.: D.C. Heath, chap. 2.

—— (1993). "Territoriality and Beyond: Problematizing Modernity in International Relations." *International Organization* 47, no. 1 (Winter): 139–74.

Ruland, L. J. and J.-M. Viaene (1993). "The Political Choice of Exchange Rate Regime." *Economics and Politics* 5, no. 3 (Nov.): 271–84.

Sack, Robert David (1986). *Human Territoriality: Its Theory and History.* New York: Cambridge University Press.

Sahay, Ratna, and Carlos A. Vegh (1995). "Dollarization in Transition Economies." *Finance and Development* 32, no. 1 (March): 36–39.

—— (1996). "Dollarization in Transition Economies: Evidence and Policy Implications." In Paul D. Mizen and Eric J. Pentecost, eds., *The Macroeconomics of International Currencies: Theory, Policy and Evidence.* Brookfield, Vt.: Edward Elgar, chap. 11.

Salin, Pascal (1984). "General Introduction." In Pascal Salin, ed., *Currency Competition and Monetary Union.* The Hague: Martinus Nijhoff, 1–26.

Salvatore, Dominick (1997). "The European Monetary System: Crisis and Future." In George S. Tavlas, ed., *The Collapse of Exchange Rate Regimes: Causes, Consequences and Policy Responses.* Boston: Kluwer Academic, pp. 171–93.

San Paolo Bank of Turin (1990). "The Commercial Use of the ECU: Invoicing and Import-Export Practices." *ECU Newsletter* no. 31 (Jan.), pp. 16–30.

Sassen, Saskia (1996a). *Losing Control? Sovereignty in an Age of Globalization.* New York: Columbia University Press.

—— (1996b). "The Spatial Organization of Information Industries: Implications for the Role of the State." In James H. Mittelman, ed., *Globalization: Critical Reflections.* Boulder, Colo.: Lynne Rienner, chap. 3.

Savastano, Miguel A. (1992). "The Pattern of Currency Substitution in Latin America: An Overview." *Revista de Análisis Económico* 7, no. 1 (June): 29–72.

—— (1996). "Dollarization in Latin America: Recent Evidence and Policy Issues." In Paul D. Mizen and Eric J. Pentecost, eds., *The Macroeconomics of International Currencies: Theory, Policy and Evidence.* Brookfield, Vt.: Elgar, chap. 12.

Savvides, Andreas (1990). "Real Exchange Rate Variability and the Choice of Exchange Rate Regime by Developing Countries." *Journal of International Money and Finance* 9, no. 4 (Dec.): 440–54.

—— (1993). "Pegging the Exchange Rate and the Choice of a Standard by LDCs: A Joint Formulation." *Journal of Economic Development* 18, no. 2 (Dec.): 107–25.

Schelling, Thomas C. (1980). *The Strategy of Conflict.* Cambridge: Harvard University Press.

Schwartz, Anna J. (1992). *Do Currency Boards Have a Future?* London: Institute of Economic Affairs.

—— (1993). "Currency Boards: Their Past, Present, and Possible Future Role." *Carnegie-Rochester Conference Series on Public Policy* 39 (Dec.): 147–87.

Schwartz, Pedro (1993). "A Market Approach to Monetary Perestroika." *Cato Journal* 12, no. 3 (Winter): 621–32.

Schweickert, Rainer (1994). "Exchange Rate Based Stabilisation: Lessons from a Radical Implementation in Argentina." *World Economy* 17, no. 2 (March): 171–89.

Scitovsky, Tibor (1958). *Economic Theory and Western European Integration*. Stanford: Stanford University Press.

Seitz, Franz (1995). "The Circulation of Deutsche Mark Abroad." Discussion Paper 1/95. Frankfurt: Deutsche Bundesbank, May.

—— (1997). "How Many Deutschmarks are Held Abroad?" *Intereconomics* 32, no. 2 (March/April): 67–73.

Selgin, George A. (1994). "On Ensuring the Acceptability of a New Fiat Money." *Journal of Money, Credit, and Banking* 26, no. 4 (Nov.): 808–26.

Selgin, George A. and Lawrence H. White (1994). "How Would the Invisible Hand Handle Money?" *Journal of Economic Literature* 32, no. 4 (Dec.): 1718–49.

Shapiro, Michael J. (1993). *Reading "Adam Smith": Desire, History and Value*. London: Sage.

—— (1996). "Introduction to Part I." In Michael J. Shapiro and Hayward R. Alker, eds. *Challenging Boundaries: Global Flows, Territorial Identities*. Minneapolis: University of Minnesota Press.

Shapiro, Michael J., and Hayward R. Alker, eds. (1996). *Challenging Boundaries: Global Flows, Territorial Identities*. Minneapolis: University of Minnesota Press.

Shelton, Judy (1994). *Money Meltdown: Restoring Order to the Global Currency System*. New York: Free Press.

Shlaes, Amity (1997). "Loving the Mark." *New Yorker*, April 28, pp. 188–93.

Sibert, Anne (1992). "Government Finance in a Common Currency Area." *Journal of International Money and Finance* 11, no. 6 (Dec.): 567–78.

—— (1994). "The Allocation of Seigniorage in a Common Currency Area." *Journal of International Economics* 37, no. 1/2 (Aug.): 111–22.

Simmel, George [1900] (1978). *The Philosophy of Money*. London: Routledge and Kegan Paul.

Simons, Marlise (1994). "Gaza-Jericho Economic Accord Signed by Israel and Palestinians." *New York Times*, April 30: 1, 4.

Soja, Edward W. (1989). *Postmodern Geographies: The Reassertion of Space in Critical Social Theory*. London: Verso.

Solomon, Lewis D. (1996). *Rethinking Our Centralized Monetary System: The Case for a System of Local Currencies*. Westport, Conn.: Praeger.

Sprenkle, Case M. (1993). "The Case of the Missing Currency." *Journal of Economic Perspectives* 7, no. 2 (Fall): 175–84.

Spruyt, Hendrik (1994). *The Sovereign State and Its Competitors*. Princeton: Princeton University Press.

Stekler, Lois E. (1991). "The Statistical Discrepancy in the U.S. International Transactions Accounts: Sources and Suggested Remedies." International Finance Discussion Paper no. 404. Washington: Federal Reserve Board of Governors, July.

Stephan, Joerg (1994). *A Political-Economic Analysis of Exchange Rate Movements*. Konstanz: Hartung-Gorre Verlag.

Strange, Susan (1971a). "The Politics of International Currencies." *World Politics* 23, no. 2 (Jan.): 215–31.

—— (1971b). *Sterling and British Policy: A Political Study of an International Currency in Decline*. London: Oxford University Press.

—— (1987). "The Persistent Myth of Lost Hegemony." *International Organization* 41, no. 4 (Autumn): 551–74.

—— (1994). *States and Markets*. 2d ed. London: Pinter.

—— (1995). "The Defective State." *Daedalus* 124, no. 2 (Spring): 55–74.

—— (1996). *The Retreat of the State: The Diffusion of Power in the World Economy.* Cambridge: Cambridge University Press.

Streissler, Erich W. (1992). "Good Money Driving out Bad: A Model of the Hayek Process in Action." In Ernst Baltensperger and Hans-Werner Sinn, eds., *Exchange-Rate Regimes and Currency Unions.* New York: St. Martin's Press.

Sturzenegger, Federico A. (1992). "Currency Substitution and the Regressivity of Inflationary Taxation." *Revista de Análisis Económico* 7, no. 1 (June): 177–92.

—— (1994). "Hyperinflation with Currency Substitution: Introducing an Indexed Currency." *Journal of Money, Credit, and Banking* 26, no. 3 (Aug.): 377–95.

Sumner, Scott (1994). "The Case of the Missing Currency." *Journal of Economic Perspectives* 8, no. 4 (Fall): 201–3.

Swoboda, Alexander K. (1968). "The Euro-Dollar Market: An Interpretation," *Essays in International Finance* no. 64. Princeton: International Finance Section.

—— (1969). "Vehicle Currencies and the Foreign Exchange Market: The Case of the Dollar." In Robert Z. Aliber, ed., *The International Market for Foreign Exchange.* New York: Praeger, chap. 4.

Taguchi, Hiroo (1994). "On the Internationalization of the Japanese Yen." In Takatoshi Ito and Anne O. Krueger, eds., *Macroeconomic Linkage: Savings, Exchange Rates, and Capital Flows.* Chicago: University of Chicago Press, chap. 13.

Tavlas, George S. (1991). "On the International Use of Currencies: The Case of the Deutsche Mark." *Essays in International Finance* no. 181. Princeton: International Finance Section.

—— (1993a). "The Deutsche Mark as an International Currency." In Dilip K. Das, ed., *International Finance.* London: Routledge, chap. 30.

—— (1993b). "The 'New' Theory of Optimum Currency Areas." *The World Economy* 16, no. 6 (Nov.): 663–85.

—— (1993c). "The Theory of Optimum Currency Areas Revisited." *Finance and Development* 30, no. 2 (June): 32–35.

—— (1994). "The Theory of Monetary Integration." *Open Economies Review* 5: 211–30.

—— (1996a). "Currency Substitution and the International Demand for Yen." In Paul D. Mizen and Eric J. Pentecost, eds., *The Macroeconomics of International Currencies: Theory, Policy and Evidence.* Brookfield, Vt.: Elgar, chap. 10.

—— (1996b). "Dominant International Currencies and the Determination of Feasible Currency Areas: An Analysis of the U.S. Dollar." Manuscript, June.

Tavlas, George S., and Yuzuru Ozeki (1992). *The Internationalization of Currencies: An Appraisal of the Japanese Yen.* Occasional Paper no. 90. Washington: International Monetary Fund.

Taylor, Peter J. (1993). *Political Geography: World-Economy, Nation-State and Locality.* 3rd ed. New York: Wiley.

—— (1994). "The State as Container: Territoriality in the Modern World-System." *Progress in Human Geography* 18, no. 2 (June): 151–62.

—— (1995). "Beyond Containers: Internationality, Interstateness, Interterritoriality." *Progress in Human Geography* 19, no. 1 (March): 1–15.

Teitelman, Robert, and Stephen Davis (1996). "How the Cash Flows." *Institutional Investor* 30, no. 8 (Aug.): 58–73.

Thomson, Janice E. (1995). "State Sovereignty in International Relations: Bridging the Gap between Theory and Empirical Research." *International Studies Quarterly* 39, no. 2 (June): 213–33.

Thrift, Nigel (1995). "A Hyperactive World." In R. J. Johnston, Peter J. Taylor and Michael J.

Watts, eds., *Geographies of Global Change: Remapping the World in the Late Twentieth Century.* Oxford: Basil Blackwell, chap. 2.

Thrift, Nigel, and Kris Olds (1996). "Refiguring the Economic in Economic Geography." *Progress in Human Geography* 20, no. 3 (Sept.): 311–37.

Thygesen, Niels, et al. (1995). *International Currency Competition and the Future Role of the Single European Currency.* Final Report of a Working Group on European Monetary Union— International Monetary System. London: Kluwer Law International.

Toffler, Alvin (1970). *Future Shock.* New York: Random House.

Tsoukalis, Loukas (1977). *The Politics and Economics of European Monetary Integration.* London: Allen & Unwin.

—— (1991). *The New European Economy: The Politics and Economics of Integration.* Oxford: Oxford University Press.

Ullmann, Owen, et al. (1993). "The Global Greenback." *Business Week,* Aug. 9: 40, 44.

Underhill, Geoffrey R. D. (1991). "Markets beyond Politics? The State and the Internationalisation of Financial Markets." *European Journal of Political Research* 19, nos. 2–3 (March/April): 197–225.

—— (1995). "Keeping Governments Out of Politics: Transnational Securities Markets, Regulatory Cooperation, and Political Legitimacy." *Review of International Studies* 21, no. 3: 251–78.

—— (1996). "Financial Market Integration, Global Capital Mobility, and the ERM Crisis 1992–1995." Paper prepared for the 1996 annual meeting of the International Studies Association.

Ungerer, Horst (1997). *A Concise History of European Monetary Integration: From EPU to EMU.* Westport, Conn.: Quorum Books.

Uribe, Martin (1995). "Hysteresis in a Simple Model of Currency Substitution." International Finance Discussion Paper no. 509. Washington: Federal Reserve Board of Governors.

Usman, Abraham A., and Andreas Savvides (1994). "A Differentiated Goods Model of Coffee and Cocoa Exports with Reference to the CFA Franc Zone." *Applied Economics* 26, no. 6 (June): 583–90.

van de Walle, Nicolas (1991). "The Decline of the Franc Zone: Monetary Politics in Francophone Africa." *African Affairs* 90, no. 360 (July): 383–405.

van Meerhaeghe, M. A. G. (1987). *The Belgium-Luxembourg Economic Union.* Tilburg, Netherlands: Société Universitaire Européenne de Recherches Financières.

Vaubel, Roland (1977). "Free Currency Competition." *Weltwirtschaftliches Archiv* 113, Heft 3: 435–61.

—— (1978). *Strategies for Currency Unification: The Economics of Currency Competition and the Case for a European Parallel Currency.* Tubingen: J. C. B. Mohr.

—— (1984). "The Government's Money Monopoly: Externalities or Natural Monopoly?" *Kyklos* 37, no. 1: 27–57.

—— (1990). "Currency Competition and European Monetary Integration." *Economic Journal* 100, no. 3 (Sept.): 936–46.

Vegh, Carlos A. (1989). "The Optimal Inflation Tax in the Presence of Currency Substitution." *Journal of Monetary Economics* 24 (July): 139–46.

Vegh, Carlos A., and Pablo E. Guidotti (1990). "Optimal Taxation Policies in the EMS." *International Monetary Fund Staff Papers* 37, no. 2 (June): 311–37.

Vernon, Raymond (1971). *Sovereignty at Bay: The Multinational Spread of U.S. Enterprises.* New York: Basic Books.

Vilar, Pierre (1976). *A History of Gold and Money, 1450–1920.* London: NLB.

Villanueva, Delano (1993). "Options for Monetary and Exchange Arrangements in Transition

Economies." Paper on Policy Analysis and Assessment PPAA/93/12. Washington: International Monetary Fund, September.

von Hagen, Jürgen, and Michele Fratianni (1993). "The Transition to European Monetary Union and the European Monetary Institute." *Economics and Politics* 5, no. 2 (July): 167–86.

Walker, R. B. J., (1993). *Inside/Outside: International Relations as Political Theory*. New York: Cambridge University Press.

Walker, R. B. J., and Saul H. Mendlovitz, eds. (1990). *Contending Sovereignties: Redefining Political Community*. Boulder, Colo.: Lynne Rienner.

Wallace, Neil (1983). "A Legal Restrictions Theory of the Demand for 'Money' and the Role of Monetary Policy." Federal Reserve Bank of Minneapolis *Quarterly Review* 7, no. 1 (Winter): 1–7.

—— (1988). "A Suggestion for Oversimplifying the Theory of Money." *Economic Journal* 98, supplement: 25–36.

Wallerstein, Immanuel (1984). *The Politics of the World Economy*. Cambridge: Cambridge University Press.

Walter, Andrew (1991). *World Power and World Money: The Role of Hegemony and International Monetary Order*. New York: St. Martin's Press.

Walters, Alan (1992). "Sterling." In Peter Newman, Murray Milgate, and John Eatwell, eds., *The New Palgrave Dictionary of Money and Finance*. London: Macmillan. 3: 549–554.

Walters, Alan and Steve H. Hanke (1992). "Currency Boards." In Peter Newman, Murray Milgate, and John Eatwell, eds., *The New Palgrave Dictionary of Money and Finance* London: Macmillan. 1: 558–61.

Wark, McKenzie (1994). *Virtual Geography: Living with Global Media Events*. Bloomington: Indiana University Press.

Watt, E. D. (1982). *Authority*. London: Croom Helm.

Webb, Michael C. (1991). "International Economic Structures, Government Interests, and the International Coordination of Macroeconomic Adjustment Policies." *International Organization* 45, no. 3 (Summer): 309–42.

Weber, Cynthia (1995). *Simulating Sovereignty: Intervention, the State, and Symbolic Exchange*. New York: Cambridge University Press.

Weber, Max [1925] (1947). *The Theory of Social and Economic Organization*. Glencoe, Ill.: Free Press.

Weil, Gordon (1983). *Exchange-Rate Regime Selection in Theory and Practice*. New York: New York University Press.

Weil, Phillipe (1991). "Currency Competition and the Transition to Monetary Union: Currency Competition and the Evolution of Multi-Currency Regions." In Alberto Giovannini and Colin Mayer, eds., *European Financial Integration*. Cambridge: Cambridge University Press, chap. 10.

Welfens, Paul J. J. (1996). "Creating a European Central Bank after 1992: Issues of EC Monetary Integration and Problems of Institutional Innovation." In Paul J. J. Welfens, ed., *European Monetary Integration: EMS Developments and International Post-Maastricht Perspectives*. 3rd ed. New York: Springer-Verlag, pp. 223–69.

Wendt, Frantz (1981). *Cooperation in the Nordic Countries: Achievements and Obstacles*. Stockholm: Almqvist and Wiksell.

White, Lawrence H. (1983). "Competitive Money, Inside and Out." *Cato Journal* 3, no. 1 (Spring): 281–99.

—— (1984). "Free Banking as an Alternative Monetary System." In Barry N. Siegel, ed., *Money in Crisis: The Federal Reserve, the Economy, and Monetary Reform.* San Francisco: Pacific Institute for Public Policy Research, chap. 11.

—— (1988). "Depoliticizing the Supply of Money." In Thomas D. Willett, ed., *Political Business Cycles: The Political Economy of Money, Inflation, and Unemployment.* Durham, N.C.: Duke University Press.

—— (1989). *Competition and Currency.* New York: New York University Press.

Wickham, Peter (1985). "The Choice of Exchange Rate Regime in Developing Countries: A Survey of the Literature." *International Monetary Fund Staff Papers* 32, no. 2 (June): 248–88.

Willett, Thomas D., and King Banaian (1996). "Currency Substitution, Seigniorage and the Choice of Currency Policies." In Paul D. Mizen and Eric J. Pentecost, eds., *The Macroeconomics of International Currencies: Theory, Policy and Evidence.* Brookfield, Vt.: Elgar, chap. 5.

Willett, Thomas D., Richard C. K. Burdekin, Richard J. Sweeney, and Clas Wihlborg, eds. (1995). *Establishing Monetary Stability in Emerging Market Economies.* Boulder, Colo.: Westview.

Williams, John H. (1947). *Postwar Monetary Plans and Other Essays.* New York: Knopf.

Williamson, John (1995). *What Role for Currency Boards?* Washington: Institute for International Economics.

Wilson, John F. (1992). "Physical Currency Movements and Capital Flows." In International Monetary Fund, *Report on the Measurement of International Capital Flows: Background Papers.* Washington, pp. 91–97.

Wisely, William (1977). *A Tool of Power: The Political History of Money.* New York: Wiley.

Wolf, Thomas A. (1994). "Currency Arrangements in Countries of the Former Ruble Area and Conditions for Sound Monetary Policy." Paper on Policy Analysis and Assessment PPAA/94/15. Washington: International Monetary Fund.

Woodford, Michael (1991). "Currency Competition and the Transition to Monetary Union: Does Competition between Currencies Lead to Price Level and Exchange Rate Stability?" In Alberto Giovannini and Colin Mayer, eds., *European Financial Integration.* Cambridge: Cambridge University Press, chap. 9.

Yamazawa, Kotaro, Yoshiaki Wada, and Takeshi Hachimura (1992). *Outlook for the Financial Markets of Hong Kong.* Special Paper no. 218. Tokyo: Bank of Japan.

Yansane, Aguibou Y. (1978/79). "Some Problems of Monetary Dependency in French-speaking West African States." *Journal of African Studies* 5, no. 4 (Winter): 444–70.

Yeager, Leland B. (1983). "Stable Money and Free-Market Currencies." *Cato Journal* 3, no. 1 (Spring): 305–26.

Zarazaga, Carlos E. (1995a). "Argentina, Mexico, and Currency Boards: Another Case of Rules Versus Discretion." *Federal Reserve Bank of Dallas Economic Review* (Fourth Quarter): 14–24.

Zarazaga, Carlos E. (1995b). "Can Currency Boards Prevent Devaluations and Financial Meltdowns?" *The Southwest Economy,* no. 4: 6–9.

Zelizer, Viviana A. (1989). "The Social Meaning of Money: 'Special Monies.'" *American Journal of Sociology* 95, no. 2 (Sept.): 342–77.

—— (1994). *The Social Meaning of Money.* New York: Basic Books.

Zevin, Robert (1992). "Are World Financial Markets More Open? If So, Why and with What Effects?" In Tariq Banuri and Juliet B. Schor, eds., *Financial Openness and National Autonomy.* Oxford: Clarendon Press.

Zimbalist, Andres, and John Weeks (1991). *Panama at the Crossroads: Economic Development and Political Change in the Twentieth Century.* Berkeley: University of California Press.

Index

Sierra Leone, 52
Simmel, George, 12
Simons, Marlise, 38
Single European Act (1986), 76
Smith, Adam, 143
SMU. *See* Scandinavian Monetary Union
(SMU).
Social institutions: governance implemented
through norms of, 146; market as, 146;
money as, 147
Social spaces, 25–26
Soja, Edward, 10
Solidus (Byzantine), 30
Som (Kirghizia), 80
South Africa, 60, 88
Sovereignty, monetary, 17; defending or re-
taining, 164–67; history of, 27–28; in
monetary alliance, 87–91; monetary bloc
subordination, 60–62; role of CI in sub-
ordinating, 93–94; subjugation using cur-
rency board, 52–55; subjugation using
pegged exchange rates, 55–59; subordination and sharing of, 48, 80–91; surrender of, 48–51
Sovereignty, state: asserted in Peace of
Westphalia, 14–15, 33; challenges to
Westphalian model of, 142–43; effect of
continued, 142; before Westphalia, 14–
16, 142; in world politics, 150–52
Soviet Union, 78
Spaces: conceptions tied to regimes of representation, 10; physical and functional
notions of, 21–23. *See also* Currency
space; Social spaces
Spain, 77
Spatial organization: of finance, 20–21; in
idea of networks, 21–23
Special Drawing Right (SDR), 57
Speculative attacks: on rupiah (1997), 121
Spencer, Michael J., 78
State, the: diminished power of, 131–32;
interaction with social spaces, 25–26; jurisdiction over money supply, 5; as
oligopolist, 5, 138–42, 148–49, 167;
power of autonomous, 14; privilege in
supplying currency, 133–34; quasi-states,
49; replacement of monopoly power, 146;
seigniorage as source of revenue for, 39–
41. *See also* Government; Sovereignty,
state

Sterling bloc, 62
Strange, Susan, 127, 139, 142–43, 146
Swaziland, 60, 73
Sweden, 70, 75, 77, 89
Switzerland, 70, 75
Symmetry theorem, 106

Tabellini, Guido, 41
Tajikistan, 49, 80
Tanganyika, 73
Tavlas, George S., 83, 96, 102, 104, 105,
107, 108, 162
Taylor, Peter J., 18
Tequila Effect, 54
Territoriality: defined, 13–14; established
by Peace of Westphalia, 14–15
Thailand, currency crisis (1997), 164
Thaler (Austrian), 31–32
Thrift, Nigel, 18, 22
Thygesen, Niels, 86, 94, 98, 104, 105, 109,
136, 156
Tietmeyer, Hans, 37
Toffler, Alvin, 21
Tolar (Slovenia), 37
Top Currency (Currency Pyramid), 116,
121, 127, 152–56
Trade: currency denomination in (1980–
96), 104–10; yen-dominated Japanese ex-
ports, 164
Transactions: costs using monetary ex-
change, 111; currencies' cross-border use,
93–97; ghost moneys in, 32; in a money
network, 12–13
Treaty of Rome (1957), 74
Trust: embodied in money, 11–12; in trans-
actional networks, 146–47
Tsoukalis, Loukas, 75

Uganda, 73
Ukraine, 80
Underhill, Geoffrey R. D., 148
Unholy Trinity, 56, 63, 75
Uzbekistan, 80

Vatican, the, 48
Vaubel, Roland, 135–38
Vegh, Carlos A., 96, 110, 120, 165
Vienna Coinage Treaty (1857), 71